A Research Agenda for Environmental Management

Elgar Research Agendas outline the future of research in a given area. Leading scholars are given the space to explore their subject in provocative ways, and map out the potential directions of travel. They are relevant but also visionary.

Forward-looking and innovative, Elgar Research Agendas are an essential resource for PhD students, scholars and anybody who wants to be at the forefront of research.

Titles in the series include:

A Research Agenda for Management and Organization Studies
Edited by Barbara Czarniawska

A Research Agenda for Entrepreneurship and Context
Edited by Friederike Welter and William B. Gartner

A Research Agenda for Cities
Edited by John Rennie Short

A Research Agenda for Neoliberalism
Kean Birch

A Research Agenda for Human Resource Management
Edited by Paul Sparrow and Cary L. Cooper, CBE

A Research Agenda for Shrinking Cities
Justin B. Hollander

A Research Agenda for Women and Entrepreneurship
Edited by Patricia G. Greene and Candida G. Brush

A Research Agenda for Entrepreneurial Cognition and Intention
Edited by Malin Brännback and Alan L. Carsrud

A Research Agenda for Entrepreneurship Education
Edited by Alain Fayolle

A Research Agenda for Service Innovation
Edited by Faïz Gallouj and Faridah Djellal

A Research Agenda for Global Environmental Politics
Edited by Peter Dauvergne and Justin Alger

A Research Agenda for New Institutional Economics
Edited by Claude Ménard and Mary M. Shirley

A Research Agenda for Regeneration Economies
Reading City-Regions
Edited by John R. Bryson, Lauren Andres and Rachel Mulhall

A Research Agenda for Cultural Economics
Edited by Samuel Cameron

A Research Agenda for Environmental Management
Edited by Kathleen E. Halvorsen, Chelsea Schelly, Robert M. Handler, Erin C. Pischke and Jessie L. Knowlton

A Research Agenda for Environmental Management

Edited by

KATHLEEN E. HALVORSEN

Department of Social Sciences and School of Forest Resources and Environmental Science, Michigan Technological University, USA

CHELSEA SCHELLY

Department of Social Sciences, Michigan Technological University, USA

ROBERT M. HANDLER

Sustainable Futures Institute, Michigan Technological University, USA

ERIN C. PISCHKE

Ecosystem Workforce Program, University of Oregon, USA

JESSIE L. KNOWLTON

Department of Biology, Wheaton College, USA

Elgar Research Agendas

EE Edward Elgar PUBLISHING

Cheltenham, UK • Northampton, MA, USA

Published by
Edward Elgar Publishing Limited
The Lypiatts
15 Lansdown Road
Cheltenham
Glos GL50 2JA
UK

Edward Elgar Publishing, Inc.
William Pratt House
9 Dewey Court
Northampton
Massachusetts 01060
USA

A catalogue record for this book
is available from the British Library

Library of Congress Control Number: 2018960567

This book is available electronically in the **Elgar**online
Social and Political Science subject collection
DOI 10.4337/9781788115193

Printed on elemental chlorine free (ECF)
recycled paper containing 30% Post-Consumer Waste

ISBN 978 1 78811 518 6 (cased)
ISBN 978 1 78811 519 3 (eBook)

Typeset by Servis Filmsetting Ltd, Stockport, Cheshire
Printed and Bound in the USA

For Avery and Ellie

Contents

Figures

Tables

Contributors

Jesse Abrams, University of Georgia

Datu B. Agusdinata, Arizona State University

Gabriela Alonso-Yanez, University of Calgary

Brad Barnett, Western Upper Peninsula Planning and Development Region, Michigan Technological University

Nathan Basiliko, Laurentian University

Kirby Calvert, University of Guelph

Diana Córdoba, University of Victoria

Jennifer L. Dunn, Michigan Technological University

Amarella Eastmond, Universidad Autónoma de Yucatán

David J. Flaspohler, Michigan Technological University

Kristin Floress, USDA Forest Service

Valoree S. Gagnon, Michigan Technological University

Amanda Giang, University of British Columbia

Hugh S. Gorman, Michigan Technological University

R. Brian Guerrero, University of Texas at El Paso

Kathleen E. Halvorsen, Michigan Technological University

Robert M. Handler, Michigan Technological University

Muhammad A. Hanif, Arizona State University

Raphael J. Heffron, University of Dundee

Josiah Heyman, University of Texas at El Paso

Lily House-Peters, California State University, Long Beach

Abhilash Kantamneni, University of Guelph

Jessie L. Knowlton, Wheaton College

Robert A. LaFave, Village of L'Anse, Michigan Technological University

Julian Licata, Bemidji State University

Heide K. Lukosch, Delft University

Ena E. Mata-Zayas, Universidad Juárez Autónoma de Tabasco

Rodrigo Medeiros, Conservation International-Brazil, Federal Rural University of Rio de Janeiro

Mayra del Carmen Fragoso Medina, National Autonomous University of Mexico

M. Azahara Mesa-Jurado, Colegio de la Frontera Sur

Daisuke Minakata, Michigan Technological University

Ali Mirchi, University of Texas at El Paso

Cassandra Moseley, University of Oregon

Tedd Moya Mose, Queen Mary University of London

Tuyeni Heita Mwampamba, University of California, Davis

Cesar J. Vazquez Navarrete, Colegio de Postgraduados

Erik A. Nielsen, Northern Arizona University

Marcella Ohira, Inter-American Institute for Global Change Research

Excel Ortega, Arizona State University

Judith A. Perlinger, Michigan Technological University

Erin C. Pischke, University of Oregon

Emily W. Prehoda, Michigan Technological University

Valentin D. Picasso Risso, University of Wisconsin-Madison

Julio C. Sacramento-Rivero, Universidad Autónoma de Yucatán

Maryam Samimi, University of Texas at El Paso

Diego Sanchez, University of Texas at El Paso

Chelsea Schelly, Michigan Technological University

Theresa L. Selfa, State University of New York, College of Environmental Science and Forestry

Rachael Shwom, Rutgers University

Roman V. Sidortsov, Michigan Technological University

Tatiana de Souza, Conservation International – Brazil

Bethel Tarekegne, Michigan Technological University

George Tchobanoglous, University of California, Davis

Noel R. Urban, Michigan Technological University

Lucía Pérez Volkow, National Autonomous University of Mexico

Shane Walker, University of Texas at El Paso

David Watkins, Michigan Technological University

Richelle L. Winkler, Michigan Technological University

Acknowledgments

This book is the outcome of the work of many authors, collaborations and research projects across a number of countries. Our group of authors is itself transdisciplinary since it includes social, natural and engineering scientists as well as individuals from other sectors. Scientists from the College of Sciences and Arts, College of Engineering and the School of Forest Resources and Environmental Science at Michigan Technological University led most of the projects described in this book. Many contribute to the Michigan Tech Department of Social Sciences' Environmental and Energy Policy graduate program. Decades of careful hiring, university investment and research agency funding helped create a Michigan Tech faculty with particularly high capacity to conduct environmentally related research across disciplinary and sectorial boundaries.

As described in Chapter 10, much of this capacity was initially created through collaborations during Tech's National Science Foundation (NSF) Integrative Graduate Education and Research Traineeship project on sustainability and later projects that built on those foundations, most funded by NSF's environmental sustainability research programs. Michigan Tech's many institutes and centers, including the Sustainable Futures Institute, Ecosystem Science Center and Center for Water and Society and the faculty who created them, also contributed greatly to this capacity. The Inter-American Institute for Global Change Research (IAI) provided key research funding. For many of us, NSF and IAI support allowed us to develop transdisciplinary research projects and teamwork skills. We thank our funders and employers, particularly Michigan Tech, for their investment in our work.

This book would not be possible without the many individuals who helped us with our research projects as survey respondents, interviewees and research assistants. A number of anonymous reviewers generously gave their time to review these chapters and their comments greatly strengthened this book. Jennifer L. Dunn, Mayra Sanchez Morgan, Jacob S. Slattery and Kyla Valenti assisted enormously through their careful work in the checking and assemblage of our references. We thank them all.

PART I

Introduction to transdisciplinarity in environmental management research

1 Introduction to *A Research Agenda for Environmental Management* –Through transdisciplinary, social science-rich environmental governance research

Kathleen E. Halvorsen, Jessie L. Knowlton, Chelsea Schelly, Robert M. Handler and Erin C. Pischke

Introduction

Forty-seven years after the first Earth Day, environmental management problems remain some of humanity's greatest unsolved challenges. Climate change, resource scarcity, air and water pollution, and biodiversity losses continue and are, in some cases, worsening over time (Berkes et al., 2003). Developing the capacity to successfully understand these problems and their solutions therefore remains an important research agenda item.

Unfortunately, environmental management research problems have more commonly been defined as predominantly natural science problems to be studied by biologists, ecologists and chemists or engineering science problems to be solved with technology. These approaches have failed to help us solve many of these critical problems. Increasingly, foundation, policy making and science funding organizations and agencies call for broader inclusion of social science in interdisciplinary (ID) and even transdisciplinary (TD) research approaches (Baerwald et al., 2016). Unfortunately, few individuals and organizations are proficient in developing and managing ID, much less TD, environmental management research teams (Halvorsen et al., 2016; Hadorn et al., 2008).

Based on experience working together and teaching on environmental management research, we believe that the best approach views environmental problems as "governance" issues. By governance, we mean issues around human relationships to the environment, including understanding the social dimensions of these problems as well as their technical components (engineered elements) and natural science elements (often embedded in the ecosystems with which humans are interacting; Vatn, 2016). Social and environmental systems interface through relationships that may simultaneously be policy-driven, technologically based and behaviorally grounded. Figure 1.1 illustrates this system including social, technological and environmental components (Vatn, 2016). As this figure shows, the nature of these relationships often has profound cultural, political, organizational, psychological,

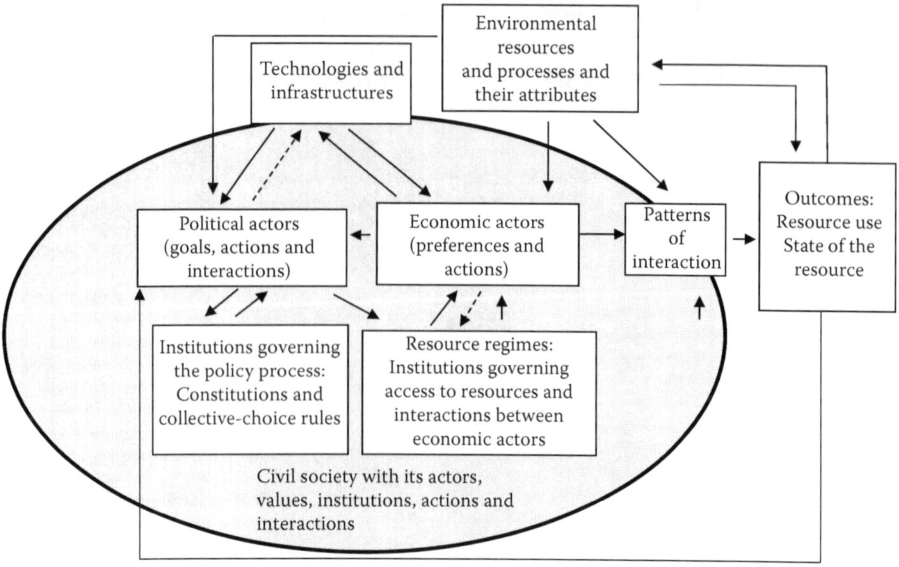

Note: From Vatn, 2016, used with permission.

Figure 1.1 The environmental governance system

historical, and spatial components – the provenance of various types of social science. As is discussed in more detail in Chapters Two and Three, understanding the fundamental basis for environmental management – the definition of the environmental problem and its solution – therefore demands the integration of social sciences with natural and/or engineering sciences.

However, as shown in Figure 1.1, approaching environmental management as environmental governance also brings us into a complex social system of groups and individuals who have defined the environmental problem, are potentially contributing to its causes, may support or oppose specific types of solutions, are affected by the problem and/or its solution(s), and will be involved in carrying out solutions (Vatn, 2016). This is the realm of diverse individuals and groups beyond science: that of industry, policy makers, non-governmental organizations, sovereign nations (tribes, cross-national contexts) and human community members.

Environmental management research that provides true understanding of problems and solutions therefore needs to include significant social science, integrated with natural and/or engineering sciences, combined with team members representing diverse types of groups. Successfully developing and managing such research teams is difficult. This research agenda book therefore focuses on three interrelated tasks as represented in the three main parts of the book: (a) establishing a rationale for a social science-centered TD approach to environmental management (Part I); (b) discussing the challenges associated with this approach as well as strategies for overcoming them (Part II); and (c) showcasing how these challenges can be overcome through the presentation of a series of case studies illustrating how this can and has been done by research teams studying different types of environmental management problems (Part III). This first chapter is an overall introduction to the primary concepts used throughout and to the book with upcoming sections detailing some of the definitions of terms, history leading to their development, and summarizing and synthesizing the main emphases of the chapters that follow.

History of the development of transdisciplinarity

The recognition of significant environmental problems arguably peaked in the 1960s and 1970s as post-World War II economic booms resulted in sharply increased air and water pollution (Kraft and Vig, 2015). Over time, scientists and governments developed new policies and professionals focused on solving these problems. The professionals tended to come from natural and engineering sciences, with, for example, the emergence of various types of ecology and the new field of environmental engineering. Much of this early environmentalism conceptualized humans as external to the biophysical worlds the field was trying to protect.

The field expanded and refined itself into the 1970s paralleling the emergence of Earth Day, the Stockholm Declaration and the development of the United Nations Environmental Program (UNEP) (Kraft and Vig, 2015). One outcome was the definition of the term "sustainability", a term that has come to be associated with many other fields, including sustainable development and manufacturing. Sustainability, defined as "development that meets the needs of the present without compromising the ability of future generations to meet their own needs" (Brundtland, 1987), was grounded in the concept of incorporating people into environmentalism equation, at least in terms of trying to satisfy human needs. This history is described in more detail in Chapter Two.

Meanwhile, traditional social science disciplines across the world began to develop new environmentally focused specialty areas from within traditional social science departments and also in natural resource and environmentally focused departments, including often cross-departmental environmental science and studies programs. Over time, environmental geography, anthropology and sociology joined environmental and natural resource social sciences as fully fledged specialty areas with graduate and undergraduate programs, professional societies, international conferences, and, increasingly, international environmental social science journals.

However, by and large social, natural and engineering scientists rarely collaborated across their fields. Two trends began to change this. One was the realization that, despite decades of trying, natural and engineering sciences alone were insufficient to solve many environmental problems. The second, interrelated with the first, was the emergence of funding opportunities from science agencies that called for ID proposals to carry out ID research and education, such as the late 1990s start of the US National Science Foundation Integrated Graduate Research and Education program and its Coupled Natural and Human Systems program that emerged from the coupled human–natural systems field (Baerwald et al., 2016).

Defining interdisciplinary and transdisciplinary

ID research links disparate disciplines to solve a common problem, by integrating the methods of each discipline and creating a shared language that leads to a more holistic approach to problem solving than a single discipline would allow (Buizer et al., 2015; Hickey and Nitschke, 2005). In the context of this book, an ID approach to solving environmental management problems refers to the required cooperation of social, natural and/or engineering scientists via integration of their various methods and development of a shared vision of both the problem and solution. TD research takes the ID approach one step further, and includes non-academics who are involved with the research topic or communities where fieldwork is taking place from the very beginning, including shared problem definition, methodology and final outcomes (Buizer et al., 2015; Hadorn et al., 2006).

Transdisciplinarity should be a reflexive, integrative, method-driven approach aiming at the solution of complex environmental management problems by differentiating and integrating knowledge from social, natural, engineering and societal bodies of knowledge (Lang et al., 2012). This definition highlights that TD research should focus on societally relevant problems, enable mutual learning processes among researchers from different disciplines and from outside academia, and create knowledge that is solution-oriented and transferable to both the scientific and societal practice (Lang et al., 2012).

The structure of this book

This book is designed to progress from fundamental concepts to strategies for overcoming common challenges to successful TD teamwork and ends by illustrating those strategies through a series of case studies of successful TD work. Part I focuses on introducing basic concepts with Chapter Two discussing underlying issues related to sustainability, governance and environmental management as well as raising key questions that justify the inclusion of strong social science capacities within TD teams. Chapter Three continues this discussion while focusing on the nuanced and difficult power dimensions associated with environmental governance questions. It is our intention that readers from diverse sectors and disciplines will find in this book a deeper understanding of how TD research can better develop environmental management solutions. We also hope that they will get a sense of the challenges of doing good TD work and strategies for overcoming them. Our case studies are designed to provide these readers with the stories of many TD research teams, how they developed, the challenges they faced and how they overcame them, and finally what taking a TD approach to studying a problem enabled the team to accomplish.

Part II focuses on discussing the challenges of successful TD teamwork in general, including, as presented in Chapter Four, strategies for overcoming them. Chapter Five discusses the challenges specific to including team members from other sectors, including non-governmental organizations. This is followed by Chapter Six with a discussion of the challenges specific to including public policy makers from all levels and branches of government. Chapter Seven delves into issues surrounding the involvement of general community members in research teams and defines a continuum of involvement that parallels that of TD teams generally. This section of the book is closed with a discussion of the challenges particular to TD teamwork across national boundaries.

Part III closes out the book with a set of case studies of research teams that span the continuum of research involvement presented in Chapter Seven. Some of the teams described in this section were deeply TD with individuals from non-science sectors included in the team from beginning to end. Others took a looser approach to TD, functioning more as ID research groups that used a more consultative approach to working with team members from other sectors. The research team described in Chapter Nine focused on understanding the causes of Lake Superior fish advisories and, through inclusion of community members in the definition of their research questions, discovered new dimensions to the issues under study.

Chapter 10 describes the challenges of a particularly large and international research team process showing how an ID group of scientists added other sectorial partners to understand tradeoffs related to renewable energy projects across the Americas. Chapter 11 delves more deeply into the community solar project described more briefly in Chapters Six and Seven to illustrate how researchers combined efforts with policy makers and community members to investigate development of local solar energy capacity. We move to a global scale in Chapter 12, illustrating the issues around TD research into diverse justice issues around conventional fossil fuel projects. Chapters 13 and 14 present the history of a TD research effort focused on understanding how household scale food-energy-water conservation can be encouraged (Chapter 13) and describing in more detail how the team took a TD approach to developing one research method – a role-playing game – to test research questions about effective behavioral interventions (Chapter 14). Finally, Chapter 15 closes out the book with an illustration of the inherently TD questions surrounding an increasingly pressing problem, supplying sufficient levels of potable water.

2 Governing sustainability and environmental management: what, why and how?

Erin C. Pischke, Robert M. Handler and Jessie L. Knowlton

Introduction

Sustainability has recently become a buzzword used by politicians, the media and corporations to garner public support. However, it has a decades-long history, with roots in the US environmental movement. Since the 1960s, sustainability has morphed from encompassing concepts that strictly focused on the economic and natural components of the environment as they relate to spaces that humans inhabit, to ones that included criteria focusing on the engineering sciences. More recently, there have been attempts at incorporating the social sciences into the sustainability concept, but such attempts have fallen short in part because they do not address difficult to measure subjective perspectives. While sustainability as a concept is central to understanding today's environmental management, this shortcoming inhibits progress toward a truly holistic approach of sustainably managing the environment.

In this chapter, we first give a brief history of the terms sustainability and sustainable development and describe how definitions of sustainability have morphed with time and depending on who is using them. We then discuss how sustainability relates to environmental management, and how the different disciplines of engineering and natural sciences have traditionally approached concepts of sustainability and environmental management, as well as how social sciences have approached such concepts over time. Finally, we argue that while there have been some important successes in solving environmental management problems using a single-discipline approach, current and future sustainability problems are incredibly complex and require transdisciplinary research to help solve them.

An emerging vision of sustainability, sustainable development and environmental management

Sustainability and sustainable development emerged as concepts of national and international interest in the 1960s, sparked by high-profile environmental issues, social movements and a sense that current development patterns would not be able to continue on their present course (Kraft and Vig, 2015). The 1972 United Nations Conference on the Human Environment was the first international meeting that focused on the interaction of people and their communities with the natural world. At this meeting, 26 principles were outlined for guiding a positive human–environment interaction, which represented the first concerted, international effort to develop a consensus on these matters (United Nations General Assembly, 1972). The term "sustainability" was not used in any of these principles, but the stage was set for an increased focus on the issues of beneficial human interactions with the natural world. This marked the start of a slow, incremental process of international efforts to define the concept of sustainability and develop strategies to implement more sustainable policies.

With the publication of the Report of the World Commission on Environment and Development, commonly referred to as the "Brundtland Report", the United Nations produced a work that thoroughly described the interconnected challenges facing countries and communities around the world relating to environmental pressures, economic development and social needs (Brundtland, 1987; World Commission on Environment and Development, 1987). Along with defining sustainable development as "development that meets the needs of the present without sacrificing the ability of future generations to meet their own needs", the Brundtland report outlined opportunities for action in ways that would align the interests of human development and environmental concerns (Brundtland, 1987: 41). The Brundtland sustainable development definition was concise and simple, but reflected many of the concerns at the time, regarding the promise of economic development to provide benefits for all people, not just the wealthy. At the same time, it was recognized that the quest for economic development should not come with irreparable harm to the natural world, thereby impacting the livelihoods of future generations.

At the 1992 United Nations Conference on Environment and Development, also known as the Earth Summit, the Rio Declaration on Environment and Development was published (United Nations General Assembly, 1992). This declaration recognized and outlined the responsibilities of government in developing policies that would reduce environmental harm by increasing eco-efficiency, or the amount of economic output or production per input unit of natural resources, thereby reducing environmental harm. The Rio Declaration stipulated that human welfare is the central concern for sustainable development and people are entitled to a healthy and productive life in harmony with nature (United Nations General Assembly, 1992). Countries were acknowledged to have a sovereign right to exploit their own resources, but not at the expense of causing damage to the environment of others.

From the 1990s onward, the term "sustainability" was used more broadly, as people attempted to translate the goals of sustainability into specific contexts, such as agriculture or transportation. As the term gained prominence, a common feature of most definitions or interpretations of the term was the focus on the relationship between social, economic and environmental (Vos, 2007). These three fundamental considerations, also sometimes envisioned as "people, profit, planet", and their relationships may be defined more specifically depending on the context, but most visions of sustainability include a conceptual model illustrating these three elements reinforcing each other in a mutually beneficial manner.

In 2000, the United Nations again advanced the common international vision of sustainability and sustainable development by publishing the UN Millennium Declaration (United Nations General Assembly, 2000). The Millennium Declaration outlined key priority areas for sustainable development to advance human well-being, environmental restoration and economic development, which would come to be known as the Millennium Development Goals (MDGs). Over the next few years, eight MDG areas were formalized for poverty, education, gender equality, child mortality, maternal health, communicable diseases, environmental issues and developing global partnerships for development. Across all of these goal areas, there were dozens of sub-targets outlining quantifiable metrics to judge improvement, with defined targets to achieve by 2015.

This process of seeking to more rigorously outline what the most pressing issues were with regard to sustainable development was a big help in making the vague term more tangible. Each country was able to outline how they would help make progress in each of these areas by stating specific actions to be taken. Countries could also develop partnerships to provide financial or other resources in order to help others improve in these areas. Progress toward these goals and targets across participating countries was tracked and shared every five years, with improvement made across many focus areas, most notably in the reduction of extreme poverty and child mortality (United Nations General Assembly, 2015). To build upon momentum generated by the MDGs, the United Nations issued the 2015 Sustainable Development Goals (SDGs), which outlined metrics to achieve by 2030 (United Nations General Assembly, 2017). The SDGs expanded the MDGs, defining 17 goals, with almost 170 quantifiable sub-targets. The SDGs placed increasing importance on environmental and economic issues, creating separate spaces for climate change, job and economic growth, and marine and terrestrial life, while retaining the human well-being focus areas of the initial MDGs.

The United Nations development goals highlight the need to define sustainability and sustainable development along multiple axes, with the overarching need to preserve our natural environment while ensuring adequate socioeconomic success and well-being for people. The quantity and quality of our natural environment has often been referred to as a stock of "natural capital", which is often utilized to produce manufactured capital in a traditional economic sense, or "human capital" when it relates to measures of human well-being (United Nations General Assembly, 2017). The Brundtland definition of sustainable development alludes to the competing demands of allowing people to utilize the current stock of natural capital to meet their own needs, while still allowing future generations to have enough capital to meet their own needs.

A situation where the total level of capital stock (natural, human and material) is maintained but the levels of individual stocks are allowed to change would be considered weak sustainability (Goodland and Daly, 1996). This would most likely arise from a situation where natural capital was reduced and material capital stocks would increase a corresponding amount and would assume a complete ability for these capital stocks to serve as perfect substitutes (i.e., a reduction in natural capital stocks of standing trees in a forest is balanced out by an increase in wood furniture as a material stock), with no loss in overall sustainability. On the other end of the spectrum would be a case of strong sustainability, where individual stocks of natural, human and material capital are considered separately and individually preserved over time, and would serve as complements to human flourishing, rather than substitutes. In the case of strong sustainability, the natural capital stocks represented by standing trees in a forest would have to be tracked independently from material stocks that the trees might be converted into, and the natural capital stock would have to be maintained over time (Goodland and Daly, 1996). In the middle of these two fixed views on sustainability, there could also be context-dependent intermediate sustainability situations, where a fluctuating mix of natural, human and material capital stocks is determined to be required, with a view towards critical thresholds that should not be exceeded when depleting a capital stock (Goodland and Daly, 1996).

Well before this coordinated international focus on formalizing sustainability and sustainable development began, many cultures and traditions incorporated elements of sustainability thinking into their beliefs and practices. In particular, the concept of organizing human society so that it is in harmony with the natural world is a central element in many indigenous traditions (Mebratu, 1998). The Iroquois Nation has governing language urging tribal members to consider impacts of all actions on future generations, recognizing the intergenerational aspects of sustainability as manifested by a societal ability to survive in harmony with their surroundings (Lyon, 1978). Several African traditions place humans within the context of a universe that has natural cycles and rhythms that are not to be dominated, but instead recognized and supported for community flourishing. The re-emergence of sustainable development thinking in the last 50 years reflects a re-discovery of the importance of these concepts and a new sense of urgency in developing a shared vision for sustainability as a common grand challenge.

Sustainability thinking in the engineering and natural sciences

The emerging view of sustainability as a guiding principle has certainly been important to the pursuit of environmental management goals, yet particular aspects or definitions of sustainability are more relevant than others in specific disciplines, which cause different actions related to environmental management in those areas. As shown in the previous section, the definitions of sustainability and sustainable development are continually changing, as new ways to define and measure related concepts are proposed. It is also important to note that practitioners working in the field of environmental management come from diverse scientific and technical backgrounds, and those different perspectives also contribute to differences in how sustainability thinking has been operationalized in the field of environmental management. In this section, we briefly discuss how environmental management concerns are typically viewed from natural and engineering science perspectives, while pointing out some successful results stemming from these viewpoints and challenges that still remain. These are generalized perspectives on very diverse areas and disciplines, but they seek to outline common themes for later reflection.

Engineering sciences' concept of sustainability

Sustainability thinking in the engineering sciences has been an important development regarding environmental management for a few reasons. Most important, it provides a firm foundation for the belief that human flourishing is linked to environmental health, and in order for human societies to flourish, attention should be paid to the condition of their natural environment. In the US, the foundation of environmental management concerns as a focus of engineering professionals is often traced to developments in the 1800s surrounding the provision of clean water to growing cities and the related issue of disposing of contaminated wastewater, most notably in the city of Chicago (Anderson, 2003). As the profession developed and formalized its underlying scientific and engineering framework for quantifying and optimizing water and wastewater treatment parameters, it also evolved from its roots in "sanitary engineering" to a wider field that focuses on environmental issues related to water, air and soil systems (Anderson, 2003).

In general, however, the theoretical framework that governs the engineering sciences' viewpoint of environmental management can most closely be tied to the idea of managing the existing stock of natural capital, which may include water resources, mineral resources, air quality, agricultural products, timber, and so on. Herman Daly and collaborators formalized definitions of sustainability related to maintenance of natural capital stocks as they relate to human capital or material capital, as discussed above (Goodland and Daly, 1996). To achieve "weak sustainability" as described above, any reductions in natural capital stocks should be mitigated by corresponding increases in human or material capital. To achieve a stronger vision of sustainability, critical thresholds in any of these separate dimensions of natural capital may be defined according to the minimum requirements needed by human societies in order to preserve human well-being over the long term. Importantly for engineers focused on environmental management, Daly and colleagues developed a set of guiding principles related to the use of natural capital stocks and introduction of waste flow into the natural environment, often referred to as the "Daly Rules" (Goodland and Daly, 1996):

1. Renewable resources should not be used at a rate which exceeds their regenerative capacity within the natural system.
2. Non-renewable resources should not be used at a rate which exceeds the

development of renewable substitutes to these resources developed by human society.
3. Waste emissions from a system should not exceed the ability of the surrounding natural system to assimilate those wastes.

This framework, especially the guidance concerning waste emissions, can be clearly seen in the engineering response to environmental management, which initially focused efforts on reducing harm to the environment by mitigating the impacts of our wastes on the natural environment that we ultimately depend on. Attempts to follow this guidance have developed from more passive strategies ("dilution is the solution to pollution") to more active strategies (primary, secondary and tertiary treatment of wastewater) over time as conditions have changed, but the basic understanding is the same. In a natural system, there is a threshold of harm that can be introduced, beyond which that system becomes less useful to surrounding human society. Efforts to determine that threshold level, and design waste treatment options to meet or exceed that design target, have traditionally been the dominant goals of engineers working within the area of environmental management.

In several domains, the application of these principles and this mental framework to environmental management has been a success. As one example, the regulation of criteria pollutants such as sulfur dioxide (SO_2) emissions in years since the passage of the Clean Air Act in the US has been successful in reducing the amount of environmental and human health impacts associated with SO_2, including acid rain and respiratory issues (US EPA, 2017). An initial scientific review was performed, which has been periodically updated, to stipulate the quantity of ambient SO_2 in the atmosphere that would result in an unacceptable level of environmental and human harm. The Acid Rain Program of the 1990 Amendments to the Clean Air Act set an annual maximum amount of SO_2 that could be emitted to the atmosphere from qualifying sources. Under this program, emitters of SO_2 were encouraged to reduce their annual emissions through a combination of market-based incentives and pollution control technology implementation (US EPA, 1990). The annual targets have been reduced periodically, in a way that was both responsive to new scientific information but also reflective of the gradual ability of emitters to install new technology or make new decisions. As a result of this management strategy, average SO_2 concentrations in the atmosphere have been reduced by more than 80% since 1990 (US EPA, 2016).

Despite the successes of the general engineering mindset in solving several serious issues related to environmental management, obvious environmental challenges remain around the world. In general, the engineering approach to environmental management has worked well to address issues where a clear link exists between a known cause of environmental harm (e.g., point-source water pollution) and an observable environmental response that is detrimental to human well-being in the relatively short-term (seasonal algal blooms, acid rain, fecal contamination of beaches, etc.). As environmental problems become more complex, with regional or global flows of pollutants, from multiple or diffuse origins, with a longer response time between emission and impact, environmental challenges become harder to address solely on the basis of an engineering sciences approach. Clear examples would be multistate contributions of agricultural runoff to eutrophication and hypoxic Dead Zones in the Gulf of Mexico and throughout the world (e.g., Diaz and Rosenberg, 2008), and anthropogenic climate change impacts brought on by continued increases in emissions of greenhouse gases. In addition, many persistent issues that have less to do with remediation of wastes, such as biodiversity loss, are more difficult to address within this framework.

Natural sciences' concept of sustainability

Unlike the United Nations' and many other groups' definitions of sustainability and sustainable development, which are anthropogenically focused as outlined in the Rio Declaration, in the natural sciences and especially the field of ecology, sustainability is often characterized as "environmental sustainability", or protection of Earth's biodiversity and ecosystems (Chapin et al., 2010; Turner, 2003). This view acknowledges the inherent value and right to exist of biodiversity and natural systems, regardless of the benefits that these systems do or do not provide to people, as is often implied when alluding to these items as stocks of "natural capital". However, whether natural scientists like it or not, humans are integral components of natural ecosystems, and both impact and respond to ecosystem processes (Berkes et al., 2003). Since the Millennium Ecosystem Assessment (MEA, 2005), these differing approaches to sustainability have been integrated to address social–ecological, or socioecological, sustainability, recognizing that efforts that fail to address the synergies and tradeoffs between ecological and societal well-being are unlikely to be successful (Chapin et al., 2010). For instance, local people are unlikely to respect rules that establish parks and restrict activities if their needs are not taken into consideration (Liu et al., 2007; Kristjanson et al., 2009). Conversely, development projects that cause ecosystem degradation are unlikely to produce a sustainable trajectory of human well-being (MEA, 2005). Along these lines, sustainable development can be defined in terms of development that is sustainable for both humans and nature, that is, an equitable advancement of human well-being that does not compromise ecosystem integrity (Kates et al., 2001; Fischer et al., 2015).

In the natural sciences, environmental management often seeks to return habitats or ecosystems to relatively arbitrary "historic" conditions before substantial human impact (Christensen et al., 1996). These ideal conditions may not be achievable in a rapidly changing world, and, more recently, "ecosystem stewardship" has been advocated (Chapin et al., 2010), which takes a socioecological sustainability approach to environmental management with a focus on preserving or restoring ecosystems and the services they provide to humans. Valuing ecosystems for their economic service-to-humans potential has also resulted in strong criticism (e.g., McCauley, 2006) and continuing debate on this issue (Spash and Aslaksen, 2015) by critics who argue that efforts to place economic values on nature may provide some benefits, but could ultimately undermine conservation goals, since those economic values may change with time or technology (Reid and Mooney, 2016).

Many critics argue that it is better to base conservation on the intrinsic and aesthetic values of nature. There is some merit to these arguments, since basing the need to preserve and restore ecosystems on the economic benefits they provide to people can lead to undesirable ecological outcomes if people's needs are met despite ecosystem degradation and biodiversity loss. For example, recent evidence points to a global increase in human well-being, despite global declines in environmental health and the provision of ecosystem services (Raudsepp-Hearne et al., 2010).

Over the last three decades the most common natural science approach to environmental management under situations with high levels of uncertainty has been "adaptive" management (Gunderson and Holling, 2002). This approach generally uses carefully designed, experimental management interventions and monitoring programs to determine outcomes of each approach and to allow managers to change course when needed owing to inevitable ecological surprises (Clark, 1980; Gregory et al., 2006). However, this approach usually fails to acknowledge economic, social, and political surprises that also can arise over the course of a management intervention, creating problems for an ecologically focused adaptive management plan (Gregory et al., 2006).

As we have shown thus far, the definition of sustainability must not be confined to an either–or focus on humans or the environment, but instead should be considered within the holistic framework of more complex systems (Berkes et al., 1998; Liu et al., 2007). This approach emphasizes that people, economies, societies and cultures are embedded parts of the biosphere and shape it at all scales (Folke et al., 2016). In the next section, we take the discussion one step further and discuss the importance of including governance in discussions of sustainability and environmental management.

What is being governed?

Management of biodiversity and ecosystem services has been extended to include *governance* through incorporation of multiple perspectives from various stakeholders (a broad range of scientists, not just natural scientists, as well as practitioners, non-academics, community members and indigenous people) and links science with policy makers and decision makers (Díaz et al., 2015). In many countries, for example, bioenergy-related policy initiatives have led to greater levels of governance by international actors through the use of public or private certification programs (Bailis and Baka, 2011; Moser et al., 2014). These certification programs, often voluntary in nature, ensure that not only are bioenergy crops being harvested in an environmentally friendly way, but that the people who are harvesting the crops are being treated fairly (i.e., through fair wages, insurance benefits, etc.).

The principles that guide the management of the certification programs attempt to secure economic stability, promote best practices and responsible production by growers, sustainability of environmental practices and responsible awareness of socioeconomic issues (Schouten and Glasbergen, 2011). These new approaches to managing human–environment interactions have begun to reverse long histories of problematic relationships in the places where crop production occurs; this is why social science research is important. Before such programs were in place, many of the people who were affected by structural changes were not able to participate in solving the problems they encountered (Escobar, 2011).

Conceptual frameworks guide holistic sustainability initiatives

Through the use of a conceptual framework such as the one that the Intergovernmental Science-policy Platform on Biodiversity and Ecosystem Services uses to characterize a socioecological system, these types of governance-based systems acknowledge that including multiple perspectives and knowledge systems in the management of natural resources can facilitate communication and understanding of complex systems (Díaz et al., 2015). Including multiple perspectives in environmental management can broaden the scope of inquiry, investigate diverse angles of environmental problems, and reframe how problems might be tackled or dealt with (Díaz et al., 2015). The Intergovernmental Science-policy Platform on Biodiversity and Ecosystem Services and socioecological systems frameworks open up the often narrow view taken of what nature is and how to protect or manage it; these systems place human beings into natural systems and attempt to depict the interactions that occur (Díaz et al., 2015). In some cases, ecosystem services are co-produced by humans and nature, indicating the tight associations and interactions between the two (Díaz et al., 2015).

Why is governance important?

As the world moves deeper into the Anthropocene, the Earth's increasingly complex and interconnected socioecological systems will be challenged in both expected and unexpected ways (Cumming and Peterson, 2017; Homer-Dixon et al., 2015). Finding means of avoiding, anticipating and reducing the negative impacts of collapses in socioecological systems should therefore provide common goals for both sustainability science and ecology (Cumming and Peterson, 2017; Raudsepp-Hearne et al., 2010). This potentially aligns well with the engineering sustainability goals for the things can be measured and quantified at the present time. If there are ecological issues, or critical thresholds, that we currently cannot value appropriately in the sense of a natural capital stock, then the engineering mindset might not be well positioned to manage these ecological issues.

Despite the various structural and technological solutions available for controlling pollution and environmental degradation, one of the underlying barriers to achieving better outcomes is human action. Individuals' actions are very difficult to control (i.e., they can wash their cars in their driveways, dump their used car oil into open waterways, etc.). Policy tools can be used to inform the public and incentivize their actions (i.e., citizens might be asked to pay more for water they use in their houses so the local water treatment plants can afford to treat increasingly polluted water). This is another reason why including a social perspective in sustainability indicators is important. Focusing on how decision makers govern is also important to consider within conceptual frameworks and socioecological systems. The institutions and policy makers that comprise such systems are those that decide how natural resources are managed or allocated, control access to resources (e.g., energy, land) and often perpetuate the status quo and existing structures of power (Díaz et al., 2015).

Importance of inclusive sustainability in policy making: incentive-based policy instruments

Social science perspectives and methods are important for drawing out local factors that may undermine natural or engineering science research methods. For example, conservation schemes like payments for ecosystem services or the Reducing Emissions from Deforestation and Forest Degradation programs use spatial and natural science data to prevent deforestation, increase carbon sequestration and support forest communities (Montalvo, 2015). If these programs' criteria ignore the local context (e.g., a local population's social norms and practices), they could result in unequal, unjust or low participation rates and unintended consequences, such as illicit logging (Balderas Torres et al., 2013; Bremer et al., 2014; Cole, 2015; Pascual et al., 2014; Rantala et al., 2014).

How should socioecological systems be governed?

Much of the extant literature on sustainable environmental management covers the positive and negative impacts of socioecological change on environmental, social and economic systems, but the established sustainability criteria and methods, such as life-cycle assessment, lack a focus on in-depth knowledge of the socioeconomic impacts that are likely to occur (Solomon et al., 2015; Stattman and Mol, 2014). In order to achieve social sustainability within environmental management, sustainability indicators should consider who is being impacted by proposed changes in a socioecological system and what the wider sociopolitical context looks like (see Escobar, 2011). The following criteria should be considered: the local human value systems that are in place; the contested and contrasting ways of current environmental management; and the institutions (governance system) that have the power to change environmental conditions (Díaz et al., 2015).

Knowing how the public and landowner-producers perceive proposed environmental management – which trade-offs people are willing to live with and ones that they deem unacceptable – is one way to gauge acceptance and long-term sustainability of natural resource management within a social system (Dale et al., 2011; Howe and Boyer, 2016; West et al., 2010). Such attention to social needs can lead to greater overall environmental management. In the next section we expand on this conversation and review opportunities and challenges for incorporating governance concepts into environmental management practices.

Benefits of including multiple perspectives in environmental governance

Sustainability frameworks can be improved through the use of interdisciplinary and transdisciplinary approaches to problem solving, where "interdisciplinary" is defined as including scientists from a range of academic disciplines and "transdisciplinary" means that non-academic social actors such as policy makers, decision makers and members of local communities are strongly integrated into the collaborations (Kirk-Lawlor and Allred, 2017). An excellent example of the need for transdisciplinary collaboration to meet both human and ecological sustainability goals for environmental management comes from research on protected areas around the world. Many protected areas have failed in terms of their goals for sustaining biodiversity and intact habitats because of pressures from nearby human populations (Laurance et al., 2012). While the debate between proponents of forcible exclusion of humans in protected areas and proponents of attempting to meet the needs of local human populations within protected areas still rages (e.g., Soulé, 2013; Marvier, 2014), there is now mounting evidence that focusing solely on biodiversity conservation goals while ignoring human needs does not work. In a recent meta-analysis of 165 protected areas using data from 171 published studies, Oldekop et al. (2016) found that positive conservation and socioeconomic outcomes were more likely to occur when protected areas adopted co-management regimes, empowered local people, reduced economic inequalities, and maintained cultural and livelihood benefits. This analysis makes clear that attempting to exclude anthropogenic influences to achieve biological conservation objectives does not often work, and that a transdisciplinary approach focusing on all aspects of sustainability in environmental management will be much more effective at achieving joint biological conservation and socioeconomic development outcomes.

Current challenges and opportunities for reform in environmental management

Environmental management today is challenged to use an adaptive, socioecological approach to address complexities, including broad scales that cross international boundaries, conflicting values and worldviews, managing for abrupt change and threshold dynamics, open system issues and institutional limitations (Polasky et al., 2011; Virapongse et al., 2016). Two of the main forces exacerbating environmental problems today are global climate change and a large human population that continues to grow and demand a larger per-capita amount of resources, including land. Core societal values, which developed when humans had a much smaller ecological footprint, still center on economic growth and the advancement of technology to solve societal and environmental problems (Martin et al., 2016). Many ecologists and conservation biologists feel that the only way to tackle the present environmental crisis will be through a fundamental societal shift in human values: from human-centric to valuing all life and the natural processes that sustain humans and non-humans alike. This transition in human values should favor biodiversity and autonomous ecological processes as central within the agenda of human activities and understanding human behavior and attitudes should be at the forefront of a "conservation socioecology" for the future of environmental management (Martin et al., 2016).

Trade-offs associated with allowing governance and human actors into the conceptual frameworks of natural systems include choosing the wrong policies, not taking action (regardless of the number of policies that outline what should be done), humans continuing to make "bad" decisions based on their needs/values (people can be wrong) and that the entire basis for what we believe to be true (scientifically or socially) can be wrong, leading us further down the "wrong" path. If the wrong incentives (e.g., fuel subsidies) are chosen, it can lead to perverse outcomes or problems in other parts of the system, while man-made boundaries (state or country borders, zip codes) can prohibit or hinder problem-solving across a geographical scale (Díaz et al., 2015).

Shove's work (2004, 2010) lends a macro viewpoint to the social science literature covered here, putting the discussion of environmental decision making into perspective. Shove (2004) argues that people (society) often ask the wrong questions when making decisions and quickly embrace "normality"; instead of asking where we can make new technological developments to solve problems, environmental managers should examine where we can make changes in everyday decision making. Research should question the broader societal norms and the practices that perpetuate and lead to poor environmental decision making. Shove (2010) writes that a focus on individual behavior reinforces the status quo and leaves radically transformative alternative solutions off the table. Transitions to sustainable ways of life and combating climate change involve a radical upheaval of the process of policy making as we know it (Shove, 2010).

Not only are environmental decisions made by politics and policy makers who may rely on research generated by academia, but social norms created and reinforced by path dependency also have a great influence on what decisions are made and what the outcomes are. Policy should not focus on personal choice because the drivers of and barriers to environmental behavior are arbitrarily chosen and can each be a driver or a barrier, depending on the context (Shove, 2010). A multitude of approaches at many levels, from the individual to the societal level through policy changes and transnationally, need to be brought together to continue to understand environmental decision making and move toward new theories and approaches to solving problems (Gardner and Stern, 2008; Shove, 2004; Shwom and Lorenzen, 2012). Moreover, solving environmental problems requires patience because values and norms change over long time scales (Heberlein, 2012). It is important to note that societal misunderstandings of science and environmental issues can perpetuate unsustainable practices (Gardner and Stern, 2008; Heberlein, 2012) and that educational campaigns are unlikely to change this (Heberlein, 2012). Owing to the diffuse nature of negative environmental management and the reluctance or ignorance to change destructive personal habits and actions, national and sub-national policies are needed to make society-wide structural changes to slow global environmental change (Gardner and Stern, 2008; Selin and VanDeveer, 2009).

Conclusion

This chapter has provided a brief overview of how sustainability has come to be defined with ever-increasing specificity in certain contexts and how those definitions are often operationalized in the pursuit of environmental management approaches. In general, natural and engineering sciences have taken different approaches to environmental management based on their disciplinary backgrounds. While each of these approaches has resulted in important successes, we have seen how more complex environmental issues still need to be addressed with a new perspective. A more comprehensive approach involving transdisciplinary thinking, as well as an increased focus on governance issues, has been demonstrated to improve environmental management outcomes in a few key contexts. We explore complex issues related to governance in more detail in the following chapters.

Acknowledgments

This work was supported by the National Science Foundation's Partnerships in International Research and Education Program grant IIA no. 1243444 and Research Coordination Network Program grant CBET no.1140152, as well as an Inter-American Institute for Global Change Research's CRN3105 grant.

3 Power within and beyond the state: understanding how power relations shape environmental management

Jesse Abrams, Diana Córdoba, Roman V. Sidortsov, Chelsea Schelly and Hugh S. Gorman

Introduction

In 2016, representatives of 195 nations signaled their support for the Paris Agreement, a global plan to reduce greenhouse gas emissions and avert the worst effects of a warming climate. Less than a year later, the President of the US (the world's second-largest greenhouse gas emitter) announced his intent to withdraw the US from the accord. In 2017, the newly installed Brazilian President abolished a protected area in the Amazon to allow for mining, arguing that the change was needed to boost a flagging economy. Following an outcry from indigenous and environmental organizations, a college professor filed a lawsuit that resulted in a temporary injunction against the abolition of the reserve. That same year, violence flared in Kenya as armed cattle herders began moving their animals onto private estates – including nature reserves – in search of forage, in some cases burning reserve lodges and shooting reserve owners and managers. Drought was blamed for pushing the herds onto areas with the best grazing conditions, but the upcoming elections were also suspected to be at play.

As these examples indicate, environmental management is an inextricably political activity. Far from being the outcome of purely technical or scientific considerations, environmental decision making reflects a complex process of environmental governance, the "regulatory processes, mechanisms and organizations through which political actors influence environmental actions and outcomes" (Lemos and Agrawal, 2006: 298). Understanding and addressing issues of environmental governance requires combinations of new knowledge, action and engagement with the myriad forms that power takes. Transdisciplinary research offers the potential to illuminate the role of power in driving environmental management and to contribute to transformative change.

This chapter provides a brief overview of the concept of power, both that emanating from formal governmental channels (including through formal laws) and that arising from outside the state. We explore the implications of power for environmental management, drawing upon theory and research from political ecology and related fields. Specifically, we ask how power relations influence environmental management, how state and non-state activities reproduce social inequalities, and how actors from both inside and outside the state contest power relations in ways that influence environmental management. Throughout, we consider the implications of power for the conduct of transdisciplinary research.

Power: a review of concepts

"Power is everywhere; not because it embraces everything, but because it comes from everywhere" (Foucault, 1980: 93). This frequently quoted passage from Michel Foucault's *The History of Sexuality* highlights the ontological place of power in social science. Russell (1937: 10) identifies power as "the fundamental concept in social science" and compares its importance with that of the concept of energy in physics. Foucault's quote also underscores the challenge of studying power: scholarship offers a multitude of divergent views on defining and operationalizing this multifaceted concept (Morris, 2012: 1). Power is a concept that has occupied (and sometimes vexed) some of history's brightest minds, from Aristotle and Plato to Hobbes and Weber (Ledyaev, 2001). Weber, for instance, found that the "concept of power is sociologically amorphous" and instead preferred to use the concept of domination, which he defined as "the probability that a command will be obeyed" (Weber, 1978: 53).

A thread that runs throughout much of the scholarship on power is a need to distinguish between overt and more subtle or invisible manifestations of power (Grewal, 2008; Lukes, 2005; Scott, 2001). Scott (2001: 13), for example, distinguishes between what he calls corrective and persuasive influence. As a more overt form of power, "[c]orrective influence operates through the use of resources that can serve as punitive and remunerative sanctions that are able to work directly on the interests of subalterns in power relations". He further identifies force and manipulation as the two elementary forms of power that comprise corrective influence. Force usually comes in the form of negative sanctions, while manipulation employs both negative and positive sanctions. From this perspective, a fitting definition of power comes from Castells (2011), who defines it as "the relational capacity of a social actor to influence asymmetrically the decisions of other social actors in ways that favor that power actor's will, interests, and values". This definition of power includes the following three elements: (a) social agents, two at a minimum, which Scott (2001) calls principal and subaltern; (b) a causal connection between the agents; and (c) the ability of the principal to act and the ability of the subaltern to resist. This definition broadly aligns with what Scott (2001: 9) terms the "mainstream" theories on the organization of power.

In contrast, the second stream (Scott, 2001) or heterodox (Grewal, 2008) theories emphasize the subtler and more pervasive techniques characteristic of persuasive influence, which "operates through the offering and acceptance of reasons for acting in one way rather than another" (Scott, 2001: 13). Scott associates persuasive influence with "cognitive symbols" and "value commitments". Accordingly, he differentiates between signification and legitimation as the two principal persuasion forms. These more invisible manifestations of power act through practices such as the generally nonviolent coercion of employees to comply with bureaucratic procedures, the framing of problems in ways advantageous to particular interests, and the deployment of symbolic resources to legitimize or de-legitimize actors, claims or social structures. For example, framing conservation issues under an "ecosystem services" approach can, at least potentially, lead to a neglect of biodiversity (e.g., by focusing efforts on altered landscapes that provide measurable benefits to human populations), and can exacerbate inequality by benefiting landowners and harming those dependent upon resources that previously existed outside of relations of market exchange (Adams, 2014). Similarly, global conservation initiatives that emphasize the problem of overpopulation place attention (and, implicitly, blame) on poor populations in the global South, whereas a focus on the impacts of industrial production and consumption shifts attention to the activities of wealthier populations in the North.

Lukes (2005) argues that non-action can also reveal evidence of power relations at play, particularly if it entails a subaltern's acquiescence to or internalization of their own oppression, or if non-action results from the ability of the powerful to set the terms of discussion so as to eliminate consideration of certain possibilities. Some second stream theories, Foucault's theory of disciplinary power in particular, fail to give full credit to human agency (Grewal, 2008: 131), thereby violating the first element of Castells' aforementioned definition. For Foucault, power is not simply a resource mobilized in service of maintaining social inequality, but rather constitutes the very fabric of all social relations, extending even to what we have come to call "knowledge".

Second stream theories raise difficult questions regarding agency, or the discretion regarding action: if power underlies fundamental components of social life such as knowledge, can it truly be considered to result from, or be vulnerable to active resistance based in, human action? Under the theory of structuration (Giddens 1984), the Foucauldian definition of power as a "complex strategical situation in a particular society" (Foucault, 1980: 93) can be traced back to human agents through an integrated account of agency and structure. For example, power channeled through ostensibly rigid legal and regulatory requirements might seem to leave an environmental manager without room to maneuver. Yet examining the process through which the constellations of power emerged, in this case, legislative history or rulemaking record, might reveal opportunities for discretion based on the legislature's or administrative agency's intent. In addition, this approach might lead to the discovery of pathways to change in the legal and regulatory regime.

The law as a manifestation of state power

Given the strong and pervasive role of institutionalized state power in governing natural resources and environmental problems, it is important to look closely at the use of power by the state and its representatives. Scholars have argued that we cannot understand the functioning of the state without necessarily understanding society and its structures, describing the state as a multidimensional phenomenon that includes institutions, practices and effects that are present at different levels in society (Sharma and Gupta, 2006). The idea of a unified entity called "the state" as a distinct and distant autonomous force is, thus, illusory (Abrams, 1988; Mitchell, 1991). Some propose, instead, to analyze the state as a social relation in which governmental actors and society are inextricably linked in order to understand the capacity of both to reproduce the existing social relations of production and attendant inequalities in society (Jessop, 2008). Under this approach, the state is both part of the social ensemble and, at the same time, is called upon to resolve contradictions that emerge in this ensemble.

Law is a principal means by which state power is exercised. Similar to power, law is not an easy concept to define; Weber (1978) saw the law as a form of "organized coercion" and he saw the state as having a monopoly on the legitimate use of violence (think, for example, of the use of armed police forces and their technologies of capture, restraint and containment to enforce domestic law). Across temporal and political settings, law generally refers to a rule or a set of rules promulgated by a sovereign entity (Prince, 1904). Yet scholars have been arguing about the meaning of law since ancient times and have yet to reach consensus. Positivist scholars see law as a "matter of what has been posited (ordered, decided, practiced, tolerated, etc.)" and thus as a social construction (Green, 2009, accessed 16 November 2018 at https://plato.stanford.edu/entries/legal-positivism/). Natural law theory sees law as "[a] philosophical system of legal and moral principles purportedly deriving from a universalized conception of human nature or divine justice rather than from legislative or judicial action; moral law embodied in principles of right and wrong" (Garner, 1999). Legal realism, in contrast, is a theory of adjudication. Leiter (2001: 279) describes it as "a theory about what it is judges really do when they decide cases". True to its name, legal pluralism is concerned with reconciling behavior according to more than one legal order occurring in the same social or institutional setting (Griffith, 1986; Merry, 1988). Although law is often seen as being an internally coherent system, in many ways it represents a diverse assortment of rules conceived and implemented at multiple scales, with roots in various political movements, historical periods and interpretations of the role of government in society. It thus represents the current and historical power of various social interests to both mete out rewards and punishments for particular behaviors and to communicate a moral code regarding appropriate and inappropriate behaviors with respect to social and environmental action (Freyfogle, 2003).

Inequality, the environment and state action

Environmental problems are inextricably linked to existing social structures and to inequality among social groups; managing environmental resources involves recognizing that environmental issues are in actuality socioenvironmental issues (White et al., 2015) and subsequently grappling with the ways in which social inequality shapes current environmental management issues. These social inequalities may involve inequitable distribution of and access to the economic, political and knowledge resources necessary to participate in environmental management decisions. They may also involve structural inequities embedded in the very institutions tasked with environmental management, which work to limit access to participation and decision making and often operate to perpetuate material inequalities in society (Downey, 2015). Attempts to reduce the environmental impacts of human activities (e.g., via improved technology) can be both shaped by and work to perpetuate social inequalities (Schelly and Banerjee, 2018) – inequalities based on culturally prescribed social status as well as materially derived social positions.

Given that the state can act as both a resource for perpetuating inequality and for addressing social demands for justice, it is worth considering how changes in the functioning of the state influence these dynamics. A broad global turn toward neoliberalization – a governing philosophy emphasizing markets and market logic over traditional state intervention in economic, social and environmental concerns – has provided additional authority to some already-powerful private actors in environmental disputes (McCarthy, 2004). While "the planetary character of the ecological crisis" has put more emphasis on varied global institutional arrangements and networks of private and civil society entities than on the state itself (Peet et al., 2011: 27), some argue that the complex nature of contemporary environmental and social problems "means that the state is coming back" (Ioris, 2015; Parenti, 2014). This is because the state's role as "mediator and a champion of the demands of groups, classes and class fractions" (Ioris, 2015: 11) is central to solving socioecological crises, and the state is often the only capable actor that can coordinate and enforce rules at higher levels to regulate the interaction and impact of society on the environment. State power, however, is experienced by society in ambivalent ways. Some segments of society may dislike state interventions because of their distributional implications or out of a broader distrust borne of prior experiences. In other cases, social groups may support and demand state interventions to address environmental crises and social inequalities. Still others, who might embrace the neoliberal ideal that practices should be governed by market forces alone and not by states enforcing the political choices of a population, seek to constrain the power of states to govern uses of the environment.

The process by which states define and execute interventions to address inequalities also needs to be considered, as the state itself is a complex assemblage of actors. Its various goals are often at least partially in conflict with one another, if not outright mutually contradictory (for example, one government agency may devote itself to conserving habitats for sensitive species while another works to promote resource extraction that degrades those same habitats). Further, achievement of these varied goals is contingent upon the coordination of a wide array of actors – not all of whom are necessarily faithful to official state aims, and some of whom may operate largely outside of the reach of the state apparatus (Funder and Marani, 2015). Research on bureaucracies shows that power struggles are often pervasive within these organizations, as well as between the organizations and the larger society in which they operate. Lipsky's (1980) study of "street-level bureaucrats", for example, details the work of government agents that directly interface with the public, finding that they cope with limitations, create routinized schemes for dealing with ambiguity and ultimately make political decisions regarding the distribution of government goods and services within a context characterized by insufficient resources, unclear policy direction and attempts by higher-level administrators to constrain their discretion. The interactions of these front-line agents of the state with the public they serve have been described as "a civil wrestling match to establish the purpose and boundaries of the encounter and the respective rights and obligations of the two (or more) principals" (Moore, 1987: 84).

At the same time, many scholars – especially in the field of environmental management – have observed a growing trend toward policy implementation based not solely in the power of bureaucracies but rather in networks of state and non-state actors. The concept of coproduction describes an arrangement in which the beneficiaries of a government good or service participate with government entities in its delivery (Ostrom, 1996), and co-management refers to a broad array of natural resource models that involve the sharing of power and authority among various state and non-state actors (Berkes, 2009). For example, collaborative processes with representation from major stakeholder groups (e.g., local government, resource users, conservation interests, recreationists, local businesses) have become especially common in the management of public lands and waters in the US West, and in many places these have been informally integrated with longstanding formal and bureaucratic decision-making procedures (Cheng and Sturtevant, 2012). However, questions of power are no less relevant in co-management or coproduction than they are in more traditional bureaucratic governance; stakeholder involvement, community-based management models and private–public cooperation do not necessarily resolve issues of unequal access to power and resources (Dressler et al., 2010). Scholars have raised critical questions regarding which interests and social groups have the resources and availability to participate in collaborative processes, which voices are excluded and whose interests are ultimately served by these new forms of network governance (Reed, 2008; Robbins et al., 2009).

Such observations suggest that it is not enough to ensure the participation of multiple perspectives in environmental governance decision making. Transdisciplinary scientists will need to attend to questions of the distribution of power not only among scales (local, regional, national) but also among those interests that have been included in collaborative processes as well as those that remain absent owing to a lack of resources or recognition, or for other reasons. Similar questions pertain to the conduct of transdisciplinary research itself: the scientists and practitioners that are able to participate in any given project are unlikely to fully represent the range of relevant interests and perspectives at play. Governmental agencies involved in transdisciplinary research may represent particular (usually powerful) societal interests, and the knowledge they produce may serve those same interests. Non-governmental organizations are also not value-neutral, and attention should be paid to what perspectives civil society participants represent and what perspectives remain absent. In a similar vein, scientists themselves are social actors and their processes of knowledge production (including the problems deemed worthy of research, the kinds of data considered legitimate and how knowledge is applied) should be seen as fundamentally social processes with all of the implications for power relations implied therein.

Power beyond the state

Power relations inevitably shape environmental management decisions, and these decisions are likely to exacerbate existing conditions of inequality unless environmental managers explicitly consider and seek to address inequitable relations of power when making decisions. However, it is also the case that individuals in society can and do organize to combat existing relations of power and to improve environmental management in both local and extra-local contexts. Civil society can be an extremely powerful avenue for exercising the ability of social groups to enact social change, particularly when individuals effectively organize into civic associations to improve the conditions of their own lives and the lives of their neighbors (Tocqueville, 1835/2004).

One of the most familiar means for individuals to organize for change in environmental management in contemporary American society involves shifting consumer purchases and collectively advocating for consumer decisions that promote environmental responsibility in resource use. In societies where individuals are heavily reliant on identities as consumers (Meyer, 2015), it perhaps seems reasonable for mobilization to take the form of consumer movements. Through campaigns targeting, for example, unsustainable logging or agricultural practices, consumer movements have the potential to shift larger-scale environmental management of production to correspond to consumer concerns or to perhaps even nudge environmental policy through altering what are considered acceptable environmental impacts (Seyfang, 2005). There is some concern that collective action focused on shifting consumption may result in less engagement with more traditional forms of political organizing or activism; however, shifting consumption choices to reflect environmental values may support rather than detract from time and energy focused on enacting change through political processes (Willis and Schor, 2012). Political mobilization and forms of collective action have certainly changed over time, as technologies now enable people to communicate rapidly across space and time in order to physically congregate as a crowd or to digitally congregate around a cause. Both consumer-based and politics-based activism can take place through technologically enabled forms of digital activism. Digital media allows for rapid dissemination of consumer concerns and information about violations in socially sanctioned forms of environmental management, and managers in both private and public spheres must now contend with forms of digital civic engagement.

Some collective forms of mobilization involve full adoption of environmentally responsible practices, alternative technologies and alternative ways of living through new means of organizing work and home life to minimize environmental harm. Adopting renewable energy technologies at the residential scale is a form of consumer engagement that has the potential to shift resource management, energy policy and electric utility business practice (Graffy and Kihm, 2014). Alternative technologies, eco-villages and other forms of sociotechnical change allow individuals and groups of individuals to live according to their values in ways that change the environmental impacts of human life (Boyer, 2016); these forms of direct social change can also result in rippling impacts as local government units grapple with new building codes and zoning regulations to allow for new arrangements in everyday life (Schelly, 2017).

Whether through consumption choices, lifestyle decisions, digital mobilization or more traditional activism, individuals and groups of individuals in society can mobilize the collective power of individuals and organizations by vocalizing concerns, offering support or developing alternative options. In each of these cases, power is operating "from below" (Piven, 2008), from the realm of civil society, and can have important consequences for environmental decision making. In each of these cases, however, the same questions regarding who gets to participate, why and how remain essential for understanding participation in "power from below" and the role of collective mobilization in creating socioenvironmental change.

Research teams that include multiple perspectives, including those from outside of academia, can improve our understandings of power dynamics by drawing attention to actors and processes that would otherwise be excluded from academic analysis. Scott (1990), for example, argues that researchers can be misled if they only pay attention to the "public transcripts" of social interaction – the performances of domination and subordination visible to the public eye and captured in formal media. He urges us to pay attention to the myriad, often invisible, ways in which even the least powerful act, alone or in concert, to frustrate the domination of resources and people by the powerful (Scott, 1985, 1990). Forms of "everyday resistance" among the rural poor range from subtle uses of language to challenge the scripts of domination employed by the powerful (e.g., calling existing power relations into question using ambiguous language that is tacitly understood by other subaltern subjects) to bolder acts such as "theft, pilfering, feigned ignorance, shirking or careless labor, foot dragging, secret trade and production for sale, sabotage of crops, livestock, and machinery, arson, flight", as well as "poaching, squatting, illegal gleaning" and other clandestine acts (Scott, 1990: 188). Although the use of these tools of resistance does not give subjugated people anything near the measure of power possessed by dominant classes, it may complicate and even foil efforts to consolidate control over resources and populations. This is yet another example of how important it is for both scientists and environmental management decision makers to be attentive to issues of inequity and power; not doing so can both exacerbate conditions of inequality and contribute to ineffective management decisions that are resisted by those who are affected in ways that are perceived as unfair.

Among other implications, this perspective encourages a critical interpretation of common environmental problems such as arson, poaching, timber theft, livestock trespassing and similar issues. Jacoby (2003) and Montrie (2011), for example, suggest that the early history of American conservation can be seen, in part, as the use of state power to criminalize traditional and subsistence uses of land among poor rural populations on behalf of the interests of the wealthy – a process that was often frustrated by the insurgent activities of poor whites, recent immigrants, African-Americans and Native American populations. This perspective also challenges us to consider the limits of state power and the potential for varied forms of resistance among even the most subjugated populations. The "moral economy" (a shared set of understandings and moral considerations based in a common structural position) of marginalized groups and their diverse conceptions of environmental "commons" (Neumann, 1998; Newfont, 2012) may, indeed, serve as resources to contest practices of domination. These concepts can also be used to develop innovative, and more effective, tools of environmental management that may be beneficial for both conservation and for addressing social inequality, as suggested by the literature on common-pool resource management (Agrawal, 2002).

Integrating power considerations into research: insights from political ecology

The interdisciplinary body of scholarship in political ecology illustrates approaches to a more explicitly power-conscious engagement with environmental management research. Political ecology is presented as an alternative to "apolitical" accounts of human–environment relations (Robbins, 2012) influenced by Malthusian and Boserupian theories that rely upon simplistic causal links between population growth, poverty, environmental degradation and social conflicts (Blaikie and Brookfield, 1987; Gray and Moseley, 2005). Political ecology is characterized by at least three common assumptions. First, it rejects the nature–society dichotomy in which nature is conceived as a separate entity from society, a view that has been predominant during the development of capitalism as the justification for the continuous exploitation of natural resources (Moore, 2015). In political ecology, on the contrary, the dynamics of what we have come to know as "nature" – from ocean environments, managed forests and the atmosphere to nature parks and preserves – operate not independently of social and political processes but rather are strongly shaped and influenced by these same processes (Loftus, 2009; Neumann, 2005). Second, nature–society relations are, thus, considered intrinsically political because they are mediated by relations of power characterized by inequitable patterns of use and access to natural resources. In the exercise of political and economic power, there are always losers and winners because ecological relationships and environmental changes produce costs and benefits that are unequally distributed among social groups such as those defined by class, race, gender and other socially constructed categories (Moseley, 2005; Paulson and Gezon, 2005). Thus, critical questions pertain to who controls access to resources and who has the power to benefit from environmental changes. Third, political ecology criticizes the view that both causes and solutions to socioenvironmental problems must be locally based. Instead, it emphasizes the variables that operate across different geographical scales and levels to explain environmental changes and explains how these variables are embedded within institutions and frameworks that exist at different geographical and political scales (Paulson and Gezon, 2005; Peet et al., 2011).

Thus, a common metaphor utilized in political ecology scholarship is that of "chains of explanation" (Blaikie and Brookfield, 1987) – referring to the ways that local interactions between social groups and their environments are explained by their connections to higher-level political–economic processes that may include such disparate influences as economic structures, the domination of resource access by government agencies, longstanding patterns of social inequality or prevailing discourses of conservation and development. Political ecologists also pay attention to how power is contested from below, for example via highly visible social movements or by more subtle forms of resistance (Zimmerer and Bassett, 2003). These concepts and frameworks suggest that both corrective and persuasive forms of influence are constantly at play in questions of environmental management. Corrective influence may be most apparent through the use of formal sanctions for particular kinds of environmental behavior. For example, a prevalent theme in political ecology concerns conflicts between powerful government environment or natural resource agencies and the peasant populations that depend on those resources for their livelihoods (Montrie, 2011; Neumann, 1998; Peluso, 1992). These state agencies may use various techniques ranging from control of scientific information to the use of deadly force to control people and natural systems. At the same time, peasant populations may resist via means that also range from subtle to overt, drawing on their own intimate knowledge of the land and on moral economies that exist outside the reach of the state. Further, political ecologists caution that we should be aware of power imbalances even in cases where such overt conflict is absent. Seemingly neutral and technocratic activities may act through "chains of explanation" to define natural and historic conditions, invisibly reinforce state justifications for control and reproduce existing inequalities. And although rural communities are typically assumed to be largely homogenous and characterized by close relations of mutual support, in reality they are often riven by internal inequalities and power struggles (Agrawal and Gibson, 1999).

Engagement with political ecology suggests the need to view environmental management decisions, policies, institutions and outcomes through multiple conceptions of power. The most overt instantiations of power may consist of threats, coercion, implementation and enforcement of laws, and other visible forms of domination and resistance. This kind of power relation is implicated in environmental management dynamics through, for example, the use of state power to craft environmental legislation or enter into intergovernmental agreements, the use of the state's "monopoly" on legitimate violence to enforce laws (e.g., environmental protection, resource extraction and waste disposal laws), the actions of environmental agencies vis-à-vis communities that depend on natural resources or that are disproportionately exposed to environmental harms, or the mobilization of publics to defend or assert rights related to natural resources and environmental quality. Subtler manifestations of power may still make themselves visible through the traces they leave in the form of claims of expertise, the use of seemingly technocratic practices that consolidate power and make competing knowledges invisible, discourses of environment and development, the symbolic components of environmental disputes and the internalization of relations of inequality on the part of subaltern populations. A key lesson from political ecology is that these and other manifestations of power are not merely relevant to the fields of sociology or political science, but instead have profound implications for environmental and resource conservation, landscape patterns, the dynamics of processes such as wildfire and soil erosion, and the functioning of global carbon cycles. Indeed, the growing recognition of the coupled nature of social and ecological systems (Liu et al., 2007) implies that environmental analyses that omit questions of power are necessarily incomplete.

Conclusion

Power in environmental management includes both the diverse tools and practices of state-led influence as well as myriad forms of domination and resistance within and between social groups regarding access to environmental goods and exposure to environmental harms. Environmental management relies upon regulatory tools of corrective influence, as well as on persuasive influence, a more indirect and, often, invisible form of power that may nonetheless face resistance from affected groups. Acknowledging the ways that environmental management can perpetuate social injustice is an essential first step, and the conceptual and methodological tools of political ecology for transdisciplinary research offer the essential next step for improving environmental management by grappling with fundamental issues of power, inequality and the environment. There is no way for transdisciplinary research – or any other research approach – to neutralize questions of power in knowledge production and application. However, by conscientiously incorporating diverse scientist and practitioner perspectives and explicitly considering the role of relations of power in the problem context, transdisciplinary research endeavors can make power relations more visible and help ensure that their influence on research processes and outcomes does not go unacknowledged. Moreover, it can help to define or redefine critical issues, empower stakeholders and encourage social engagement.

A serious treatment of the role of power in environmental management carries a number of implications, some of which may discomfort those accustomed to a less explicitly political approach to analysis. It implies the need to pay close attention to patterns of inequality – including unequal access to the harms and benefits associated with environmental decisions – and the myriad social processes that reproduce patterns of inequality. It implies the need to look beyond what Scott (1990) terms the "public transcripts" of social interactions to discover the sometimes-hidden ways in which social groups wield power and resist domination.

It implies considering not only the overt manifestations of power but also the subtle and indirect means by which power is exercised. And it means taking a critical perspective on the research process itself to analyze ways in which it, too, may be implicated in patterns of domination. Despite presenting challenges to research as usual, contending with issues of social power can make for better environmental management and better scholarship.

Acknowledgments

This work was supported by the National Science Foundation's Partnerships in International Research and Education Program grant IIA no. 1243444 and Research Coordination Network Program grant CBET no. 1140152.

PART II

Integrating diverse sectors and disciplines into transdisciplinary environmental management research

4 Integrating across sectors and disciplines: transdisciplinary teamwork challenges and strategies

Kathleen E. Halvorsen, Jessie L. Knowlton, Robert M. Handler, Chelsea Schelly and Erin C. Pischke

Introduction

As discussed in Chapter 1, transdisciplinary (TD) research groups by definition include interdisciplinary (ID) sets of scientists working together with representatives of groups from other sectors. These sectors can include industry, government, communities (geographic, indigenous, etc.), and non-governmental organizations (NGOs) from the non-profit realm (Bornemann et al., 2017; Kooiman et al., 2008; Hadorn et al., 2008). We define ID environmental research groups as those that include members from two or more of the following disciplinary types: social, natural and engineering sciences (Conrad, 2002; Halvorsen et al., 2016). TD environmental research teams are, at their core, small or large groups of people working together (Levi, 2016).

Sociological research on human groups reveals that successful groups must interact over time, have a social structure, share a common purpose and self-identify as a group (Babbie, 1994; Stokols et al., 2008). The stages of group cohesion and effectiveness development are often referred to as "forming, storming, norming, [and] performing" (Kirschner et al., 2015: 63; Levi, 2016) drawing from Tuckman and Jensen's (1977) early work. Tuckman and Jensen's (1977) findings point us to the fact that the development of an effective group is a process that takes time, a finding supported by many in the TD research field (Turner et al., 2016).

These factors become more important *and* more difficult to achieve as groups become more heterogeneous (Halvorsen et al., 2016; Turner et al., 2016). Effective, cohesive ID research groups of some mix of social, natural and engineering scientists are difficult to create owing to high heterogeneity along many variables, including norms, cultures and epistemologies (O'Rourke and Crowley, 2013; Pischke et al., 2017; Reid and Mooney, 2016). However, they at least share an emphasis on research and scholarship and probably have at least a few members working in the same types of organizations, whether universities or research institutes. Moving beyond ID to TD brings together team members with none of these things in common from very different types of organizations with even more variable norms, cultures, and epistemologies (Buizer et al., 2011; Hadorn et al., 2008; Lang et al., 2012; Norris et al., 2016; Stokols et al., 2008).

This chapter explains why successful TD groups must have Babbie's (1994) characteristics that only develop over time (Hadorn et al., 2008; Halvorsen et al., 2016; Hollaender et al., 2008; Lang et al., 2012; Tuckman and Jensen 1977). It also discusses the particular challenges inherent in creating tightly integrated TD research groups (Harris and Lyon, 2013). We explain why social scientists bring invaluable expertise to such groups and why they are uniquely trained to facilitate their integration and success. The chapter concludes with a discussion of strategies that can increase the probability of shepherding research groups to high levels of TD environmental management integration.

In the sections and chapters that follow, Part II moves into a deeper discussion about including different types of sectors in TD research, including industrial and NGO staff (Chapter Five), government employees (Chapter Six) and communities of various types (Chapters Five and Seven). It also expands the discussion in this chapter to international TD teams that are doing cross-national research together (Chapter Eight). The chapters in Part III present case studies of TD research teams studying a variety of environmental management problems. These case studies explain how the teams applied some of the strategies described in this chapter, what challenges they encountered and how they dealt with them, and describe the outcomes they were able to create because they were TD.

Group dynamics

When one or more people come together to work, they must have a reason for committing time and energy to the group (Babbie, 1994). In work settings, having multiple tasks to balance and having limited resources both reduce the amount of time that individuals can devote to activities that do not meet personal, professional or organizational goals (Levi, 2016). It is fundamental to creating a successful TD environmental research group that members have a reason to join the group that corresponds to their existing professional identity and perception of the scope of their work (Hadorn et al., 2008; Halvorsen et al., 2016; Steingröver et al., 2010). Reasons can include a personal or professional commitment to understanding and solving the environmental problem described as the preliminary reason that the group has been formed.

In order to function as a group, a successful TD science team must also have some form of social structure (Babbie, 1994; Klein 2008; Turner et al., 2016). Social structure includes the positions held by group members (for example, leader, initiator, or specified subgroup leader) and the roles or behaviors associated with these positions. Without clear social structure, members will find it difficult to know what roles they are expected to adopt and internalize. A lack of leadership will problematize the group's ability to conduct work in a high-quality and timely manner. The development of social structure, including positions and roles, will typically be iterative, with an initial leader or leaders convening the group and with the evolution of additional positions and roles over time, ideally in response to group needs. Identifying those needs requires group interaction, whether in person or remotely via computer and other technology (Hadorn et al., 2008).

Relatedly, groups require shared norms or understood rules for behavior in order to interact efficiently (Babbie, 1994; Halvorsen et al., 2016; Harris and Lyon, 2013; Klein 2008). For instance, there are choices to be made about deadlines and how people will know what they are, rules about how work products will be shared, and expectations of how the group leader will behave and communicate their expectations to other group members. Some norms may be implicit because everyone understands them without discussing them. For instance, even though they come from diverse backgrounds, all team members probably understand everyone is going to have to do some form of work in order to achieve their objectives. Their personal and organizational norms around when work is done, how deadlines are set and enforced, and how shared goals will be defined and chosen, are however, unlikely to be shared across a diverse group (Hadorn et al., 2008). This means that some of these norms may need to be made explicit through discussion and explanation, and even formal documents, such as memoranda of understanding between the organizations members represent.

While individuals will have chosen to join the TD research group based on their understanding of the group's purpose, that purpose will probably change over time (Halvorsen et al., 2016; Hollaender et al., 2008; Levi, 2016; Tuckman and Jensen, 1977). Joining a group focused on studying a regional water scarcity problem may be initially enough for many members with water scarcity interests. However, such a broad topic will generally need to be refined, narrowed and explained based on context, funder requirements and group interests. Successfully developing an evolving focus that continues to interest all members and suit their needs requires sustained hard work and interaction (Babbie, 1994; Halvorsen et al., 2016; Steingröver et al., 2010). If the purpose of the TD collaboration evolves too far away from member needs, including real and perceived professional interests and commitments, those individuals will probably reduce their commitment to the work and may even leave the group.

Finally, although it seems elementary, members must identify as a group and share some sense of themselves as such (Babbie, 1994). If some members see the group as focused on economic development research and others see it as a water scarcity group, this will probably lead to challenges over time when those goals come into conflict or fail to be successfully integrated. Similar to the group objectives, an initial sense of group identity will typically evolve over time, but in order to retain all of the members, the individuals must interact to discuss and determine who they are and what type of work they are doing.

These key elements of successful groups may seem straightforward and even obvious. However, it has been our experience that they are often ignored when putting together TD or ID teams, especially when group leaders are inexperienced or funding deadlines loom. We assert that the sustained interaction to develop a shared purpose, identity and structure is even more important and more difficult when the group is diverse, as with a TD group (Halvorsen et al., 2016).

Imagine a group of physicists coming together to define a research problem, develop a proposal and implement a project. While the field of physics is inherently diverse, with some physics departments housing individuals studying everything from quantum particle physics to astronomy, the field itself is certainly less diverse than a group of researchers that includes geographers (social scientists), astronomers (natural scientists) and environmental engineers. Most PhD physicists probably trained in physics departments as both undergraduate and graduate students, attend physics conferences, publish in physics journals and apply for funding to physics programs. We would expect that they would often be housed in departments next to other physicists, teaching classes to physics students and sitting on committees with other physicists. In short, most of their training and professional career is likely to take place through working closely with other physicists. They will thus have thousands of hours of instruction from and interaction with other physicists, allowing them to develop an identity as a physicist, to understand the typical social structures, roles, norms and positions developed within large and small physics groups, and to develop a sense of shared goals with other physicists.

Now imagine this physicist sitting down to work with a geographer. If both are faculty, there will typically be some shared norms between them, but many others will be unknown and unfamiliar (Andersen, 2016; Buizer et al., 2011; Conrad, 2002). How do geographers design their research and what research problems do they study? To what agencies do they apply for funding? Do they tend to use hypotheses in their research conducted in a laboratory setting or do they use research questions and collect iterative data from qualitative interviews for the purpose of inductive analyses? Where do they publish? What underlying epistemological assumptions ground their research? What are their expectations with regard to authorship? The two individuals cannot presume shared answers to these questions (Landon et al., 2015).

We can now add a rural city manager to the TD group. While they probably have some form of university training, they may not have a graduate degree and probably have little exposure to research as a participant. Their day-to-day work probably involves managing employees who fix and clean streets, collect and treat waste, and carry out construction projects. Crises may be frequent, budgets tight and timeframes short. They are supervised by and subject to the year-to-year priorities of their mayor and city council. While they may share great passion for solving the environmental management problem upon which the TD research team is focused, incorporating them into a group with scientists is likely to be quite a foreign process for everyone involved (Agger, 2002). These effects may multiply if the team includes even more sectors (Buizer et al., 2011; Wiek and Walter, 2009).

In addition, issues around power dynamics complicate the picture. Scientists are often high-status professionals in our society with PhDs and many publications. Some are arrogant about their knowledge and expertise and look down upon people without similar years of academic training. Team members from other sectors may feel intimidated and disrespected. For instance, a TD environmental management team may include a community member with no college education and an NGO staff member with "just" a bachelor's degree. When TD team members talk across these sectors and professions, it is normal to have to work to get to shared language, yet that may be unclear to participants with less status or education who may feel less intelligent or valuable to the team if they do not understand every term that is discussed (Lang et al., 2012).

These issues come up between scientists as well. Traditional views of science may define social sciences as "HASS" (Humanities and Social Sciences) and physical sciences as "STEM" (Science, Technology, Engineering, and Mathematics), not so subtly suggesting that geography is a "soft" or "social" science whereas physics is "hard" or "real" science that requires no qualifier – it is just plain "science". This already sets up a power dynamic where one form of expertise is defined as "hard" or "real" and the other as "soft" or less than "real". It is inherent in the development of a successful collaborative work group that norms of effective communication across sectors and disciplines and, perhaps even more importantly, mutual respect be followed to ensure that all members feel valued and like full members of the team. These power dynamics threaten these norms.

It is therefore important that the leader of an ID team understands these challenges and has experience with strategies for overcoming them (Hadorn et al., 2008; Halvorsen et al., 2016; Hollaender et al., 2008; Knowlton et al., 2014). As described in Chapter One, social sciences are inherently critical to successful understanding of environmental problems and development of effective solutions to them. Social scientists therefore bring invaluable expertise to TD environmental research teams (Baerwald et al., 2016; Peters and Wals, 2013; Vatn, 2016). Moreover, their training in studying and understanding human systems, including the areas of social structure, culture and power dynamics common to many fields of history, geography, sociology, anthropology, policy sciences and political science can make them particularly skilled in acting as the glue in diverse work teams (Klein, 2008; Landon et al., 2015). These skills and training in understanding how groups function and learning to scientifically interrogate points of view different from their own makes many social scientists well positioned to be sensitive to and able to navigate work with diverse sets of colleagues.

Effective interdisciplinary and transdisciplinary research teamwork strategies

Finally, we recommend a series of strategies that can help overcome the challenges of working within an ID or TD environmental research team as described more fully in Halvorsen et al. (2016). First, it is important to begin to work together early. If it takes three months for a group of environmental engineers to create a successful proposal or publication, then it is likely to take twice as long for a group that includes social, natural and engineering scientists, for all the reasons described above. The group leader must prepare for this and expect to build in extra time to define and refine group norms, objectives, language, structure and identity (Babbie, 1994; Landon et al., 2015; Levi, 2016; Tuckman and Jensen, 1977).

Along those lines, it is helpful if the group leader has experience working within ID and/or TD research teams (Baerwald et al., 2016; Halvorsen et al., 2016). This experience will help them more deeply understand the challenges and feel more comfortable with strategies for overcoming them. Similarly, training in ID and/or TD teamwork, such as the Professional Development Seminars organized by the Inter-American Institute for Global Change Research (Pittman et al., 2016), Future Earth (Mauser et al., 2013) and the workshops organized and offered by the National Socio-Environmental Synthesis Center (Palmer et al., 2016) and other groups can go a long way toward ensuring that group leaders and members are more comfortable working within this challenging setting.

It can help if the core of the group has some experience working together on past initiatives or projects (Halvorsen et al., 2016; Harris and Lyon, 2013; Landon et al., 2015; Wiesmann et al., 2008). For instance, if the group will ultimately have 10 members, having two or three with existing positive relationships can set the tone for the larger group, especially members less experienced in TD work. In many ways, professional work, perhaps especially research-focused work, exhibits high levels of reciprocity (Hadorn et al., 2008; Levi, 2016). A healthy, collaborative relationship based in mutual trust and respect will enable core group members to jump-start the group as it moves toward more complex, abstract tasks and works through inevitable conflicts and challenges (Halvorsen et al., 2016; Harris and Lyon, 2013).

Relatedly, it is important to choose TD group members carefully (Halvorsen et al., 2016). Over time the research group will identify and refine necessary scientific expertise, but social skills are arguably equally important. Ability to feel comfortable and confident operating in an unfamiliar environment with very different disciplines is essential to TD research work. Some scientists are very much loners, used to having nearly complete control over processes and products. This will not be the case in an ID or TD research group. Not every scientist is well suited to such work. If the team leader plans to bring in a member known to be most comfortable with solo work, they should do so because their expertise is essential and they should have a plan for accommodating their work style. The creation of a successful larger TD research group will therefore often happen over time as core members identify new members with both valuable expertise and the social skills to work successfully within the group (Harris and Lyon, 2013). It is difficult to judge the social skills of an individual with whom someone has never worked – informal discussions with one or more team members who already know the prospective member may, in those cases, be particularly helpful. It is important to keep in mind that such discussions can also bring in explicit or implicit biases leading to the group losing a potentially valuable member – the two always need to be balanced. Finally, cultures and practices differ across disciplines with some disciplines being more likely to attract individuals that prefer to work alone. For instance, anthropology has a tradition of solo research and authorship. While social skills are important, team leaders should also be aware that they may need to compromise on this issue in order to include individuals with expertise vital to a particular research project.

It is particularly useful to ensure that a critical mass of the team members are known by one or more of the core members (Halvorsen et al., 2016; Harris and Lyon, 2013). Working within ID and TD research teams is difficult. Conflicts will develop. Members will be in situations where their professional identity is challenged. They may encounter rude or hostile questions and challenges to their expertise. Having a group where at least some of the members are comfortable enough to tolerate such difficulties can be very helpful (Harris and Lyon, 2013). Individuals being able to tolerate a trusted colleague asking a pointed question in the interest of advancing discussion and integration or having the skills to smooth over hurt feelings in those kinds of situations involving other members are abilities that are essential to building a well-integrated team product.

Conflict in ID and TD research teams is common (Conrad, 2002; Hadorn et al., 2008). As with other issues around group norms and coordination, it is important to discuss the group's preferred decision-making process early in their work together. For instance, some TD groups may prefer to take a majority rules approach to deciding issues when there is conflict. This approach risks alienating some, but also facilitates efficient decision making. Others may prefer to take a consensus approach, continuing discussion about an issue until a decision is crafted with which everyone can live. It is critical that the team leadership has the ability to work successfully across different modes of decision making (Turner et al., 2016). In the end, there are multiple modes for making group decisions; it is probably most important to discuss this early and agree which mode a particular research team will use rather than waiting until a fractious issue arises and tension is high.

Finally, it is particularly valuable to be explicit in terms of group positions, roles, norms and objectives when the group is particularly heterogeneous, especially since heterogeneity means that there is no presumption of shared norms around these elements (Halvorsen et al., 2016; Klein, 2008). Developing strategies for working together across time and space, as will generally be the case with TD research teams, and communicating those strategies and the accompanying expectations clearly and transparently is vital. Computer-based conference calling systems, cloud-based file storage, online scheduling tools and software that helps groups organize complex tasks can all be valuable tools for TD research work. However, the leader or leaders need to identify or work with support staff or other team members to identify these tools before or early in the group's work together. Similarly, having a clear structure for the different positions and responsibilities members will contribute is essential. Rules around deadlines matter; for instance, will a 24-hour reminder be sent out before group meetings? Where and how will the group meet? If they are working across many time zones, how will meeting times be communicated? All of these mundane but important work decisions become increasingly important when forming a TD research team.

In conclusion, although it is certainly more complex and time consuming to work within an ID or TD environmental research team, our experience in these groups has been overwhelmingly positive, with many group members continuing to work together on new projects after the original projects end. Aside from the personal and professional growth that comes with working in these teams, the complexity of today's environmental management problems necessitates ID and TD approaches. We hope that this chapter and book as a whole motivate other teams to undertake this important work, and that by sharing our experiences other teams can avoid some of the common stumbling blocks that come with ID and TD collaboration.

Acknowledgments

This work was supported by the National Science Foundation's Partnerships in International Research and Education Program Grant IIA no. 1243444 and Research Coordination Network Program Grant CBET no. 1140152, as well as the Inter-American Institute for Global Change Research's CRN3105 grant.

5 Transdisciplinary research teams: broadening the scope of who participates in research

Erin C. Pischke, Kathleen E. Halvorsen, Tuyeni Heita Mwampamba, Lily House-Peters, Amarella Eastmond, Lucía Pérez Volkow, Mayra del Carmen Fragoso Medina and Marcella Ohira

Introduction

Conducting environmental governance research with teams that intentionally include a wide array of social actors allows different sets of interests, experiences, skills, values and knowledge to contribute to the research process (Nasiritousi et al., 2016). Such transdisciplinary teams are much more likely to explore the multiple dimensions of environmental governance as understood and experienced by different social actors, and to develop an understanding of the problem that, from the onset, is better suited to addressing its social and ecological system complexity.

Research teams comprising diverse social actors must, by their very nature, invest more time and resources into communication, debate and negotiation than more homogeneous teams (Jasanoff, 2004; Lemos and Morehouse, 2005; Kirk-Lawlor and Allred, 2017). Indeed, a large component of transdisciplinary (TD) research is about managing the numerous, and often conflicting, expectations of its participants (Simon et al., 2003). However, it is precisely this process of co-creation of knowledge (Lemos and Morehouse, 2005) that stimulates social learning and innovation at the boundaries and intersections of traditional silos (Sillitoe, 2004). From the moment of identifying and framing the research question or problem to the point of agreeing on the appropriate methods of data collection and analysis and, finally, to building consensus on the most appropriate solutions to promote, the TD process must – first and foremost – ensure that a conducive environment exists in which research participants can deliberate and negotiate effectively and equitably (Phillipson et al., 2012).

In this chapter, we highlight the importance of expanding the range and diversity of social actors who participate meaningfully in TD research teams that address environmental governance issues, to include groups traditionally omitted in research, such as industry, non-governmental organizations (NGOs), private landowners, local community members and indigenous groups. For clarity, although scientists are social actors, we distinguish between team members with doctoral training in the social, natural or engineering sciences, referring to them as "scientists", and to representatives of the above types of groups as "social actors".

A key characteristic of TD research teams is the multiple working styles and cultures that each participating member brings to the collaboration, and the distinct sets of expectations that each member has of the process and outcomes of the research (Bammer, 2008). Consequently, while diversity is a key strength of TD teams, it can also create challenges. Managing expectations and developing a working culture that is conducive to all members and which achieves project objectives is, perhaps, one of the biggest challenges of managing TD research teams.

Our chapter is organized as follows. After explaining why diversity in research teams is important, we then describe the culture and expectations of each social actor type. We follow this with a discussion of the challenges of managing the diversity of such research teams, which include ensuring that all scientist and social actor perspectives are given equal standing or credibility; balancing and integrating across multiple and non-aligned objectives; taking into account cultural and language differences; performing parallel play instead of integrated efforts; and managing multiple motivations and expectations. Before concluding, we offer recommendations for overcoming these challenges.

Importance of including diverse actors in TD research

Deciding which sectors to include in a TD research team is almost entirely context driven; the nature of a governance problem to be addressed, including its geographic, institutional and thematic scope, determines who the relevant actors are. For example, a research team addressing the social and environmental impacts of a natural gas extraction project (the governance problem) might include members of communities likely to be affected by the project (geographic scope), civil society and NGOs working in the project area who might influence or be affected by the project (geographic and institutional scope), staff from the company implementing the project (thematic scope) and various levels of governmental officials or agency staff (Buizer et al., 2011; Hadorn et al., 2008; Klein, 2008).

A preliminary stakeholder analysis that identifies all of the possible social actor groups that could affect or be affected by the research topic (i.e., the governance issue to be explored), followed by a characterization of the groups in terms of their relevance and influence, can be useful for understanding the full array of potential participants to invite, how groups are related to one another and the implications of including or excluding each of them in the research team. Given the shared characteristics of most environmental governance issues (e.g., complexity, cross-sectoral or international nature), it is possible to develop a preliminary list of likely candidates for the team that is improved with increasing knowledge of the local context. Indeed, an ideal team should include a combination of representatives from various sectors, resources for each social actor group so that they can participate equally in the TD project and sustained and equal participation across groups throughout the project.

Types of transdisciplinary actors

Because the challenges of including policy makers in TD research are discussed in Chapter Six, in this chapter we focus on NGOs of various types (environmental, but also community development, human health, etc.), business (industrial and commercial entities), private landowners (forest, farmland owners) and communities (indigenous, geographic, municipal, neighborhoods) (Agger, 2002; Kooiman et al., 2008; Hadorn et al., 2008; Harris and Lyon, 2013; Landon et al., 2015; Lang et al., 2012; Madsen and Ulhøi, 2015; Steingröver et al., 2010). The types of social actors appropriate to any given TD team will depend upon the type of environmental problem being studied and its context.

NGOs of various types focus on solving particular problems and protecting specific interests. They may provide valuable resources, such as staff and budgets to carry out projects, and they possess in-depth knowledge related to the problem in question. However, NGOs are constrained by needing to promote and advance their mission/agenda, must obtain funding to keep operating and they generally take a specific position, either in support or opposition to policy.

There are many examples of interest-specific NGOs that might be involved in TD research. Trade union NGOs are responsible for defending their members' interests (Nasiritousi et al., 2016). Their vision of society includes, amongst other things, civil and democratic rights for all, the elimination of poverty and the rule of law. By helping to improve working conditions, they serve the interests of society generally. By representing their interests, youth NGOs aim to empower young people to participate actively in society and improve their opportunities and living conditions (Nasiritousi et al., 2016). Environmental NGOs are organizations that often receive donations to carry out their work (Nasiritousi et al., 2016). Their goals include solving environmental problems and providing training and assistance related to conservation, agriculture and rural affairs. By acting outside the formal processes that government institutions must abide by, NGOs are often able to achieve more satisfactory solutions.

Business partners are generally market-driven, non-state actors who may offer unique perspectives to enhance understanding of and provide innovative solutions for problems, and they can provide financial resources or staff support to research agendas (Mantel et al., 2007). They work with industry to develop pro-business policies, strengthen trade and influence public opinion regarding the importance of markets. Their ultimate goal is to protect and further the nature of their economic interests.

Private landowners are individuals or groups with vested interests in how land and environment are managed and often exercise influence independently of governments (Cocklin et al., 2007). Varying greatly in structure, size and interests, the latter operate largely by influencing public opinion. Both types of groups may either be contributing to the existence of a problem and/or be impacted – negatively and positively – by business practices and environmental governance decisions. These groups can also provide valuable local knowledge to problem-solving efforts. They may be motivated to understand solutions to problems so as to minimize some undesired impacts and also to protect their interests.

Local community members are often better able to understand local problems than researchers because they experience them directly (Fischer, 2000). They are also well positioned to identify viable solutions for reducing the negative impacts they experience or could experience with a change in governance. Indigenous groups are a unique subtype of community groups; they often face additional challenges not experienced by other groups, experience unequal power relationships and are not able to exercise self-determination (Nelson et al., 2001). They may be the victims of discrimination and marginalization and, frequently, live in impoverished conditions that lack adequate access to public services. Moreover, their voices are rarely heard in decisions that directly concern them or their territories; yet, indigenous communities can provide valuable local knowledge to environmental governance projects. When the environmental problem being researched involves indigenous territories and/or communities, it is essential to include indigenous participation in a respectful and ethical way throughout all stages of the research process. Indigenous Peoples Organizations can play an important role by advocating for indigenous rights and sovereignty, encouraging participation, improving access to justice and widening opportunities for ethnic minorities (Nasiritousi et al., 2016). They often partner with NGOs to build capacity to successfully navigate the communication and negotiation platform dominated by other groups.

Aligning work cultures in TD research teams

Scientists and social actors involved in TD research often bring their own expectations and work cultures to the larger team. Work (or workplace) culture refers to various characteristics of their professions, disciplines or work environments that culminate in determining what is expected within that environment (behaviors and products), what are acceptable processes to follow (protocols), the ideologies and principles to uphold and the reward system at play (Hall, 2005). A professional culture communicates and reinforces its shared values, beliefs, attitudes, customs and behaviors learned during educational experiences and socialization processes (Hall, 2005). Professional cultures also share a common language (jargon), organizational structure and problem-solving approaches (Hall, 2005). The work culture of a sector or scientific discipline can be reflected in written and unwritten rules, such as the appropriate time to show up for a meeting, dress codes, gender roles, how to address superiors (e.g., by first name or professional title), how team leaders are selected (elected or assigned), the structure of teams (hierarchical or distributed) and working hours (e.g., whether overtime is expected or not). Even when team members originate from the same national culture, such as American or Mexican or European, important distinctions usually exist between team members owing to their training (e.g., natural versus social scientists) or the sectors they represent (corporate versus government versus academia). These disparities may need to be discussed and negotiated so that members' working requirements are acknowledged and an agreed-upon working culture prevails. Achieving a shared, acceptable work culture in which team members feel valued, respected and relevant to the team is necessary for effective TD research.

Challenges related to incorporating diverse social actors in research teams

While TD practitioners espouse the strengths of their research methods, they must also acknowledge that there are many challenges to incorporating diverse actors into TD research teams (Hadorn et al., 2006). Researchers venturing into TD research often underestimate how difficult it can be (Jahn et al., 2012). In this section, we review five key challenges related to incorporating diverse social actors into research teams along with scientists: conflict among diverse actors; equity among TD actors; cultural and language differences; parallel play; and managing multiple motivations and expectations.

Conflict among diverse actors

Epistemic differences, characterized by knowledge diversity and different ways of knowing, are a hallmark feature of TD research, where teams are composed of members from diverse scientific, practitioner and social actor backgrounds. Bringing together multiple, even conflicting, perspectives has been directly linked to achieving scientific innovations (Cooke and Hilton, 2015; Paletz and Schunn, 2010). Many scientists and social actors are motivated to participate in TD research owing to its potential to produce innovations, such as departures from pre-existing theories and thought patterns and the emergence of new behaviors, practices, policies and routines to resolve current problems and meet future challenges. Yet, while drawing competing worldviews into conversation via collaborative science can result in productive theoretical, methodological and empirical breakthroughs, it also offers a serious potential source of conflict within TD teams that can hinder their success.

Intra-team conflicts can be separated into multiple categories, including relationship conflict, process conflict and task conflict. In the literature, these categories of conflict have different correlations with the outcome of innovation. Relationship conflict (e.g., interpersonal incompatibility) is generally associated with negative TD research outcomes, while carefully managed process conflict (e.g., disagreement about how to do a task) and task conflict (e.g., dispute about the task being performed) have been associated with productive outcomes (Paletz and Schunn, 2010; Paletz et al., 2016). For example, well-managed conflicts in team research settings can produce positive long-term outcomes, including increased creativity and problem-solving success and decreased subsequent disagreements (Paletz et al., 2016).

Equity among TD actors

Participation can reinforce existing forms of privilege and relations of power and group dynamics may discourage the expression of some perspectives (Reed, 2008). When research extends beyond universities, it is difficult to ensure that scientist and social actor perspectives receive equal standing or credibility (Leavy, 2016). Scientists often lead TD research teams. Research priorities are not always aligned between scientists and their social actor collaborators (Schmidt and Pröpper, 2017). Furthermore, the process of building a TD research team and conducting TD research can reinforce existing forms of privilege, and relations of power and group dynamics may discourage the expression of dissent and minority perspectives (Reed, 2008). The credibility of TD research has also been questioned because many interested parties, especially local, non-scientist community members, may have insufficient experience to engage meaningfully in what are often highly technical debates (Reed, 2008).

For non-scientist participants, additional obstacles may complicate the extent of their participation in TD research. For example, NGOs typically have a fairly narrow mission, which may make it difficult for them to work with TD research teams more wedded to answering scientific questions using scientific methods rather than aiming to get any particular answer. It may be difficult for community members to participate and represent their community because there may be conflicting views on the issue that the TD team is studying. Furthermore, a working-class forest landowner may feel her knowledge is inadequate when working with highly trained scientists. The process and language of writing a research proposal for funding may be foreign and uncomfortable for many members of non-scientific organizations, making it harder for them to fully participate in a TD team (Schmidt and Pröpper, 2017).

Cultural and language differences

One fundamental problem is the lack of a consensual language to generate appropriate ways to handle transcendental frameworks, fundamental to TD research, while maintaining the usefulness of the disciplinary perspectives that are to be adopted (Attwater et al., 2005). The question of the orientation of TD research through philosophies and methodologies in different cultural contexts is another critical challenge (Attwater et al., 2005). There are cultural differences between how and when diverse social actors are meant to interact; when there are misunderstandings that arise, it can lead participants to feel as if they are part of unequal partnerships (Simon et al., 2003). Moreover, difficulties in overcoming differences in language, culture and scientific jargon can lead to turnover in participants and stakeholders (Schmidt and Pröpper, 2017).

Parallel play

A common obstacle to knowledge integration and convergence in research collaborations is parallel play, where individuals and/or subteams work side by side, but never achieve integration (Bailey et al., 2015). This is a trap recognized by Max-Neef (2005), who warns that accumulating diverse visions is not equivalent to achieving an integrative synthesis. Barriers to TD team formation can be seen across the diverse interests of actors involved, which may explain why successful integration is difficult. For example, unequal division of labor between scientists and social actor partners in TD research (different goals, outcomes and expectations) can create tensions; realizing that every partner country and individual has different tasks to do and interests related to the project, especially if they are not aligned, is especially difficult (Schmidt and Pröpper, 2017). Furthermore, paying lip service to the concept of TD research (saying you are doing it, but not actually doing it in practice) leads to a lack of ownership among research partners (Schmidt and Pröpper, 2017). For example, all actors who are involved in the process in theory or on paper may in reality not be equally incorporated into the process or be involved at all.

Managing multiple motivations and expectations

Arguably, TD research is very much about managing the expectations of the different participants, including the research process, timelines and desired outcomes. Social actors usually participate because they hope to gain something from the research process or the outcomes, even if it is only to confirm or dispute existing hypotheses about the research problem. Participation may be motivated by personal, institutional or other group-level objectives that are not part of the TD research objectives and which might not align with the common objectives either. Discrepancies might also exist between expected implementation timelines of different actors, such as the short-term agenda of government representatives, versus the long-term vision of NGOs, scientists and local communities (Schmidt and Pröpper, 2017). Making these contradictions explicit is highly recommended to increase the understanding of each actor and their position within the research project.

Social actor partners often have different agendas and problems to solve than scientists (Schmidt and Pröpper, 2017). While many research projects have commercial and industrial partners, involving them may be particularly challenging when the project conflicts with or does not lead to clear financial benefits for these organizations. In a competitive environment, corporate managers must always weigh their commitments and their ability to protect their organization's bottom line. Business values, cultures and interests may conflict with those of other team members, such as environmental NGOs who prioritize environmental protection over other goals (Simon et al., 2003). Industry may be more accustomed to working in research settings with scientists who receive industrial contracts to pursue a narrowly conceived research question with clear benefit for the funding company.

Overcoming TD research challenges

Challenges and obstacles that arise as a result of the diverse actors who participate in TD research must be effectively addressed. If not, collaboration may not succeed and the ability to achieve the research objectives and knowledge co-production outcomes may be compromised. The dynamics of the process of collaboration is an emerging area of research. This research attempts to better understand the best practices teams employ throughout every stage of the research process to overcome challenges, especially related to incorporating diverse social actors across the life of a project. In this section, we elaborate on strategies to mitigate the challenges discussed above. The strategies are: managing conflict and overcoming cultural barriers; constructing shared conceptual frameworks; boundary spanners; utilizing guided dialogue; and consilience workshops.

Managing conflict and overcoming cultural barriers

The ambiguity of outcomes associated with intra-team conflict requires attention to strategies and best practices for constructively managing conflict (Hinds and Bailey, 2003; Paletz et al., 2011). In particular, three types of conflict – epistemic, process and task conflicts – commonly arise in collaborative settings (Cooke and Hilton, 2015; Paletz et al., 2013). The goal of implementing these strategies is to minimize the potential for destructive forms of conflict while maximizing the potential for innovation and effective TD research outcomes. The extent to which collaborators are able to understand each other's perspectives, minimize misunderstanding and exchange knowledge via informal, unstructured dialogue serves to reduce the potential for more dangerous forms of conflict to emerge and persist (Pennington, 2008).

Effective group communication is also critical for managing conflict and transforming it into productive outcomes. Group communication is composed of both the effective transfer of information and collective relationship and identity formation, which can be especially helpful for groups from different cultures (O'Rourke and Crowley, 2013). Using intentional, structured dialogues focused on epistemology, team members can enhance their mutual understanding of the diverse ways of knowing that each actor brings to the team, and potentially mitigate future destructive forms of epistemic conflict from occurring (O'Rourke and Crowley, 2013). Other useful strategies include establishing a team rhythm through regular meetings and a predictable schedule and distributing information to all team members (e.g., meeting notes), in addition to the need for strong leadership to prioritize tasks and integrate materials (Crowston et al., 2015).

Constructing shared conceptual frameworks

Strategies that help teams construct shared conceptual frameworks may mitigate tensions associated with bringing together diverse actors with different ways of knowing and multiple perspectives, objectives, motivations, expectations, work cultures and languages in TD research. Research suggests facilitating constructive modes of diverse knowledge integration. Knowledge integration can occur across multiple stages of the research process, including idea generation and idea implementation. These strategies are effective as they stress collective learning and thinking and collaborative action focused around well-defined problems (Pennington, 2008). Recognizing that values and practices of scientific fields of knowledge are grounded in and serve to reproduce specific epistemologies, collaboration success depends on the cultivation, facilitation and management of environments conducive to ongoing cross-disciplinary interactions (Pennington, 2008; Pennington et al., 2013).

The early exploratory phase of collective thinking is important because this is the stage where participants construct shared conceptual frameworks in an attempt to become aware of and begin to understand one another's perspectives (Pennington, 2008). Strategies, such as joint planning and integrated execution of group activities, help to achieve collective intentionality, a characteristic of successful collaborations (O'Rourke et al., 2014). Finally, team actualization may occur when different perspectives are recognized and valued and the team evolves to accommodate the different perspectives into a shared common vision, making full use of all the expertise available within the team (Pennington, 2008).

Boundary spanners

To overcome the TD research problem of knowledge/information inequity among participants, group leaders can involve boundary spanners in their project. Research suggests that the presence of knowledge brokers (e.g., people trained in library sciences and information sciences) has a positive impact on team relationships as these people act as effective knowledge facilitators, helping to orchestrate information exchange across disciplinary boundaries (Crowston et al., 2015). These knowledge brokers, or boundary spanners, are important because they know how to effectively ask questions about disciplines that are not their own. Thus, knowledge brokers assist with creating continuities across diverse knowledge systems and can help reduce challenges related to communication frustrations, maintaining momentum between big meetings and ongoing uncertainty of project goals, misunderstandings and language barriers associated with transcending disciplinary boundaries (Crowston et al., 2015). To overcome other types of inequity, such as power or financial inequity, Pischke et al. (2017) suggest trust-building exercises to facilitate congenial working relationships; boundary spanners could be used to facilitate this as well. While overcoming financial inequality can be a difficult hurdle to overcome because of the legal and institutional restraints that may exist, Pischke et al. (2017) suggest finding ways to provide all research participants with their own subcontracts and funds as a way to provide all participants with some autonomy to spend funds.

Utilizing guided dialogue

Recognizing that "the epistemically multicultural character of collaborative cross-disciplinary research creates many challenges for those involved", O'Rourke and

Crowley (2013: 1938) also identify communication challenges as central obstacles to achieving interdisciplinary success. The authors introduce "guided dialogue" as a method of intervention to improve cross-disciplinary communication. Guided dialogue can lead to decreased difficulty of combining expertise from different worldviews and can facilitate diverse perspectives being brought into alignment. In cases where the strength of a problem and the similarity of the underlying values are strong enough, local dialogue between disciplinary interests can endure a process through which transcendence can occur (Attwater et al., 2005). As a common language grows based on recognized common values, disciplinary languages can become less dominant (Attwater et al., 2005).

Consilience workshops

Consilience is defined in the team science literature as according equal value to different perspectives and knowledge systems (e.g., natural sciences, social sciences, local knowledge). The objective of consilience workshops is for each team member and/or subteam to gain appreciation of the relevance of other members' expertise to their own work (Bailey et al., 2015). Conducting a series of consilience workshops over the life of a collaborative research process can facilitate a deeper understanding of individual team members' work and expertise, including the time, financial and intellectual demands of that work; the policy relevance of the work being done; and the importance of communicating findings to the broader world of policy makers and local stakeholders. This process may begin to break down former relations of power that disadvantage some groups' standing over others (Reed, 2008).

Recommended strategies for including diverse actors in transdisciplinary research teams

In this section we offer several recommendations for including a variety of TD actors into the environmental governance research process (see also Pischke et al., 2018). First, misunderstandings can be reduced by requiring scientists and social actors to spend time at the research site to gain firsthand knowledge of the research context (Wickson et al., 2006). Allowing the TD research project to be an iterative process by revisiting data and knowledge from different actors throughout the process can help facilitate an integrated understanding of the problem and how it might be addressed (Wickson et al., 2006). One recommendation is to find where different epistemologies overlap and focus on those areas of common ground in the research (Wickson et al., 2006).

Recommendations for overcoming barriers to cultural and language differences include using clear, non-jargon-laden communication so that all parties can understand and benefit from TD research collaborations and their outcomes (Brandt et al., 2013). Engaging with an indigenous community in a culturally appropriate way and ensuring clear benefits from the research project from the outset are important first steps for gaining trust and establishing good cross-cultural communication.

Ideally, the indigenous team member's role is that of a boundary spanner, facilitating the collaboration, smoothing over potential conflicts and negotiating an outcome, which, as far as is possible, meets everyone's expectations. This can include being respectful of differences in how people communicate (i.e., language and vocabulary) and the use of guided dialogue (Attwater et al., 2005).

TD teams can overcome existing power imbalances by ensuring that all actors involved set and agree on the terms of the collaborative partnership (Simon and Schiemer, 2015). This process should be culturally appropriate, relevant for the context in which the research takes place and sensitive to past imbalances between stakeholder groups (Simon and Schiemer, 2015). Another way this can be accomplished is to organize different opportunities for all participating actors to conduct fieldwork so: (a) all participants get a general impression of the place, conflict, geography, etc. (Simon et al., 2003); (b) they make concrete connections between theory and practice; and (c) they become comfortable working with each other.

Conclusion

TD research teams need to find a workable balance between appreciating and benefiting from the diversity inherent in the team while also cultivating a shared vision (Harris and Lyon, 2014). Leveraging the wide diversity of problem perspectives, skills and team member capacities is crucial for TD teams to work. Yet, for the team to function and deliver timely results, they need to have a homogenous understanding of the problem, synchronize their expectations, develop a common vision and generate a shared working culture (Meyer, 2014).

Recent trends suggest that TD research has several benefits, including the ability to approach problems with multiple methods and analytical frameworks, the integration of diverse and local perspectives, the capacity to view problems holistically and the integration of social actor partners. TD approaches often lead to robust project outcomes and direct, context-specific solutions to challenging socioenvironmental issues. Working in large, diverse teams can be also be time consuming and frustrating. Scientists and social actors need to agree on what values and types of knowledge they have, what they have in common and where they differ (Jahn et al., 2012). The challenges of incorporating diverse social actors into research teams fall into several categories: conflict among diverse actors; equity among TD actors; cultural and language differences; parallel play versus integrated efforts; and managing multiple motivations and expectations.

The focus of TD research on ensuring that no single discipline is automatically prioritized makes negotiation between the members a necessity. Negotiation with full understanding of the multiple perspectives that exist, in and of itself, is a key ingredient for stimulating innovative problem solving that generates outcomes that are more likely to be relevant to society. They also generate solutions that have been developed through democratic and transparent processes (Nowotny, 2003). The process of bringing different actors into a discussion can facilitate an understanding of why people act in the ways they do or identify cultural (or other) reasons for certain practices (Hadorn et al., 2008). Scholars should share their experiences so we can collectively work towards improved processes and outcomes.

Acknowledgments

This work was supported by the National Science Foundation's Partnerships in International Research and Education Program grant IIA no. 1243444 and Research Coordination Network Program grant CBET no. 1140152, as well as the Inter-American Institute for Global Change Research's CRN3105 grant.

6 Administrative roles in environmental governance research: scientists incorporating policy makers

Robert A. LaFave and Jennifer L. Dunn

Introduction

Involving policy makers in scientific research is an emergent issue as policy makers and managers increasingly require specific scientific expertise to solve complex problems and scientists increasingly understand the importance of working with policy makers to craft science more likely to contribute to solving these problems. Policy makers often describe scientists as lacking understanding of their particular situation or challenges and therefore see their research as irrelevant (Gibbons et al., 2008). However, the increase in complex environmental problems has started shifting this from what each party can achieve independently to how they can work together in a collaborative process. Roux et al. (2006) argues that criticism between the two parties comes from a mutual understanding of their dependence on one another. For instance, a number of studies have enhanced understandings of how to structure institutions so that policy actors and scientists can better interact and collaborate (Cortner, 2000; Dovers, 2005; Briggs, 2006). The results can help research teams better anticipate the research needed to inform policy.

During the process of writing and summarizing the literature three lessons about effective environmental governance and administrative engagement emerged. They are:

1. earlier engagement;
2. engagement as a way around organizational constraints (i.e. funding, lack of knowledge);
3. trust amongst actors can lead to future engagement (reciprocity).

In this chapter these three themes will continue to be highlighted in case studies and discussions of the barriers, benefits and challenges, and solutions to engagement.

Who are policy makers?

As Table 6.1 shows, policy makers are diverse in their positions, roles, and tools. Policies include a broad suite of tools used to "...influence citizen behavior and achieve policy purposes" (Schneider and Ingram, 1990: 511). These authors identify policy tool categories: authority, which assumes the ability to control behaviors; and the remaining four types (capacity, incentive, symbolic, and learning), all of

Table 6.1 Types of policy actors and tools, outputs, roles and barriers related to transdisciplinary research teamwork

Policy actors	Outputs	Policy tools	Role of research	Role of actor in research	Constraints to actor's participation in research
Federal and state legislators	Federal and state statutes	Authority (laws), provides power to administrative agencies to enforce law; for policy compliance	Research is used to inform legislators to propose or support bills in the legislature	Request for research findings	Time, lack of knowledge about the research process
Federal and state administrative agencies	Rules/regulations, plans, programs	Authority (regulations), capacity, incentive, learning	Research is used to inform legislators and follow agency missions	Conduct and request research	Funding and occupational constraints
Local legislators and administrators	Local statutes	Authority (regulations), power to enforce local ordinances, local dollars to fund research on problems	Research is used to help with fixes to local problems	Street-level bureaucrats are in a position to utilize their administrative discretion to engage with scientists, but may be limited owing to constraints from legislators	Funding, networks and knowledge

which assume that behaviors are not completely under the control of a given entity and that they must be encouraged or barriers to them must therefore be removed. These connections closely interconnect understandings of crafting effective public policies with social science fields that study the motivations for human behavior.

Policy actors at each level and stage in policy development and implementation processes include both visible and hidden participants (Kingdon, 2011). Visible participants are those who set agendas and receive media attention, particularly when formulating formal law, while hidden participants are more likely to be agency staff, scientists and others who contribute to policy solutions. For instance, policy entrepreneurs working to address problems with public policies may be hidden or visible, but all tend to catalyze actions and take advantage of opportunities to advance particular solutions.

The Clean Water Act: role of policy actors and research

Policy makers at various levels need to be able to draw on research findings to develop effective policies. This will sometimes necessitate their involvement in transdisciplinary (TD) research teams. For example, the Clean Water Act of 1972 (CWA), while leading to improvements in water quality impairments that resulted from point source pollution, was largely unsuccessful in reducing non-point source pollution (NPSP; Mandelker, 1989; Zaring, 1996). In 1987, further amendments by Congress (elected officials) to the CWA included Section 319, a program intended to support states and tribes in their work to reduce and remediate NPSP. The law, an authority policy tool, required states to develop a program to manage NPSP and meet water quality standards. Through section 319(h) of this program, the United States Environmental Protection Agency (US EPA) provides funding to states to support their NPSP management programs, largely through developing and implementing numerous other, non-authority, policy tools (33 C.F.R. §1329). Federal policy actors (often regional US EPA administrators) are responsible for ensuring that states have approved NPSP programs and are making satisfactory progress toward NPSP goals. Legislators, while typically not engaged in research, use research findings when developing policies to incorporate the state of science into policy solutions (instrumental use of science; Weible, 2008). They also may use or distort science for political purposes to support their policy solutions or simply absorb knowledge over a longer period of time, which alters their opinions about policy solutions (Weible, 2008).

Since the mid-1990s, the US EPA has encouraged the use of watershed-based planning and implementation, developing guidance and tools for states and projects to use. Because, in general, there are very few authority or regulatory tools in place that require individuals to engage in behaviors that prevent or remediate NPSP, non-regulatory policy tools provide the primary means of achieving NPSP goals (US EPA, 2011). For instance, Hardy and Koontz (2008) note how states have used their 319 funds to support collaborative watershed groups. Collaborative watershed groups often partner with specific entities who can provide research skills and other technical assistance to help them achieve their goals (e.g. Floress et al., 2011).

Each state, within the boundaries of their NPSP program, distributes their funds to support staff responsible for administering 319 funds and to distribute to NPSP activities within their state (US EPA, 2013). Some states fully or partially fund activities through their own state-funded programs, using 319 funds solely (e.g. New York) or partially (e.g. Wisconsin) to support staff. Regardless, a combination of federal, state, local and private funds is used to plan and implement watershed-based NPSP activities, including monitoring and evaluation. States generally solicit proposals from projects for their activities (US EPA, 2011). Thus, policy actors from administrative agencies include, at a minimum, state-level administrative agency personnel who develop broad policies for the distribution of such funds along with protocols for monitoring, evaluation and reporting, and local staff who coordinate and help lead NPSP activities. Local staff may convene meetings to garner support to apply for funding, or alternatively, are contacted by other local actors to participate in scoping and proposing a specific project. Once a project begins, watershed plans are commonly developed to guide the project's activities, once again by planning a variety of non-authority policy tools (capacity, incentive and learning) intended to support behavior change. At each step, there are opportunities for fully engaging with agency staff on research that supports this work. This example shows how meeting a specific agency mandate can provide an incentive for staff to work with TD research teams. However, that does not mean that the process is easy.

Barriers to engagement

Woodrow Wilson, one of the founders of the modern public management movement in the US, believed in the power and necessity of collaboration between scientists (experts) and managers (or policy makers) (Roux et al., 2006). The benefits of such engagement seemed evident to him, yet over time, barriers have grown between these two groups, hindering the creation of effective TD research teams that include both scientists and policy makers, to the detriment of both groups and their ability to solve societal problems. The barriers that exist today have professional, institutional and political aspects that need to be understood in order to overcome them.

Some barriers stem from a simple lack of mutual understanding. A scientist is interested in a research question, expanding scientific knowledge within a given field, and providing fixes (although these fixes may not be considered useful or relevant by policy makers). A manager/policy maker is interested in "fixes" (practical solutions) or the application of knowledge within the realm and context of their particular responsibilities and challenges (Roux et al., 2006). Thus, both groups often view each other with suspicion.

Many scientists believe that they have the answers to problems, if managers would only ask them, and managers believe that scientists do not offer anything practical

(Roux et al., 2006). This often leads to a lack of trust, which unsurprisingly contributes to a lack of engagement and finger pointing between both groups. Managers/policy makers may view scientists as potentially self-serving, focused only on career advancement related to their own research results, unable to communicate information in a useful way, and not concerned with the practical world in which the policy maker works. Likewise, scientists can view policy makers as largely ignorant, too focused on day-to-day operations to consider long-term planning, research and development, and the complexity of ecosystems (Roux et al., 2006). Both of these views are problematic, and harmful to effective TD research team building.

These perspectives are shaped by the institutions within which policy makers and scientists are embedded. Scientists are often employed by research organizations with reward systems very different from the public agencies and governments that employ policy makers. Scientific success is measured through numbers of peer-reviewed publications and citations and for garnering competitive research funds (Gibbons et al., 2008). Managers and policy makers are part of more formal top-down power structures where philosophy may be dictated, practicality is valued, many competing interests need to be accounted for, time horizons are critical, and fiscal constraints limit the breadth of options that can considered (Gibbons et al., 2008). Differences between the goals of their organizations mean that scientists and policy makers must deliver very different outcomes to their employers. This can exacerbate misunderstandings between the two groups.

Lastly, politics can be a barrier between scientists and policy makers. Legislators can exert control over public agencies, which can restrict managers/policy makers from engaging in TD work, through rule changes, reduced budgets for certain activities and changes in government objectives (Wilson, 2000). As a result, an agency is charged with performing a service, but in the delivery of that service policy makers are well aware of what they cannot do in the performance of the service. While politics are ubiquitous at all levels of government and within agencies and bureaucracy, constraints are seen more commonly in agencies, particularly federal agencies, which have less administrative discretion and are more beholden to the priorities of the legislature (Rosenbloom, 1983). Typically those with more administrative discretion are found at the local level, in what Michael Lipsky calls the "Street-Level Bureaucrat". Street-level bureaucrats are defined as "public service workers who interact directly with citizens in the course of their jobs, and who have substantial discretion in the execution of their work" (Lipsky, 1980: 3). Street-level bureaucrats are more likely to have the political freedom and fewer constraints to partnering in TD teams than upper-level managers or policy makers. These limitations can be frustrating to work through, but overcoming them is necessary to impact change. Understanding these forces can help scientists understand where policy makers are coming from and how to move forward in creating practical solutions to problems.

Scientists and policy makers have differing goals, incentives, pressures and supervisors. Professional, institutional and political forces create barriers that can seem difficult to overcome and thwart progress. By better understanding these barriers and appreciating each other's perspectives, paradigms can shift and meaningful change in policy and our society can take shape (Gibbons et al., 2008). What was evident to Woodrow Wilson nearly a century ago is still relevant and holds as much promise then as it does today, if scientists and policy makers can work to overcome their barriers to engagement.

This section highlights the barriers between policy makers and researchers that can be serious threats to successful solutions. However, engagement between these groups holds the power to alleviate barriers and create mutual understanding. It can lead to understanding that not only produces practical solutions, but can also help scientists find necessary funding to help make meaningful impacts. In order to overcome professional and political barriers that stand in the way of collaboration, engagement of policy makers early in the TD process is key. While this can be difficult, the benefits of this engagement and collaboration can unleash the potential to craft meaningful solutions.

Benefits and challenges to policy maker–research team collaborations

Involving policy makers in TD research has its benefits (i.e. knowledge transfer, establishment of new relationships and consensus decision making) and disadvantages (politics and power struggles, and uncertainty; Ross et al., 2003). Working together to solve complex environmental problems is a difficult task in itself as the barriers to engagement are expansive; however, collaboration can lead to narrowing of the gap between science and policy (Gibbons et al., 2008). By involving policy actors in the decision-making process, they can build their understanding of the state of the research and problem over time, rather than through a single report.

This can lead to more buy-in from the political actors, a transfer of knowledge and more informed decisions in the political arena about a given problem (Walshe and Rundall, 2001). A vested interest in the research process leads to the policy makers being less critical of the process and more trusting of the results that the process yields (Lomas, 2000). However, this can be a reciprocal relationship, whereby involving policy makers in the research process also opens the doors for scientists to better understand the policy process. This reciprocity can lead to more authentic dialogue between political actors and scientists and can ultimately lead scientists to be better advocates in policy settings. Those who take on this role are more likely to develop practical solutions to policy problems in their research that take into account institutional, budgetary and legal constraints (Pannell, 2004). Collaborations of this nature allow for policy actors and scientists alike to become more effective communicators (Gibbons et al., 2008; Pannell, 2004). Actors become more adept at overcoming the technical language barriers between the two fields and start to agree on a common language to explain each of their positions and the overall problem they aim to solve (Briggs, 2006).

Collaboration can directly lead to establishment of new relationships between policy actors and scientists, and indirectly lead to cooperation on other projects or policy problems once trust is built. Trust can be a significant barrier to collaboration as each actor works to establish themself as a credible source of information and decision maker (Gibbons et al., 2008). Successful partnerships are built on shared motivations, which entail more than just a common commitment to a goal; they also require mutual trust, internal credibility and agreed commitment (Emerson and Murchie, 2011).

The dissemination of TD research findings through multiple mechanisms can be an advantageous outcome of collaboration between scientists and policy actors. By involving policy actors in the research process, the tangible outcomes of the project are spread beyond the relatively closed circle of scientific publications. The findings are likely to be spread through several levels of government involving both policy makers and managers. This provides the scientists with the opportunity to have a greater impact with their results and has the potential to provide them other opportunities owing to the increased visibility of their research (Uzochukwu et al., 2016). Additionally, it helps build trust among the policy makers and scientists as they begin to develop a set of common language and understanding about a given problem.

While there are many benefits to involving policy makers in TD research, it can bring additional challenges, such as in communication. For instance, scientists are generally trained to emphasize the limitations and uncertainties associated with their findings. Policy makers, on the other hand, need to act regardless of these limitations. Finding a common language to explain and overcome these issues can be difficult.

Limited time and budgets can also create barriers to policy maker involvement in TD research (Lavis et al., 2003). Time scales for scientists and policy makers are also different, based on funding cycles and legislative sessions, which can make cooperation between them impractical (Lavis et al., 2003; Walshe and Rundall, 2001). Scientists have to stay attuned to the changing political climate and understand the policy process to be able to effectively present findings to policy makers in a timely manner (Stevens and Depper, 2016). Scientists may view policy processes simplistically, assuming that findings supported by research should automatically translate into policy outcomes without understanding the underlying complexities of garnering support for new public policies (Day and Gunton, 2003).

Other potential problems can arise because scientists and policy makers have different target audiences to which they must appeal (Lavis et al., 2003). TD research driven primarily by policy makers will tend to accommodate political agendas and climates and be very problem-focused. Scientists tend to be more open to innovative or exploratory research based on the state of science and the problem at hand (Uzochukwu et al., 2016). Often, failures in collaboration are due to organizational constraints rather than a lack of motivation or funding (Ansell and Gash,

2008). They both have to work within their own organizational frameworks. If these organizations disincentivize participation in TD research, this reduces the likelihood of success (Freeman, 1997; Lavis et al., 2003). Policy makers must be able and motivated to use the evidence-based research outcomes of the collaboration and scientists must be able and motivated to craft research designs sensitive to policy agendas (Leach, 2006; Newig and Fritsch, 2009; Ross et al., 2003).

Mutual respect and trust are critical. If either scientists or policy makers believe that their position, organization or resources are not valued they are less likely to be engaged in the research process (O'Toole and Meier, 2004). One failed TD research collaboration can prevent future work together, just as one successful collaboration where both parties meet their distinct needs can build trust, an important currency for establishing future collaborations.

Solutions

Engagement between scientists and policy makers is critical to helping scientists understand the challenges and constraints of policy makers and vice-versa, which enhances the ability of both groups to use science to benefit the public. While this challenge is not new, the challenges facing both scientists and policy makers make engagement more important than ever. Many studies have found that collaborative engagement between both groups throughout the research process brings benefits to both that far outstrip any of the costs of such involvement (Ross et al., 2003). Keeping scientists grounded in the reality of managers' and policy makers' worlds may require longer research processes, but benefits of the new knowledge creation that can be used to solve complex problems may outweigh the costs (Ross et al., 2003).

The L'Anse solar project

We have been involved in a promising TD research effort that illustrates the potential benefits. The village of L'Anse and its municipal electric utility worked with a team of social and engineering scientists from Michigan Technological University (Michigan Tech) on a community solar program being developed for village residents and businesses. The collaboration began with a grant to the village to erect a solar array at its water treatment plant. This solar project will allow the community to reduce energy costs, while providing the environmental benefits associated with green energy production. In this case, the Village Manager, acting with the administrative discretion his office has as a street-level bureaucrat, worked as a policy entrepreneur to bring this solution to his village board.

The use of the solar array project as evidence of the successful application of this technology led to discussions of potential wider community adoption. This led to an effort to provide wider benefits of this technology to residents and businesses in the community. The Village Manager developed a collaboration with Michigan Tech scientists with expertise in the area of solar technology adoption and together they developed a successful multiyear TD research collaboration (described in more detail in Chapter 11) that includes the Village Manager (who works for the Village Council), the Western Upper Peninsula Planning and Development Region and scientists. The team has been able to overcome initial barriers to collaboration through careful development of mutual objectives and shared trust. This L'Anse project recently inspired the creation of a parallel project in a neighboring community.

Engagement between policy makers and scientists began early in this project, which has been essential for effective collaboration. While there are many moving parts associated with this research, the possibilities for practical application are strong, and the commitment and trust between the two groups make this project an example of what is possible with successful engagement in TD research.

Conclusion

The three lessons identified in environmental governance and administrative engagement are on full display in the L'Anse case. First, engagement at the earliest stages between policy makers and scientists was critical to building successful solutions. Second, the development of successful partnerships and the navigation of barriers were achieved through sustained engagement. It is through engagement that barriers, such as finding appropriate funding sources and a lack of shared incentives, can be overcome. It is also through engagement that the third lesson, trust among actors, is highlighted. The reciprocity that trust creates between policy makers and scientists makes future efforts possible, such as the new efforts in an adjacent community. By being mindful of the importance of engagement and the benefits it can bring, successful TD research partnerships can be created to solve important societal challenges.

Acknowledgments

This work was supported, in part, by the National Science Foundation's Partnerships in International Research and Education Program grant IIA no. 1243444.

7 Incorporating community: opportunities and challenges in community-engaged research

Abhilash Kantamneni, Richelle L. Winkler and Kirby Calvert

Introduction

Scientists increasingly realize that involving community members in understanding and resolving environmental problems can improve research project outcomes. Community involvement can increase the relevance of research questions (Hacker, 2013; Israel et al., 2018), bridge the gap between science and practice (Balazs and Morello-Frosch, 2013), increase public understanding of science and environmental learning (Bonney et al., 2009; Ballard and Belsky, 2010) and raise attention and empowerment around environmental issues (Bacon et al., 2013; Stoecker, 2009). Moreover, community partnerships can help researchers explore the complexities and nuances of local context and incorporate local knowledge and expertise into project design (O'Fallon and Dearry, 2002). Such partnerships help build legitimacy towards proposed solutions and galvanize local support for their implementation (Northmore and Hart, 2011). Still, research teams continue to struggle to successfully integrate community partners in meaningful ways.

We see two key reasons for this struggle that are particularly troublesome for transdisciplinary (TD) teams. First, the broad literature on community-engaged research includes multiple terms, standards and approaches, which often vary by discipline. This means that any team looking to follow engaged principles must first develop a common language and understanding of exactly what it is they seek to do. Second, principles about how to do community-engaged scholarship get messy in practice. There is not a clear road-map or training program for implementation, and there remain relatively few researchers experienced in implementing partner projects. This is especially difficult in TD teams where disciplinary-based epistemologies and methodological differences may already challenge project integration. Ultimately, few researchers feel prepared or supported for knowing how to apply community-engaged research principles in practice and manage a partnership project.

This chapter aims to help scientists and practitioners catch up on what it means to do community-engaged research and provides examples from our own projects to illustrate how principles might be applied. The first section deals with defining and conceptualizing what it means to do community-engaged research. The second section focuses on some challenges for incorporating community in research teams along with practical examples drawn from our own experiences. Ultimately, we hope this chapter offers some hints for overcoming the definitional and practical hurdles described above, and in doing so opens the door to more research teams to meaningfully incorporate communities in environmental research.

Conceptualizing community-engaged research

Community-engaged research is a research paradigm that creates space for communities, community members and community-based organizations to work in collaborative partnerships with academic researchers. It aims to produce research outputs that benefit the community, while also meeting the rigors and standards expected of academic research. It is about building, maintaining and sustaining relationships – within communities and between communities and scientists. Under this broad understanding, however, are multiple terms with sometimes similar meanings, that tend to vary by discipline. Here, we use "community-engaged research" as an interdisciplinary umbrella term meant to encompass the range of more specific concepts and practices that fall under this broad conception. Based on our own experiences implementing community-engaged projects with transdisciplinary teams, we recommend that teams begin conversations at this broad conceptual level, and then collaboratively focus on more specific terms/concepts depending on project goals. We hope that this discussion and the conceptual graphics included below will help teams to overcome language barriers, understand their different conceptual assumptions, and establish common language and goals.

As we see it, the rhetoric in the growing scholarship around community-engaged research varies along what we might think of as three dimensions. First, there is the "participation" dimension, which is about the depth of community involvement and what practices community members engage in. Second, there is the "disciplinary" dimension, whereby vocabulary varies by discipline and sometimes research methodology. Third, there is the "power/action" dimension, which is about the degree to which research projects are designed and used to facilitate shifts in power differentials and drive socioecological change.

Figure 7.1 illustrates the range of community involvement along these first two dimensions (moving from left to right in terms of increasing depth of participation) and common labels used to describe each level. In the health and social sciences, scholars generally use "community"-based language, whereas in the natural and computer sciences, "citizen science" language is more common. The citizen science tract is also more likely to use more quantitative methods, especially those that incorporate geographic information systems or computer applications.[1] In Figure 7.1 and throughout this chapter, we mean to represent participation as a *continuum*. The figure and discussion that follows represent ideal types rather than discrete categories. The borders between different types of projects are often blurry.

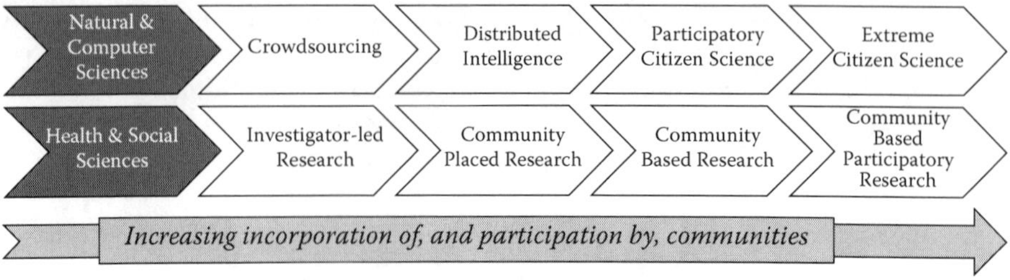

Note: In the health sciences and social sciences, scholars generally use "community"- based language, while natural sciences and computer sciences use "citizen science". The borders between different types of projects are often blurry. The sections below describe each label in greater detail (adapted in part from Hacker and Taylor, 2011; Haklay, 2013).

Figure 7.1 The continuum of community involvement in research projects in terms of increasing depth of participation, and the common labels used to describe each level

Interestingly, the literature has evolved in parallel such that there is almost no overlap between "citizen science" versus "community-based" scholarship, making it difficult to integrate and synthesize the literature around doing community-engaged research (Rowbotham et al., 2017 is a rare exception). Language differences can also contribute to misunderstandings between research team members. For example, Winkler recently co-developed a research proposal with community organizations, geographers, anthropologists, computer scientists, cognitive scientists and engineers for a project that would use participatory geographic information systems to identify and understand community-based environmental problems. In this effort, considerable time and misunderstandings were wasted on parallel communication between those on the team seeking to do "extreme citizen-science" and those seeking to do "community-based participatory research". Communications between community partners and some of the co-investigators were strained by competing understandings of the proposed work. Multiple drafts of the project proposal suffered until the team was finally able to come to a clearer understanding, recognizing that we all wanted to accomplish the same (or very similar) objectives, but had just been using different language.

From either disciplinary perspective, we conceptualize projects placed farther to the right on this graphic to fall under the community-engaged research umbrella. These offer deeper participation, more meaningful engagement for community-members and more equal power relationships between researchers and community members. It is these kinds of projects that we refer to in "The practice of incorporating community" section below.

Investigator-led/community-placed or crowdsourced/distributed intelligence

The research process is driven by the (academic) scientist who asks questions *of* the community, and collects data *from* the community. The data are analyzed, information processed and results synthesized by researchers into a body of

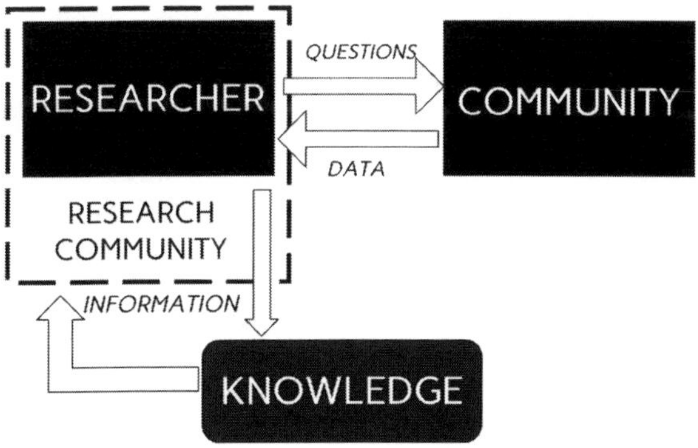

Note: Questions flow from researchers to community, data flows from communities back to researchers while information is synthesized into knowledge with relevance mostly for the researcher community.

Figure 7.2 Investigator-led/community-placed or crowdsourced/distributed intelligence research projects

knowledge most relevant to researchers. Community members or "citizens" are not included in most stages of the research process. Some research may take place *in* communities, with community members or citizens playing a data-collection role, such as responding to surveys or collecting *in-situ* data. In crowdsourced research, the participation of community members is limited to data provision, and they do not have control or ownership over collected data. In addition to data gathering, "Distributed Intelligence"-based research projects leverage the cognitive powers of participants by having them perform basic interpretative tasks like sorting or classifying data (Haklay, 2013). A classic example is Galaxy Zoo – an online platform that trains members of the general public to seek and identify galaxies from data collected by deep-space telescopes (see Zooniverse, 2018). In most cases, the community is not intended to be the target audience for publication of results, and little knowledge (if any) is transferred (back) to the community. This more traditional and common approach is illustrated in Figure 7.2.

Community-based research/participatory citizen science

Community members participate in key aspects of the research process, most often in data collection, and have some autonomy and opportunity to analyze data (i.e., focus groups/community meetings or data collection programs that allow some decision making or interpretation from citizen scientists). They also work with researchers to help identify problems and prioritize research questions. Partnering with researchers helps communities receive timely updates and feedback from the research project. This can enhance local understanding of problems, strengthen local practices and support new strategies for addressing local needs (Cargo and Mercer, 2008). However, researchers maintain control over research design, processing information and synthesizing it for academic knowledge. Communities/citizen groups do not often have a say in how this knowledge is mobilized; yet

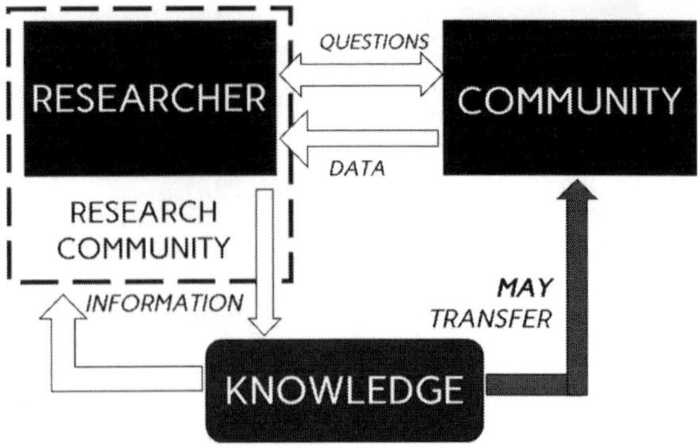

Note: Questions are developed collaboratively by researchers and community members, while data continues to flow from community to researchers. Information is synthesized into knowledge that is mostly relevant for the research community. However, the gray arrow at the bottom represents how some research knowledge may be transferred back to the community through public outreach programs and information sessions.

Figure 7.3 Community-based research/participatory citizen science

often some knowledge is transferred for the benefit of the community through "outreach" programs, reports and public information sessions (see Figure 7.3). For a detailed treatment of community-based research, see Halseth et al. (2016); for reviews of participatory citizen science in environmental research, see Couvet et al. (2008), Conrad and Hilchey (2011), Dickinson et al. (2012) or Newman et al. (2012).

Community-based participatory research/extreme citizen science

Community-based participatory research and *extreme citizen science* aim to incorporate communities as full partners in the research process (for reviews see Minkler and Wallerstein, 2008; Hacker, 2013; Haklay, 2013; Stevens et al., 2014). The work is highly collaborative and strives for equal representation and equal participation between communities and researchers recognizing the value in skills and knowledge from both directions and blurring the line between "researchers" and "community members". Projects are designed to be important to communities and to benefit communities. Research questions and priorities typically originate from the community itself. Research design is a collaborative process where the full group works together to determine the research approach and methods. Data is collected by the community to the extent possible and feasible (see Figure 7.4). Ownership is shared with the community to the extent that it is appropriate and ethical to do so. Knowledge is synthesized by researchers working in collaborative partnerships with community organizations and community members, and both researchers and community members serve as authors. Democratizing knowledge and improving conditions are key goals (Strand et al., 2003; Hacker, 2013). The community itself is the primary audience for the research outputs, and academic publications are not prioritized more than community-based outputs.

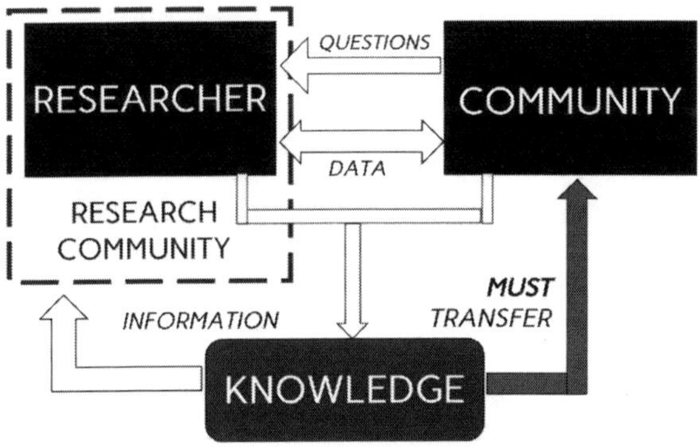

Note: Questions and issues originate from the community while data ownership is shared between project partners. Communities play a larger role in synthesizing information into knowledge that must have relevance for all project partners.

Figure 7.4 Community-based participatory research (CBPR) and extreme citizen science

Action research

Beyond the participation continuum and disciplinary distinctions described above, projects also vary by the extent to which they seek to disrupt power relations and facilitate transformative socioecological change (Kimura and Kinchy, 2016). Action research (AR) is a constellation of research methodologies that seek to expose problems and identify and intervene with solutions through an iterative and cyclic process of action and reflection (Ferrance, 2000). The fundamental aim is to improve practice (address social and ecological problems) rather than to produce knowledge for its own sake (Brydon-Miller et al., 2003; Bradbury-Huang, 2010). Another goal is to empower disadvantaged communities and give "voice" to new categories of knowledge that are based on local realities and expertise (Gaventa, 2004; Gaventa and Cornwall, 2006). Transformative socioecological change toward just and balanced socioecological systems is often a longer-term philosophical goal. Specific goals range from solving specific instances of local problems, to developing knowledge and tools to address broader socioecological problems.

AR often, although not always, engages communities as key participants, and some community-engaged research projects incorporate AR methods and philosophy. These include projects labeled as "community-based participatory action research" (see Stoecker, 2012), or just "participatory action research" (see Whyte, 1991), and some conceptualizations of "extreme citizen science" (see Kimura and Kinchy, 2016; Stevens et al., 2014). AR promotes practices where the boundaries between "researchers", "community members" and "citizen scientists" are completely blurred. Academics, practitioners, community members and citizens act as co-researchers *participating* in developing solutions while *acting* on problems as they experience them. This involves an iterative process of experimentation (action/intervention) and inquiry (reflection – see Figure 7.5).

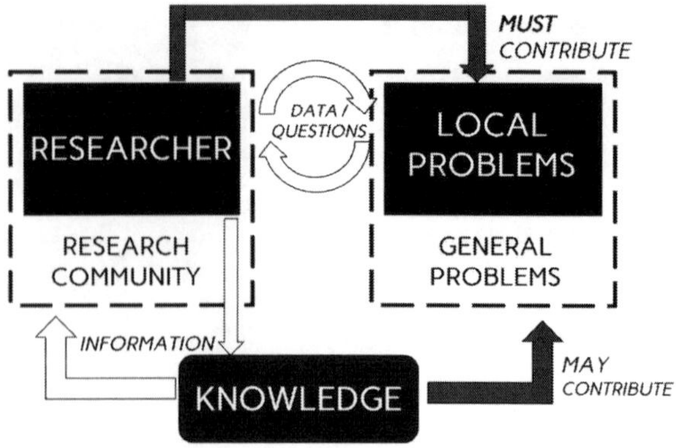

Note: Researchers collect and analyze data to solve specific instances of local problems (gray arrow on top). While generating knowledge is secondary to addressing local issues, researchers may still synthesize their experiences into knowledge. This knowledge base can then be used to develop tools and methodologies to address broader societal problems (gray arrow at bottom), for instance, through policy documents or lobbying decision makers. Figure adapted in part from concepts described in Goldkuhl (2008, 2012).

Figure 7.5 Participatory action researchers use an iterative, reflexive and cyclical process of asking questions

The practice of incorporating community

This section reflects on some key principles and practical challenges important to the practice of doing community-engaged research, drawing from the literature and our own experiences. The issues we tackle here are normative goals to strive for when working to incorporate communities into research projects, challenges associated with them in practice, and some suggestions for implementation. We present this section as a starting point. It is by no means exhaustive (for fuller reviews, principles summaries and practical guidance see Isreal et al., 1998, 2005; CTSA, 2011; Strand et al., 2003; Hacker, 2013; Stoecker, 2012; Minkler and Wallerstein, 2008; or Bonney et al., 2009).

Defining the community

Communities reflect collective and individual identities, forged through social interactions, shared interests, common goals and collective destiny (Israel et al., 1992, 2005). In the context of community-engaged projects however, what constitutes a community? How do teams decide who will be included and who will not? How do teams identify and differentiate between stakeholders, partners and participants, especially in environments where such identities might be overlapping? How do they manage and incorporate multiple voices? These decisions are particularly challenging when communities are divided or agendas contested. How a community is defined, or defines itself, will affect the focus, direction and goals of community-engaged research projects. An important consideration for teams is to develop an early and shared definition of "community".

An equally confounding question is *whom* to partner with? Through experience, we have learned to work with communities that are already fairly well organized into specific organizations. Working with a group that is not already organized means that someone has to do the organizing, and community organizing is a considerable effort for which scientists are not adequately prepared. At the same time, teams should beware that partnering with well-established organizations can sometimes mean perpetuating power imbalances and status-quo. Relatively powerful actors (community organizations) have more skills and resources that can facilitate effective partnerships, but then projects may only serve to empower those who already have power. Teams should consider this tension and attempt to balance competing project goals.

Team power dynamics and decision making

Developing equitable partnerships allows project teams to take full advantage of the myriad skills, knowledge and resources that each partner brings (O'Rourke and Dearry, 2002; Cargo and Mercer, 2008; CTSA, 2011). Yet balancing power is difficult in practice, particularly when communities include underrepresented or marginalized populations and research teams are constituted by people from relatively privileged class, gender or race/ethnic backgrounds. Researchers generally have more training and experience conducting research than community partners, who may feel inadequately prepared. These dimensions of positionality will necessarily create power imbalances. The challenge is to navigate differentials so as to reap the benefits of having a diverse team without perpetuating inequalities. Three specific strategies we suggest are:

1. *Recognizing and legitimating the specific skills and knowledges that each partner brings.* For instance, Winkler introduces research teams (including community partners) by openly discussing what resources each member brings to the team being careful to point out that all members bring certain skillsets. In this way, she emphasizes the importance of different ways of knowing, and that all members have weaknesses that others can help fill. Because labels can diminish or perpetuate power imbalances, our teams do not distinguish between "community partners" and "scientists", but rather all are "research partners".
2. *Taking intentional measures to equalize voice and to share decision making.* Teams should design strategies to ensure that all partners' voices are heard and valued and to determine how decisions will be made inclusively from the very start. Winkler finds that community partners often diminish their own thoughtful contributions by prefacing them with statements such as "I don't know very much about this" or "I'm just a [crazy old lady/other derogatory term]". Such comments indicate power imbalances and point to the

importance of reaffirming each partner's value to the team. We recommend that team leaders, in particular, reflect on and intentionally mitigate potential differences in voice that may arise.

3. *Balancing institutional rewards and responsibilities.* When research teams write grant proposals to conduct research, they should incorporate community partners as Principle Investigators or Co-Principle Investigators and seek resources to pay community researchers, who would otherwise be volunteering their time, for their labor similarly to students or faculty summer salaries. These institutional signals reaffirm value and formalize partnerships.

Ultimately, scientists generally lead research projects and provide necessary direction. However, teams will have to struggle with determining what degree of community ownership of the research process is appropriate and necessary and how to reconcile divergent visions for research goals, methods and solutions. Group dynamics research has identified characteristics of effective groups and strategies for facilitating cooperation (i.e., Johnson and Johnson, 2003; Halvorsen et al., 2016) and other studies have suggested specific strategies for managing group dynamics in community-based research teams (see Becker et al., 2005). We recommend that teams (and especially team leaders) review these principles.

Trust and mutual respect

Scientists can gain community trust and confidence by defining clear goals of engagement; communicating the basic purpose of research; developing realistic and achievable objectives; articulating the value of community participation; ensuring that project goals are tangible, valuable and achievable for all project partners; and clearly identifying roles for all team members (OCEP, 2015). Understanding a community's culture, socioeconomic conditions, social networks, power structures, demographics, norms and values, and prior experiences with research partnerships can help guide program design and development (CTSA, 2011). Knowing and respecting community diversity and securing commitments from community champions and key leaders is essential for mobilizing community participation (Campbell-Voytal, 2010). In return, local communities can help advance the research process by sharing power, local knowledge and key responsibilities with scientists (Horowitz et al., 2009).

In practice, however, trust takes time to build, and teams must invest time in developing relationships. It may take several meetings and several months (to years) before teams accomplish tangible outcomes or even start to come to common understandings. Given the nature of research grant proposals and academic institutions' pressure to publish and secure funding, the time to develop these relationships can be challenging to find. Communities also face strenuous time demands, often are working with volunteer labor and need to accomplish tasks on a shorter time scale than academics are used to operating under. Teams should seek institutional resources and specifically carve out time for relationship building before they expect real progress to occur and well in advance of research proposal deadlines (we plan for a year with new teams).

Knowledge mobilization

The broad goals of community-engaged research are to (a) integrate knowledge and practice for benefit of all partners and, in the case of AR, to (b) mobilize research results in support of community change efforts (Figure 7.6; Stoecker, 2012). To deliver effectively on the latter half, teams must "get the right information to the right people in the right format at the right time" (SSHRC, 2017). Balancing public scholarship with academic journal publication can also be a challenge, although not insurmountable. We explore how this balance may be achieved in practice:

1. *Right information.* Teams must develop a shared understanding of what knowledge is *valid* and *useful* for community change efforts. Validity of knowledge might be contested owing to epistemological, historical and cultural differences. Usefulness might be debated based on experiences and preferences. In some cases, community members might not be willing to make some findings about their community public. Partners should collaboratively determine the key messages they would like to share.
2. *Right people.* Who is the target audience and what are they likely to contribute to community change efforts? What is their power position and how can they broker knowledge/findings? Perhaps they have already been engaged in developing arguments for a certain position. How do the research team's findings fit in that story? We recommend targeting and connecting each target audience with a key message.
3. *Right format.* To have an impact, findings must be disseminated in language that is understandable, accessible and appropriate for the intended audience (see Figure 7.3). Even when teams specifically target their work to public audiences and action efforts, there is often still room to write academic publications. In our experience, it requires additional writing, but there is very often generalizable and theoretically grounded knowledge generated from community-engaged research that is appropriate for academic journal publication (i.e., Winkler, 2013; Winkler et al., 2016).
4. *Right time.* Rather than creating products one after another as the project cycle completes, teams should use knowledge mobilization materials to get involved in key debates happening in relevant circles in relevant topics. In other words, craft messages to tie directly into current events or ongoing debates, and use these opportunities to drive community change efforts. We recommend the following resources: Barwick, 2013 and OCEP, 2015 as toolkits for developing knowledge mobilization plans.

Commitment and sustainability

Community-research partnerships work best when they last long enough for trusting and coordinated efforts to develop. While sometimes this can happen in a matter of months, it usually takes years of sustained effort. Goals for systemic socioecological change require long time horizons, and often there is not a clear

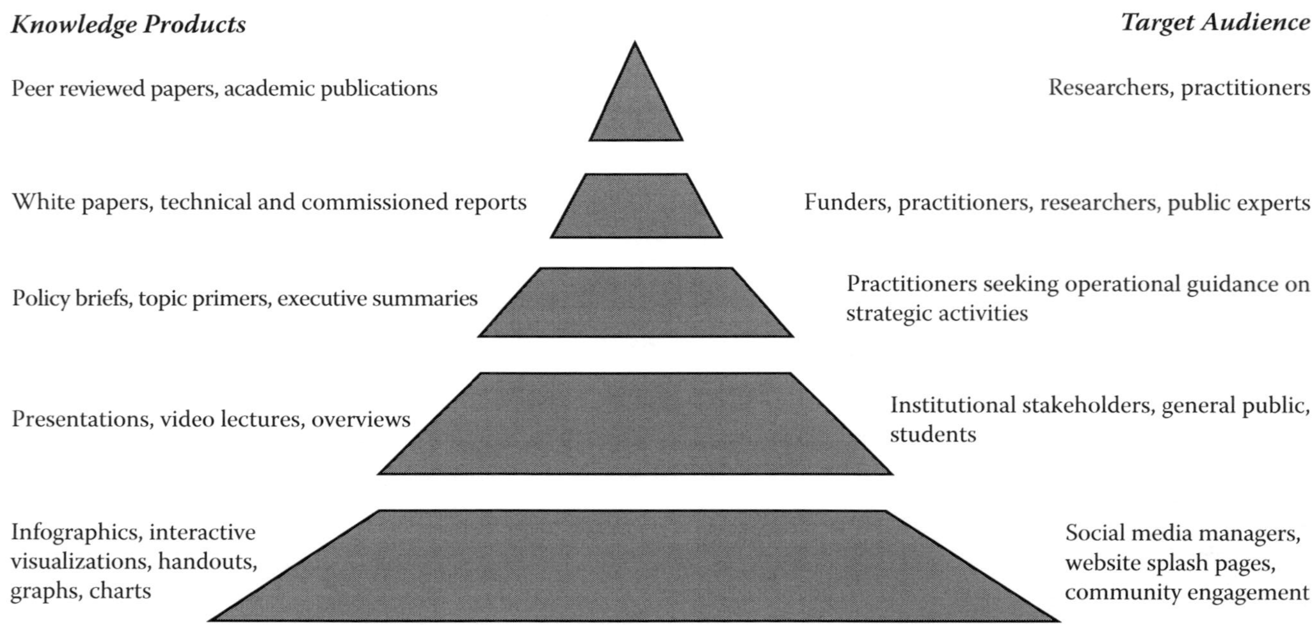

Note: At the first levels, publications are for public audiences, with key decision makers getting more in-depth information, and finally room for academic publications at the top. (Originally developed by Kantamneni and Calvert, and operationalized through their Community Engaged Knowledge-Action Partnership, CEKAP).

Figure 7.6 An example of how knowledge can be mobilized into outputs appropriate for specific audiences

ending point as answering one research question usually only leads to recognizing others. Long-term partnerships need to be resilient to weather cycles of change in politics, socioeconomic and socioecological conditions. In this context, it can be difficult to end projects or even to remove key individuals from a team.

Most partnerships die the slow death of attrition. Early excitement is high and momentum grows as projects are envisioned and teams build trust. Over time, some partners may lose motivation (burnout), get disillusioned or face personal or institutional constraints that cause them to leave the project. Their expectations may not be met or team goals and visions may have diverged. When people drop out, it puts more pressure on constrained resources within the partnership. Teams must commit to being flexible and willing to rely on a variety of unconventional methods to meet changing community and research needs (see Strand et al., 2003; Flicker, 2008; Duran et al., 2012; or Belone et al., 2016 for suggestions). Other partnerships come to an abrupt end, owing to sudden changes in political leadership, the end of funding or career changes of key personnel. We recommend that teams identify the potential for these risks early, and develop contingency plans.

The partnerships that survive those two challenges face the biggest of them all – planning for and timing the exit strategy. Where does "drive-by research" end, and "overstaying-your-welcome" begin? This can be particularly important in small communities that might suffer from research exhaustion. When is a good time to walk away? Ideally, when a community is empowered to carry out its own visions.

Conclusion

While academics are increasingly realizing the value of incorporating communities into research projects, few research teams have much experience integrating community partners, and many groups don't know where to start. This chapter identifies two key reasons for this struggle – disciplinary challenges, owing to multiplicity of terms, standards and approaches, and implementation challenges, owing to lack of clear road-maps or training programs on employing concepts in practice. These challenges are likely to be more pronounced in TD teams where integration may already be stifled by prevailing disciplinary-based methodological and epistemological differences. Our goals are to help research teams to understand and navigate these challenges by offering a broad understanding and raising important factors that teams should consider. We offer a start, and encourage teams to dig deeper into literature that specifically offers methodological guidance and core principles before embarking on a community-engaged research project.

The burgeoning literature around core principles for doing community-engaged research is particularly well developed in the health sciences, but socioecological projects (and citizen science teams) can borrow from these for guidance in designing and implementing their own projects. Table 7.1 summarizes the concepts, terms and practices associated with different styles of community-engaged

Table 7.1 Summary of community-engaged research labels and practices

	Investigator-led or crowdsourced	Community-placed or distributed intelligence	Community-based or citizen science	Community-based participatory research or extreme citizen science	Action research	Participatory action research
Research goals	Knowledge building	Increasing "awareness"	Increasing ownership of research goals and outcomes	Empowerment. Socioecological consciousness	Power to shift discourses or achieve small wins	Transformative socioecological change
Identifying research questions	Driven by researcher interests in testing theory; and filling knowledge gaps	Still driven by researcher, minimal community input	Community helps identify and prioritize locally relevant issues	Full community participation in identifying and prioritizing issues of local significance	Prioritizing the need for understanding, and simultaneously addressing local problems	Researchers address local problems encountered in practice
Research design	Based on feasibility, funding opportunities, epistemological position	Based on researcher's interests, but takes place in a community setting	Researchers consult community to ensure design is acceptable to community members	Community representative involved with every stage of research design	Design based on plan of action that will make a change and enable researcher study of the change	Intervention-based design developed in partnership with local practitioners
Data collection methods	Those appropriate to answering research questions with negligible to minimal input from the community	Data collected from, within and with the endorsement of the community	Community members involved in some aspects of data collection	Conducted by community members to the extent possible, capable and feasible. Capacity building	Any methods and sources appropriate for problem being addressed	Any methods and sources appropriate for problem being addressed

Data ownership and analysis	Researchers own data, conduct analysis and interpret results	Data owned and analysis driven by researchers	Analysis and results conducted with feedback from community	Data ownership shared with community; researchers work with community members to analyze and interpret findings	Researchers interpret data, act on evidence and evaluate results of intervention in an iterative, reflexive process	Researchers interpret data, act on evidence and evaluate results of intervention in an iterative, reflexive process
Disseminating results	Results published in academic and peer-reviewed outlets	Results published in academic and peer-reviewed outlets, but knowledge may be mobilized for community	Results disseminated in public/community venues in addition to peer-reviewed outlets	Community identifies appropriate avenues for disseminating results and transferring knowl-edge, in addition to academic outlets	Results may or may not be published, with priority on improving local practice and solving local problems	Priority on improving local practice, but knowledge may help improve general problems – through policy documents

Note: This table is meant to help transdisciplinary teams understand the subtle differences between, and develop common understanding of, terminology in community-engaged research. It summarizes and integrates the concepts and practices described through this chapter. We hope that readers won't see these labels as discrete categories, but rather as a continuum with blurred boundaries whereby specific projects might ultimately borrow from multiple boxes as partners work collaboratively to define their own goals and interests in the face of practical constraints.

research that we have reviewed. These principles are important for providing basic guidelines and for illuminating best practices. Still, we hope that teams will be flexible and recognize that this is no "all-or-nothing" game where a project either follows all core principles of *community-based participatory action research* or *extreme citizen science* to a "t" or it shouldn't incorporate communities at all. These guiding concepts and tools offer models, which each individual team will need to adapt to best suit its needs and practical constraints.

Acknowledgments

The authors would like to recognize all of the community partners with whom they have shared many of these experiences and learned some of the lessons summarized here. These include the young adults of Crow Wing County, MN and the Brainerd Lakes Area Community Foundation; Main Street Calumet and the people of Calumet, MI; the Houghton Energy Efficiency Team and the other energy justice advocates in Michigan's Upper Peninsula; the Copper Country Recycling Initiative; the Keweenaw Bay Indian Community and Keweenaw Bay Ojibwa Community College; Manitoulin-Sudbury District Services Board, Community Energy Knowledge–Action Partnership; and Our Energy Guelph. We would also like to thank Patrick Wittmann, Leah Levac, Mavis Morton and the Community Engaged Scholarship Institute for discussions and resources on community-engaged research. Winkler would like to thank Don Lafreniere, Valoree Gagnon and Robert Pastel for discussions about community engagement in large transdisciplinary teams.

NOTE

1. We caution readers against drawing too many parallels between our continuum of community participation in transdisciplinary research projects (Figure 7.1), and Arnstein's ladder of citizen participation in public planning and policy (Arnstein, 1969). On one hand, our views are informed by Arnstein's conceptualization of community participation as a ladder of increasing community power and agency to make decisions. However – and for transdisciplinary teams in particular – Arnstein's focus on power as the sole measure of participation does not adequately account for the diversity of knowledge and expertise of both scientists and community members (Tritter and McCallum, 2006).

8 Crossing boundaries: cross-national, transdisciplinary research and teamwork

Erin C. Pischke, Amarella Eastmond and Gabriela Alonso-Yanez

Introduction

As the extent of rapid global environmental change and its cascade of socioenvironmental problems gain international recognition and visibility, funding agencies and academic research and private sector organizations increasingly focus on recruiting, assembling and working within large international teams composed of scientists and non-scientists, including in the Americas (Pittman et al., 2016). These large projects require large-scale, long-term project funding, attention to group dynamics and an awareness of the challenges germane to cross-national research efforts (Börner et al., 2010; Collins et al., 2011; Goring et al., 2014; Mauser et al., 2013; Mahdizadeh et al., 2015).

In this chapter, we discuss the importance of international scientific collaboration and draw on the authors' experiences as members of transdisciplinary (TD) research teams, successes achieved in terms of international scientific collaboration and the challenges faced while conducting such research. The authors come from varied backgrounds: one has British and Mexican citizenship and has lived and worked in Mexico for decades, another is a Mexican citizen who lives and works in Canada, and the other is an American who works in Mexico. Each of the authors also works with researchers from North, Central and South America. These distinct backgrounds allow the authors to present a unique perspective on the successes and challenges they have faced while conducting TD research in multiple countries.

The importance of international scientific collaboration

TD research offers a possibility for transforming how environmental management research and sustainability science are conducted. Developing shared language, theories and methods can enhance and streamline disciplinary research (Barlow et al., 2011; Strober, 2006); similarly, such practices can also enhance international research by facilitating a common understanding of a shared problem (Pittman et al. 2016; Simon and Schiemer, 2015). For instance, researchers coming together in TD multinational research projects can better identify cross-disciplinary questions and linkages that address a gap in current understanding of a given sustainability topic. They are also more likely to be able to foster intercultural dialogue that generates research outputs with global impacts. The process can reveal different perspectives of a component of the research in multiple places and integrate and incorporate them into the research process.

Wagner et al. (2017) found that international collaboration in science is a growing trend that positively affects the impact of such research groups. These collaborations can build capacities and transfer knowledge from one country to another (Simon and Schiemer, 2015). Countries with fewer resources and limited funding access can gain from collaboration with wealthier countries able to share research resources across borders (Simon et al., 2003). Shared resources can include research funding and expensive scientific equipment and journal subscriptions (Simon et al., 2003). These collaborations may benefit all in diverse ways, for instance, Glänzel and Schubert (2001) showed that international publications have higher-than-expected citation rates in all scientific fields, a finding supported by others (e.g., Narin et al., 1991; Persson et al., 2004; He, 2009).

TD and cross-national research enables locally attuned, action-oriented research with increased likelihood of having a practical impact. It also develops intercultural competence among participants through negotiations and the creation of shared repertoires to collaborate. Part of that process entails personal efforts on the part of the research participants to be willing to engage in cultural exchanges as well as bridge building and mentorship between students and researchers from different countries.

Challenges of TD research across academic systems and countries

One of the challenges in cross-national TD research is that many academic cultures do not value it. Changes in academic labor markets and higher education policy and management, largely informed by neoliberal ideologies and marketing discourses, have affected the development of socially and locally engaged scholarship (Davies et al., 2005; Glazer-Raymo, 2008; Morley, 2007; Van den Brink and Benschop, 2012). These changes can have unequal effects across regions; for instance, Latin American scientists operate in a system structured by values shaped by power asymmetries, selection biases and a multitude of career barriers. Together, these factors create fierce competition for financial resources, recognition and scholarly publication (Alonso-Yanez and Davidsen, 2014; Sarthou, 2013; Silva Payró et al., 2016). New research evaluation systems in many countries assess the productivity and quality of scientists working in universities. In some Latin American countries these systems award significant economic incentives on top of their regular salary to individual scientists depending on their measured scientific performance (Alcantara et al., 2011).

Excelling in these systems ensures not just academic distinction, but also significant extra financial support in the form of research grants. For example, a rare and interesting study by Castillo and Toledo (2000) about the involvement of Mexican scientific researchers in applied, TD research found that only a small number of projects contributed to the larger development of applied ecology and conservation research within the country, and that research questions were often designed more to meet academic reward system metrics rather than to achieve scientific or conservation goals. It is not surprising that these systems create fierce competition among those scientists aspiring to be included in the system, as well as immense pressure on those who are already included. Nonetheless, some analysts see these traits as positive for Latin American scientific development, arguing that the system has created higher scientific standards and capacities (Alonso-Yanez and Davidsen, 2014; Loaeza, 2005).

Reports on the failure of such programs have only recently started to be published (Didou Aupetit and Gérard, 2011; Ibarra Colado, 2009). They show that additional reward mechanisms created an academic elite by relying on standardized, exclusively quantitative, measures of scholarly production. The system also gave preferential treatment to scientists with degrees from countries outside the region (mostly American and European) who therefore found it easier to publish English-language articles in international journals (Didou Aupetit and Gérard, 2011; Ibarra Colado, 2009). When working with participants from areas of the global North and global South, those from the North often dominate the framing and direction of the research problems, which can exacerbate the existing inequities (Engels and Ruschenburg, 2008).

Sometimes, science outcomes are prioritized over policy outcomes owing to three, often-interrelated variables: time, financial and institutional constraints (Alonso-Yanez, 2013; House-Peters et al., 2015). Furthermore, funding agencies lack true understandings of the challenges of international, TD research. In order to generate successful TD proposals and teams, funding agencies must understand that TD projects take more time than "normal" science projects, and this must be incorporated into their timeframes and more comprehensive reviewing criteria.

There are often additional barriers for researchers outside of the US and Canada. The specific reward mechanisms that exist in some Latin American university and research centers create a context in which this type of research is particularly challenging for scientists: researchers often depend on frequent academic assessments so as to renew their employment contracts or access additional financial support, and obviously this kind of research agenda makes that difficult. Managing institutional differences can be fraught with difficulties and that gives rise to feelings of inequality among participants from different countries (Moran et al., 2007). When working with intercultural teams, the benefits of a diverse team can be lost if a dominant culture becomes overbearing or takes control without letting nuances of the group emerge (Kirk-Lawlor and Allred, 2017). However, patience and sensitivity to these problems – what Perz et al. (2010) call long "courtships" – helped reduce such issues. Spending quality time together in all of the different countries promotes social learning, bonding and goodwill amongst all scientist and non-scientist team members.

Underappreciation of the international dimensions in global change research programs

Much of the extant literature about the challenges of conducting global change research focuses primarily on the vagaries of interdisciplinary and transdisciplinary integration (recent examples include Baerwald et al., 2016; Pittman et al., 2016; Simon and Schiemer, 2015, among others). Little published work focuses on the particular additional challenges of cross-national or international interdisciplinary or transdisciplinary research (cf. Pischke et al., 2017). Many researchers who conduct global environmental governance research cross national borders in their scientific pursuits, but descriptions of the problems they encounter in doing so are largely missing from the discussion.

For example, Pittman et al. (2016) outline the interdisciplinary aspects of the Inter-American Institute for Global Change Research's (IAI) funding programs, but say less (almost nothing) about the international component. It is obvious that the inclusion of researchers from different countries with similar global change problems helps tackle those problems from different angles in different contexts (and helps such funding organizations live up to their names). However, the question remains: what are the challenges and rewards associated with working across borders? Furthermore, other "global" or "world" funding programs – the US Global Change Research Program, The World Climate Research Program and the International Geosphere-Biosphere Program – have focused on comparing intra-disciplinary interdisciplinary research, as well as comparative research focusing on urban–rural contexts and across-disciplines interdisciplinary work, but have not focused on cross-national or explicitly international collaborations (Baerwald et al., 2016).

For instance, in their discussion of their Sri Lankan fisheries work from which they draw lessons about successful TD research, Simon and Schiemer (2015) take time to discuss the importance of culturally appropriate research guidelines without describing how and why they chose to conduct their research in another country (the researchers were European). In international contexts, the mundane might seem exotic and more readily noticeable, but it is important to note that even in a researcher's home country, such cultural awareness between rural and urban or indigenous and non-indigenous groups should be considered. Simon and Schiemer (2015) miss the opportunity to discuss their experience of working across national borders and to say why doing so is necessary for their research goals.

Not all researchers or funding organizations neglect to report on the international nature of their research. Indeed, the IAI requires that research proposals submitted to its organization show collaborative efforts among four or more nations from their member countries in the Americas. IAI proposals are screened for "equity in participation between countries" (Pittman et al., 2016), showing that it is a priority for the organization. However, this does not mean that researchers see it that way; they may be simply complying with funding requirements.

Furthermore, there may be good reasons for researchers not discussing the cross-border nature of their work in their publications. Some of the reports by researchers who work in multiple countries present one aspect of their work (e.g. the challenge of integrating across disciplines) and intentionally do not report on how or why they work in the countries where they do. In other cases, when researchers discuss other aspects of their international collaborations (e.g. lack of resources), they may be discussing similar challenges and successes in multiple countries without specifying where they have experienced such challenges.

Addressing the gap in the literature

In order to address the gap in the literature regarding why international research is vital and necessary, as well as the successes and challenges that come with such efforts, we present two projects in which the authors of this chapter were involved. Both were funded by the IAI and involved researchers from multiple countries from the Americas.

International scientific collaboration: experiences from the field

The first project, Teamwork for Effective Research Action in the Americas (TERRA), in which author Alonso-Yanez was involved, brought five researchers from Canada, Chile, Mexico, Uruguay, and the US together to generate new empirical knowledge to advance understanding of team dynamics and improve the current science–policy interface. The research project conducted in 2015 examined 22 interdisciplinary teams addressing global change in the Americas (see House-Peters et al., 2015). Their focus was to generate data about the broader factors that lead to enhanced collaboration among scientists.

The second project we present and discuss here, which authors Eastmond and Pischke were involved in, comprised approximately 20 people. The broader research project that the core group was studying involved over 130 social, natural and engineering scientists and students across six countries over six years: Argentina, Brazil, Canada, Mexico, Uruguay and the US. The larger project (referred to here as BIOPIRE) was focused on the sustainability of Pan-American forest-related bioenergy development and impacts that such bioenergy production systems have on socioecological systems, while the IAI group was interested in better understanding and building effective trans/interdisciplinary teamwork skills. As discussed in more detail in Chapter 10, the BIOPIRE project had funding from the IAI and the US National Science Foundation's Research Coordination Network and Partnerships in International Research and Education (PIRE) programs.

Advances made by international scientific collaboration in the IAI-funded projects

Beyond the obvious reasons for conducting research in multiple countries, there are also advances in scientific knowledge and collaboration that can only be made by conducting cross-national research. We review three ways in which our IAI-funded projects were enhanced by their international components.

Alonso-Yanez's TERRA research team found that these multinational collaborative networks increasingly focus on providing actionable knowledge that on-the-ground stakeholders and policy makers can use. Importantly, producing this knowledge depends on continually engaging local stakeholders and co-designing research activities that are responsive to local needs. Another significant finding of this pilot research was that global change research in South and Central America is largely supported and enabled by strong research ties with countries in North America, specifically Canada and the US. These geographically dispersed research networks often make it possible for low- and middle-income countries in the Americas to conduct socioenvironmental change and climate change research, and thus serve as central support structures to expand understanding of pressing global challenges in the region.

Beyond the perks of traveling to other countries, researchers get the opportunity to see how, for example, one type of oil palm bioenergy feedstock production system is grown in various contexts (Brazil and Mexico). Comparing cases across countries allows researchers to see how the same plant growing in similar climatic conditions can be best managed and where tradeoffs are necessary (to find compromises when there are differences in socioeconomic conditions). Furthermore, the experience on the BIOPIRE project demonstrated that, without the participation of a key member of the Mayan community involved in the project, researchers would not even have known about some of the important socioecological impacts caused by the jatropha plantations that were being investigated.

Researchers found in the BIOPIRE project that including researchers from different countries as well as from distinct disciplines and social sectors allowed them to establish an international research network which proved successful in carrying out socioecological research, enhancing cross-cultural understanding and contributing to knowledge about bioenergy development and sustainability issues in the Americas. Although extra time was required initially to learn how to communicate satisfactorily across traditional lines, the rewards fully compensated for the additional efforts made. The network proved to be an extremely efficient way of sharing knowledge, skills and work so that collectively it was possible to accomplish far more than any one country's team could have achieved by itself. By combining local, national and international theoretical perspectives, sharing resources and constantly analysing and debating each step of the project, everyone benefitted both personally (through travel and experience) and intellectually, through joint publications.

Carrying out fieldwork in new regions, learning new techniques or testing old ones with foreign colleagues and students added diversity and richness of experience which only come with large, inclusive research teams and a willingness to experiment and innovate. Participating in our multinational team was particularly valuable for young scientists who took the opportunity to broaden their capacities, make new connections, meet potential future employers and develop their leadership skills. The authors' own experience of working in the cross-national BIOPIRE project has led to a more profound understanding of how bioenergy and sustainability issues can affect local and global communities and how regional, national and international policies might mitigate the negative impacts of trade-offs.

Challenges faced in conducting international scientific collaboration in the IAI-funded projects

The mainstream model of scientific knowledge production embedded within neoliberal agendas is a core challenge that hinders effective TD, place-based research. Academic organizations require their faculty to be engaged in both education and research activities within the organization and faculty are more often than not evaluated in terms of productivity (number of papers, projects, classes, etc.). In an increasingly competitive work environment with scarce resources at stake, these drivers push faculty to be engaged in as many projects and publications as possible to maintain a competitive position while also juggling their teaching responsibilities. On a practical level, in the BIOPIRE project a great deal of sharing of technical and cultural knowledge across national boundaries was necessary in order to navigate through the complicated legal, administrative and banking regulations in the different countries. In this context, embarking on a long-term, highly demanding and time consuming TD place-based research process can be more than challenging, because on top of having to deal with the pressing timeframes of the funding agencies as stated earlier, they must also juggle multiple work obligations. These competing demands on time may lead to conflicts, project failures and desertion of the research project.

Some of these challenges are due to language and communication barriers. These barriers encompass different meanings or levels. First, there must be basic communication across colleagues with different native languages. Language was a barrier in BIOPIRE fieldwork when the team members were not reasonably fluent in at least two languages (English and Spanish and/or Portuguese). When foreign researchers tried to communicate with local community members, not only were they seen as foreigners from other countries, but they were also representing the academic world and discussing unfamiliar topics and vocabulary words at times (e.g. bioenergy).

TD, place-based research inherently involves the participation of diverse social actors and stakeholders, but the degree to which these actors are involved is often not commensurate with the requirements of social learning and co-production and convergence processes. In many cases, stakeholders are involved as research participants, rather than partners, engaged as providers of sources of information, rather than as companions in learning and co-production of knowledge. It is rare to see stakeholders engaged constantly from the very start of the project through its completion, and included in the decision-making matrix of the project. This "token" participation delegitimizes the name of TD research. However, including stakeholders in the decision-making structure of the project, starting from the problem-framing and research design through to project evaluation, adds complexity to decision negotiations, thus potentially further slowing down the progress of the research, which is often under tight time restraints.

In TERRA's research, respondents consistently described how their universities' and research institutes' policies discouraged pursuit of locally embedded, community-engaged projects. Institutionalized incentives pushed them to instead focus on short-term, generalizable research that is of interest to international audiences and publishable in top-ranked journals. Throughout the data collection process, scientists told researchers that locally relevant sustainability research, such as local monitoring, assessment, and forest and landscape restoration projects, took more time than more easily publishable laboratory research (House-Peters et al., 2015). Even within TD projects that addressed highly complex problems of societal relevance, institutional restraints obstructed progress, including the forms of institutional assessments to which individual team members were subjected. Many institutions placed enormous value on numbers of publications in tenure and promotion processes, thereby devaluing work more focused on generating policy impacts. Such institutional practices thus prevented individuals from directing time and resources toward more policy-relevant TD research.

In the BIOPIRE project, researchers experienced 11 different types of challenges to conducting international research (Pischke et al., 2017). Not all barriers were experienced by every team member or were found in each of the six countries involved in the research, but they were all mentioned by a number of students and scientists during a study of the team conducted in the third year of the project. The barriers they experienced included: budgetary concerns; issues with government or industry, paperwork, permits; difficulty understanding others and coordinating effectively; challenges in coordinating across time zones and temporal seasons; danger and safety issues; misunderstandings owing to cultural differences; barriers to collaboration and understanding between disciplinary groups; inability or difficulty communicating in another language; frustration with coordinating complex housing, transportation and time in field; complex interpersonal relationships and working with and depending on many people; time commitment to fieldwork; and interdisciplinary collaboration (Pischke et al., 2017). Not all of these challenges are germane to conducting international research; often challenges such as these are experienced in a domestic context but are exacerbated when placed in an international context (see Pischke et al., 2017 for a complete discussion).

Discussion

Recent research concludes that training interventions offer a promising opportunity to improve the performance of international TD teams by teaching skills and competencies necessary to enable multicultural and multi-institutional collaborations (Gewin, 2015). These training interventions are particularly relevant for a variety of audiences working on practicing and promoting TD, "namely, those who make policy, who fund science, who carry out research and who organize and implement institutional systems" (Cornell et al., 2013: 62). Professional development designed specifically to improve and sustain TD work is just beginning to emerge (Aronoff and Bartkowiak, 2012; O'Rourke and Crowley, 2013). Addressing policy-relevant global change issues of the twenty-first century demands novel capacity-building approaches as well as novel approaches to conducting research on case-specific TD collaborations. Such research could offer insights into the challenging institutional constraints, which often make it difficult to fulfill TD goals and provide valuable ideas, precedents and guidelines for cases where similar collaborative TD initiatives are anticipated or being established.

Relationship-building activities can help overcome international TD research challenges. Involving international colleagues in the decision-making process and budgeting and establishing power sharing arrangements with partner institutions can facilitate greater group investment and deepen relationships (Cheruvelil et al., 2014). Collaborating with local partners in the field can ensure that the research is sensitive to local cultural norms and political situations that may be difficult for outsiders to perceive. Cheruvelil et al. (2014) point out that having a philosophy that international partners are integral members of the team and should therefore share in the responsibilities, decision making and communications is essential to overcoming cultural barriers.

Di Castri (1976) suggests promoting the exchange of information and personnel between countries to facilitate training and cultural understanding. Furthermore, to build trust, it should be a priority to hold face-to-face meetings, make TD and intercultural training a priority (Morse et al., 2007; Goddard et al., 2006) and identify outside mentors who can help the team focus on integration (Morse et al., 2007). Mistrust must be overcome during the first phase of these collaborations by devoting efforts to building a consensus, making continual adjustments and creating an atmosphere conducive to collaboration (National Research Council, 2008).

The authors' experiences suggest discussing the problem and questions of study with all parties involved before designing the methodology or obtaining field data. Project leaders must plan for extra time to encourage and build communication channels and design interactive experiences for the team members, rather than assuming that this process will occur on its own. Formal and informal communication strategies should be established at the start of the project, and issues of temporal and spatial scales must be dealt with before beginning field work (Morse et al., 2007). To avoid having language be a fundamental obstacle in TD research, team members should be selected on the basis of their language as well as disciplinary skills.

Conclusion

Attention to the ways in which collaborative scientific research is institutionalized is growing (Klein and Falk-Krzesinski, 2017). Over the last three decades, research on teams and collective work has considerably expanded understanding of team effectiveness and the conditions that enable effective collaborations. However, much of this research has investigated contexts outside of science. More recently, the emerging field of Science of Team Science has provided evidence-based conceptual and methodological approaches from multiple disciplines to study how scientific teams function, how their research can effectively be translated to non-scientific communities, and how universities can create the conditions that foster interdisciplinary collaboration and responsive science (Bresman and Zellmer-Bruhn, 2013; Hilton and Cooke, 2015; Fiore et al., 2010; Little et al., 2016; Newman, 2001; Shea and Mozafari, 2014; Stokols, 2006; Stokols et al., 2008). However, most of these studies are done by researchers outside of the collaborative teams, who consider "scientific collaborations" as an object of study.

Evidence-based conceptual and methodological approaches from multiple disciplines are needed to study how scientific teams function, how their research can effectively be translated to non-scientific communities, and how universities can create the conditions that foster TD collaboration and responsive science. Here, by presenting our experiences on the TERRA and BIOPIRE projects, we have attempted to fill the gap in the literature by sharing findings of an examination of the process of research driven by an equitable partnership that is formed between diverse TD teams and academics who include team members trained in learning and pedagogy and whose research program has focused on examining the intersections between sustainability, international collaboration and processes of learning.

Which elements of international TD research are considered to be barriers is highly influenced by the cultural background of the researchers. In the same way, strategies to overcome them can differ from country to country and between disciplines. Although it is important to be aware of all the potential barriers and blockage points, good TD international research should concentrate on getting an adequate mix of cultures, disciplines and languages in order to help the flow of communication and therefore make it easier to overcome the difficulties as and when they arise.

Finding solutions to global challenges requires research teams and processes capable of crossing disciplinary, organizational and international boundaries (Perz et al., 2010; Perz, 2016) and bridging multiple differences – legal, political, cultural, economic and linguistic – which, if not adequately addressed from the outset, can create obstacles (Lang et al., 2012; Ross, 1984). Successful international TD teamwork requires scientists to produce actionable socioenvironmental solutions by engaging in interdisciplinary and TD research. TD work involves a challenging process of breaking through individual epistemological and ontological beliefs; further, it entails acknowledging and integrating different, and often conflicting, ways of perceiving and knowing the world. What is more, these processes are nested within broader institutional, organizational, cultural, political and economic environments. These multiple layers add to the complexity of operationalizing transdisciplinarity, yet they are essential to truly integrative research and applications. In this context, the scientific practice underlying TD work across multiple countries is shaped by social and institutional factors; understanding them is as critical as insights into scientists' experiences.

Acknowledgments

This work was supported by the National Science Foundation's Partnerships in International Research and Education Program grant IIA no. 1243444 and Research Coordination Network Program grant CBET no. 1140152, as well as the Inter-American Institute for Global Change Research's CRN3105 grant.

PART III

Case studies of transdisciplinary, social science-rich environmental management research

9 Policy, science and transdisciplinary research: when will it be safe to eat as much fish as desired?

Hugh S. Gorman, Valoree S. Gagnon, Amanda Giang, Judith A. Perlinger and Noel R. Urban

Introduction

Health officials in the Great Lakes Region have been issuing fish consumption advisories since the early 1970s, which is when researchers first discovered compounds such as mercury, polychlorinated biphenyls (PCBs) and various pesticides in fish tissue at concentrations high enough to be a health concern. Initially, these advisories were perceived as being temporary, necessary only until regional sources of the problematic compounds could be identified and eliminated (O'Neill, 2004). However, 45 years later, advisories are still in place, with mercury and PCBs still being two of the most problematic contaminants, even though intentional production of PCBs has been banned in most countries.

We now know that these compounds disseminate globally through cycles of atmosphere–surface exchange – that is, by continual cycles of deposition and reemission (Wania and Mackay, 1996). Regardless of where on the planet they are released, these compounds tend to spread throughout the world. Furthermore, past releases are stored in soils, water bodies and on many types of surface, giving rise to secondary emissions that contribute to what can be visualized as a global background concentration. The implication is that even if all new emissions of a particular contaminant stopped today, secondary emissions would continue. Only as compounds already in circulation are buried in sediment, sequestered in ice or are otherwise taken out of circulation will the background concentration decrease.

This chapter examines the transdisciplinary (TD) aspects of a project that examined the fate, transport and governance of pollutants responsible for fish consumption advisories in the Great Lakes region. Efforts by the project team to address the question of when communities in the Great Lakes region most affected by fish contamination will be able to safely consume as much fish as desired provide insight into the value and challenges associated with conducting TD research. The main purpose of the project, titled "Managing Impacts of Global Transport of Atmosphere-Surface Exchangeable Pollutants (ASEPs) in the Context of Global Change" and funded by the National Science Foundation program "Dynamics of Coupled Natural and Human Systems," was to develop better tools for forecasting the transport and fate of these compounds to guide policy choices. The NSF program that funded the project explicitly expects the research to examine "dynamics of a natural system," "dynamics of a human system," and the interactions between the two. The natural system, in this case, is the atmosphere through which these compounds are transported and the surfaces, soils and bodies of water on which these compounds are deposited and from which they re-volatize. The human system is the activity associated with releasing these compounds into the environment, monitoring their concentration in the environment, assessing and communicating the risks of contaminated fish, and governing practices that result in new releases of these compounds. The human system also consists of the social structures and cultural practices that influence fish consumption levels.

To examine relevant aspects of the social system, the Principle Investigator (PI), an environmental chemist with strong ties to the atmospheric modeling community, consulted colleagues in the social sciences who study various aspects of environmental policy. The project team that was eventually assembled included researchers from several universities (Michigan Technological University, Massachusetts Institute of Technology, University of Massachusetts-Boston, Boston University, and the Desert Research Institute) with training in various disciplines (chemistry, atmospheric modeling, systems engineering, limnology, cultural geography, environmental policy and policy history).

The social science researchers emphasized the value of having a component of the research guided by the interests of community partners in the area where the project was geographically grounded, the Keweenaw Bay area of Lake Superior in Michigan's Upper Peninsula. Toward this end, the proposal included a commitment to incorporate stakeholder and decision-maker participation in research design, with the intention being to formulate an additional research question with community partners who wrote letters for support. Therefore, soon after the project started, the team met for a two-day workshop in Michigan, with the second day including representatives of local organizations (such as the Keweenaw Bay Ojibwa Community College (KBOCC), the Friends of the Land of the Keweenaw (FOLK), and the local chapter of Trout Unlimited) and agencies having responsibility for managing aspects of fish contamination at different scales (such as the Great Lakes Indian Fish and Wildlife Commission (GLIFWC), the Keweenaw Bay Indian Community Natural Resources Department (KBIC NRD), state-level environmental and health agencies, the US Environmental Protection Agency (EPA) Great Lakes Program, Environment Canada, and the Stockholm Convention on POPs).

Out of this meeting emerged themes that led to the formulation of a seemingly straightforward question: "When will people in the Keweenaw Bay area be able to safely consume as much fish as they desire?" (Gagnon et al., 2017). This seemingly straightforward question was not part of the original inquiry and answering it became one of the goals of the research team only because of the commitment to TD engagement at the very beginnings of the project.

Four years after the first workshop, the project team held a closing event in which five of the researchers, the co-authors of this chapter, presented the project team's best answer to the question of when it will be safe to eat the fish without worrying about health risks posed by mercury contamination. The following summary of that workshop serves as an overview of the project. Then, we focus on the benefits and challenges of including a component of TD research in this particular project.

The closing workshop

In the autumn of 2017, a one-day closing workshop was held with the project's community partners at the KBOCC. Approximately 35 individuals were present, including four resource managers and four youth interns from the KBIC NRD, two members from the GLIFWC, a member of the KBIC Tribal Council, eight students and faculty from KBOCC, two members of the grassroots organization FOLK, and a handful of community members representing local organizations. Several of the KBOCC students had engaged directly with team investigators during the project as research assistants.

Two leaders from the Keweenaw Bay Indian Community opened the workshop. They first welcomed everyone to their homeland and then introduced themselves in Ojibwa and English. Together, they engaged participants in a smudge ceremony while singing a traditional opening song in their native language. Next, one of the investigators placed the purpose of the day in context by reminding attendees about the themes that had emerged at the first workshop four years prior, as well as reminding participants of the research question that had been articulated in response to those themes.

The question was "How many years will it take (under three different policy scenarios) before the most sensitive populations in Keweenaw Bay are able to safely consume the amount of fish that they desire without any health risks due to contamination from mercury?" The project PI noted that the question was articulated in a way that allowed it to be broken into researchable components, which included: (a) translating three scenarios of chemical governance into future emissions of mercury; (b) modeling the fate and transport of that mercury to forecast future atmospheric concentrations under the different scenarios; (c) translating the forecasted atmospheric concentrations into fish tissue concentrations; and (d) translating those tissue concentrations into health risks, with the goal being to reach a concentration below the threshold of risk for the most vulnerable fish consumers. Project investigators presented on each of these research tasks before facilitating a discussion about the implication of their findings. Here, we next present a brief summary of each task. Then, we turn to the challenges experienced and insights gained in executing this TD component of the project.

Translating scenarios into future emissions of mercury

The major sources of current mercury emissions from human activity are coal-fired power plants and small-scale gold mining. So, how much mercury will be released into the environment each year for the next 50 years, and where will these releases take place? Characterizing the spatial and temporal patterns of future releases of mercury depends, of course, on what humans do to reduce (or increase) those emissions.

Therefore, the project team examined three scenarios: aspirational, policy-in-action and failure-to-govern (Perlinger et al., 2018). The main goal for using three scenarios was to get a sense of the range of potential outcomes. Defining the aspirational scenario was simple: new releases of mercury were assumed to steadily decline, reaching zero in 2050. Likewise, the failure-to-govern scenario assumes that no action to reduce mercury emissions occurs. In the policy-in-action scenario, we assumed that new emissions of mercury will decline according to the goals set by the Minamata Convention on Mercury, the US Mercury and Air Toxic Standards rule and the Great Lakes binational virtual elimination strategy. Among other things, the Minamata Convention expects mercury control devices to be installed on power plants and for nations to help small-scale gold miners conduct their operations with significant reductions in emissions of mercury (Selin, 2014). Atmospheric modelers also took into account changes in mercury emissions owing to factors such as the changing patterns of wildfires and vegetative cover because of climate change (Kumar et al., 2017; Zhang et al. 2016).

Modeling the fate and transport of mercury releases

What future atmospheric concentrations of mercury can we expect to see in the Great Lakes region based on these policy scenarios? Essentially, the atmospheric modelers used a computational model (GEOS-Chem) that divides a representation of the atmosphere into many small boxes and simulates the chemistry and movement of compounds within and between each box. Given the pattern of mercury emissions associated with a certain policy scenario, GEOS-Chem allows one to forecast the quantity of those emissions reaching Lake Superior or other locations over a particular timeframe.

Translating atmospheric concentrations into fish tissue concentrations

What is the relationship between concentrations of mercury in water (which can be quite low) and concentrations of mercury in fish tissue (which can be much higher owing to bioaccumulation)? Given that the food chains in which mercury compounds bioaccumulate vary from location to location in Lake Superior and in the many inland lakes throughout the area, no single model can be used to represent that relationship. Furthermore, only methylated forms of mercury bioaccumulate, which means that watersheds with greater bacteria-driven methylation will experience, all else being equal, greater levels of fish tissue contamination. In this project, the biogeochemists placed the various types of lakes in the region into different categories and then correlated those categories with different levels of bioaccumulation (Urban et al., 2016). Then, using these correlations, they estimated future fish tissue concentrations based on the forecasted levels of atmospheric contamination.

Translating fish concentrations into health risks

The project defined safe consumption as fish tissue concentrations that result in doses below the US EPA's reference dose for toxic substances. For mercury, the US EPA's threshold is 0.1 mg of MeHg per kilogram of body weight per day. The project defined the most vulnerable populations as women of child-bearing age, children and those who depend heavily on marine diets. In the Great Lakes region, Indigenous communities consume fish and the associated toxic substances at rates that are well above human health criteria (O'Neill, 2004).

How much fish would individuals in these populations consume if no health risks existed and what types of fish would they consume and from where? During the project, researchers participated in a Talking Circle event to learn about the importance of fish and fishing in the tribal community so as to help identify the fish species and quantity of fish that members of the tribal community might consume if toxicity were not an issue, as well as the bodies of water from which they might obtain the fish (Gagnon, 2014). The researchers learned that the "desired" level of fish consumption at the height of the spring *ogaa* (walleye) spearfishing harvest was two 8-ounce meals per day. This rate is consistent with the desired rates in the literature for communities in the Pacific Northwest and in the northeast (Donatuto and Harper, 2008; Ranco and Suagee, 2007), but much more than the recommended safe level of two 8-ounce servings per month (MDHHS, 2016).

Facilitated discussion

The workshop ended with a discussion of the finding that the forecasted atmospheric concentrations of mercury in the Great Lakes region for the policy-in-action scenario will not be sufficiently low to eliminate the need for fish consumption advisories by 2050. Reaching the goal of safe fish is clearly a long-term goal, on the order of generations rather than years. Among other things, attendees discussed what they believed to be the most important points to communicate to others about efforts to eliminate the need for fish consumption advisories and what the next steps might be, both in terms of policy and science and in terms of action and research at the local level.

Transdisciplinary research: challenges and insights

Conducting research that involves investigators from multiple disciplines systematically examining the same issue presents a number of challenges, especially when a project includes researchers from both the social and natural sciences (Rodela and Alašević, 2017). Adding the participation of non-academic stakeholders further magnifies those challenges. This section describes the main challenges that emerged in the TD aspect of this particular project and provides insights into ways to facilitate this type of research as well as the benefits of doing so.

Challenges at the proposal stage

In the absence of pre-existing relationships, forming an effective interdisciplinary team can be difficult, especially one that includes social and natural science researchers, with complicating factors being differences in methods, theoretical frameworks and funding opportunities (Bennett et al., 2017). Indeed, many social science researchers have had the experience of being asked by PIs in the natural sciences to participate in a project shortly before a proposal is due and long after the main research questions have been framed. In such cases, the likelihood of assembling a truly interdisciplinary research proposal (much less a TD one) is low. A second important factor involves funding. Conducting effective interdisciplinary research is difficult when researchers in some disciplines (usually the natural sciences) are well funded while researchers in other disciplines (usually the social sciences) are not, limiting the contributions of the latter to what can be accomplished without the support of a PhD student.

In this project, the PI, an environmental chemist, established a budget that acknowledged the value of research performed by investigators in all disciplines. All co-PIs received enough funds to support a PhD student for three years. Furthermore, the PI asked the social science researchers to join the team early on, providing them with an opportunity to shape the project from the beginning. Given the early participation of social science researchers, they were able to advocate for a commitment to leave space in the research plan for addressing questions or concerns raised by non-academic communities. The funding of graduate students also allowed co-PIs to maintain a higher level of commitment to this aspect of the project than they otherwise may have. After all, when competing research, teaching and service demands vie for one's unfunded time, the need to mentor and advise graduate students keeps one's attention focused on the project that is funding those students. Without this level of commitment, efforts to engage non-academic communities would have been lessened as well because members of the social science team (including one funded PhD student) were the main facilitators of that engagement.

Bringing together investigators from both the natural and social sciences early in the proposal stage may be crucial to effective interdisciplinary (and TD) research, but doing so also presents challenges (Romero-Lankao et al., 2013). One of the challenges in this project involved the social science co-PIs being unfamiliar with the tools and processes of atmospheric modeling, leading to several instances of miscommunication that distracted from substantive discussion. Another challenge involved the social science researchers approaching the question of how to examine the dynamics of the "human system" in a slightly different way than the PI initially envisioned.

One example of miscommunication occurred when atmospheric modelers employed the term "policy scenario" in referring to the pattern of mercury emissions expected to occur under the Minamata Convention. The two social science co-PIs did not realize that translating expectations associated with the Minamata Convention into a pattern of emissions represented a task central to the epistemic community to which the modelers belonged. Indeed, a great deal of effort goes into constructing such scenarios, and forecasts of emissions including those associated with a successful Minamata Convention already existed (Streets et al., 2009). However, given that industrial activity responsible for mercury emissions could be seen as part of the "human system", the social science co-PIs were not sure who was expected to contribute to the creation of these "scenarios" and what types of data were available to accomplish this task.

This particular point of confusion led to another. In the description of a proposed research direction, the phrase "feedback on the human system" was used in association with atmospheric modeling efforts. The social science researchers were concerned that the natural science researchers hoped to build a model that included algorithms for predicting human actions based on their response to contamination levels. In actuality, the proposed methodology was relatively straightforward. The intent was to iteratively adjust emission scenarios to reflect a range of potential policy responses, and then to run the mercury transport model for each. Although this misunderstanding can be dismissed as a minor point of confusion, the presence of such misunderstandings complicated communication between the various investigators and reduced the opportunity for more substantial discussions.

Discussions of how best to analyze the "dynamics of the human system" were also complicated by having to communicate across disciplines. The PI initially envisioned a quantitative approach, such as assessing the value of ecosystem services to communities and assessing the effects of contamination-related degradation on that value. Neither social science co-PI saw such an approach as being central to the question of how and why policies and practices related to fish contamination change over time. Instead, they wanted to examine the capacity of the existing multijurisdictional system of chemical governance to respond to concerns at different scales. The team reached a consensus on how to proceed relatively quickly, but one can imagine how such differences, especially if the social science researchers had not shared a common vision, could cripple a project.

The issue of valuation also emerged in another context. One component of the proposed research involved translating a successful Minamata Convention into an estimate of the economic benefits to the US economy (Giang and Selin, 2015). In this case, there was no need for substantial discussion because much of the methodology had already been worked out and nothing was expected of the social science co-PIs. However, they expressed concern that this approach might suggest that reducing mercury contamination was justified only if doing so had positive effects on the economy. But what if a competing economic analysis showed that reducing contamination to a level protective of heavy consumers of fish (including birds and sea mammals) was not economically justified? Wrestling with this concern set the stage for a parallel question framed in non-economic terms.

The commitment to conduct a TD component of research emerged while discussing the impacts of fish contamination on affected communities and the ecosystem services available to them. The social science researchers advocated for making this aspect of the project a community-engaged research component, rather than one in which affected communities were an object of study. After all, socioecological issues come with multiple interpretations of what the problem is and the way in which one frames the problem matters (Holifield et al., 2010; Nadasdy, 2004). Having the affected communities, rather than the researchers, shape the framing of the problem would help ensure that the community was less an object of study than the beneficiaries of the research.

The framing of issues is especially important in research that engages Indigenous communities, who have a history of being researched by investigators unfamiliar with their values and perspectives (Geniusz, 2009). In the Great Lakes region, it is also fundamentally important to have knowledge of the treaties between Indigenous people and the federal government. For example, as the oldest and largest federally recognized Indian tribe in Michigan, the KBIC Ojibwa people retain treaty-protected homelands and hunting, fishing, and gathering rights across millions of acres in the Lake Superior watershed (Treaty with the Chippewa 1842, 1854). Furthermore, interactions with tribal communities need to be built on trust rooted in existing relationships and a commitment to prioritize the interests of a community in aspects of the research that request their participation (Battiste, 2008). Indeed, engaging members of the KBIC in a substantial way was only possible because one researcher on the team had already established those relationships.

Execution-related insights and challenges

For the TD component of this project, the plan was to hold a one-day workshop with project partners to identify a research question (beyond other questions explicitly spelled out in the proposal) that might be of interest to local stakeholders affected by fish contamination and/or to decision makers who had some role in the governance of concerns associated with contamination. In the absence of direct stakeholder involvement during the proposal phase, including this space in the project design is essential because steps to engage community partners have to be intentional and taken early on (Denzin et al., 2008; Minkler and Wallerstein, 2008). Otherwise, little opportunity for partners to influence the direction of research will be possible.

Conducting TD research also required the project team to pay more attention to issues of power. For example, to facilitate communication across disciplinary and organizational boundaries during the one-day workshop, the social science researchers intentionally designed the workshop with the goal of flattening the power dynamics at work in interactions between project investigators, agency personnel and community members (Gagnon et al., 2017). Guided by community-engaged and Indigenous research scholarship (Hart et al., 2017; Marshall and Batten, 2004), the strategy employed by the social science team involved ensuring that counter-narratives could be articulated and non-dominant voices heard. Toward this end, more time in the one-day Community and Partner Workshop was devoted to presentations by community partners than presentations by investigators. In addition, more time was devoted to group meetings and general discussion than to presentations, with each group balanced (as much as possible) in terms of gender, role in the project (investigator, agency partner, community partner) and expertise.

The question "when can we safely eat as much fish as we desire?" emerged out of themes generated at the opening workshop. These themes included the value of adopting a "seven generations" perspective and assessing whether societies were making progress toward safe fish consumption or, in the words of one participant, scientists, health officials and policy makers were just "producing lots of paper". Or, more simply, when will it actually be safe to eat fish without worrying about the effects of mercury and other contaminants. Phrasing the question in terms of "when" emphasized the goal of eliminating the need for fish consumption advisories and determining what might be required to achieve that goal.

As it turned out, integrating a TD component of research into the project increased the interaction between the social and natural science researchers. In the absence of the project's commitment to incorporate stakeholder and decision-maker participation in research design, investigators could have executed much of their research within their own broad disciplinary boundaries, without the need to cross those boundaries. Investigators involved in modeling could have proceeded independently with improving models and the scenarios that drive them. Likewise, the social science researchers could have proceeded with their governance mapping and assessment of the emerging, loosely connected, multijurisdictional system of chemical governance (which was another aspect of the project) without much interaction with other disciplinary groups. However, the commitment to engage non-academic actors in the research necessitated a greater level of coordination and cooperation. Although the social science team had the experience to facilitate community engagement, they could not address community-based questions related to the fate and transport of mercury without the natural science team. For community partners to shape a portion of the research trajectory, cooperation and working across disciplinary and TD boundaries was essential.

Addressing the question of when it will be safe to consume as much fish as desired meshed well with the general goals of the project. Addressing such a question required the contributions of all team members. Atmospheric modelers and chemists were needed to forecast mercury deposition levels in the Great Lakes Basin and to pass that information on to lake modelers. The lake modelers, in turn, required information about local fish consumption patterns, which led to their participation in the Talking Circle event. And for the social science researchers to make a meaningful assessment of the existing system of multijurisdictional and multiscale governance, knowing how long it would take, under various policy scenarios, to eliminate the need for fish consumption advisories was crucial.

Not unexpectedly, executing a project that included natural science and social science researchers as well as community partners presented challenges associated with coordinating the flow of information between the various subgroups and keeping everybody aware of what others were doing. Although communication is necessary in any multi-investigator project, even if all investigators are trained in the same discipline, the challenges are greater in TD projects. A benefit is that the relationships created (or strengthened) in the course of a project can lay the foundation for further, more focused, TD research, which was one outcome of this project.

The formal structure for facilitating communication came in the form of regularly scheduled project meetings. The first several meetings were in-person gatherings for researchers on the Michigan Tech campus, with others joining in by video conferencing. Eventually, all researchers started attending by video conferencing. Not everybody could attend each meeting, but somebody from each subgroup was usually in attendance. A routine emerged in which the PI arranged for one of the researchers to open with a research presentation and take a few questions. That was followed by a discussion of issues requiring some level of coordination. At the end of each meeting, project members briefly described what they had been working on and/or what they would be doing in the coming weeks. Project partners did not attend this meeting, but if something relevant arose, someone would volunteer to communicate with the appropriate partner.

Most issues raised in the meeting were later discussed in detail by a smaller group. A simple example of such an issue involved a plan to represent the atmosphere over the Great Lakes region with a finer "grid" than elsewhere, with questions being how fine a grid and whether the Great Lakes region should be defined as the Great Lake basin or the area occupied by all states and provinces bordering on the Great Lakes. After a brief discussion, the question was later posed to several project partners. The PI also played a coordinating role outside of the meetings, facilitating discussions and decisions as the need arose, which is how much of the detailed communication occurred.

A less visible coordination-related process involved graduate students needing to carve out a piece of research that each could claim as their own to meet the requirements of their degree program, especially students operating near or across disciplinary boundaries. Although co-PIs defined the general area of each student's contribution, informal negotiations took place between graduate students doing similar work and between students and their project supervisor. After all, if one were not careful, he or she could end up straddling several areas without any one area being associated with their individual contributions. The pursuit of a community-engaged component of research further complicated matters. How much time, for example, should one spend on the community-engaged component of the project as compared with other components, especially if one area of research promised to contribute more to one's dissertation?

One study of interdisciplinary projects involving teams of graduate students suggests that such projects are most successful when courses, comprehensive exams and dissertations have interdisciplinary components (Morse et al., 2007). In our project, funded students did participate in at least one of two interdisciplinary courses centered around the theme of social and natural scientists collaborating to address "wicked problems". In addition, the project provided funds for students to present at conferences, with all students and co-PIs attending the same conference in the second year. In addition, each co-PI served as the outside member of a dissertation or thesis committee of a student from a different department, and students generally attended each other's defenses. These courses and experiences appeared to facilitate informal processes of communication, coordination and relationship building over the course of the project.

Coordinating publications and deciding who should be included as a co-author is an issue for all projects having more than one investigator, with the challenge being greatest in diverse, highly interdisciplinary projects (Elliott et al., 2017). For the most part, the strategy taken in this project was to leave decisions involving publications to each subgroup – that is, the environmental chemists, the atmospheric modelers, the biogeochemists and the social science researchers. In the end, of the many publications generated by this project, only a few included authors from both the social and natural sciences. Two such publications were an early over-arching paper that included all co-PIs as authors (Perlinger et al., 2016) and a paper reporting on an integrated assessment of future mercury deposition in the Great Lakes region, which included all co-PIs and a number of graduate students as authors (Perlinger et al., 2018).

Involving non-academics in the co-production of knowledge also presents challenges, including issues of funding (Schmidt and Pröpper, 2017). In this project, the main points of formal engagement with project partners were the opening workshop, a Talking Circle event and the closing workshop. These events were not especially costly; still, if funds had been available, it would have made sense to reimburse participants (some of whom lived a good distance away) for their travel costs. Among other things, it would have communicated the value placed on their participation. Funding was available to engage undergraduate students from the KBOCC in project-related research, and several students took advantage of this opportunity. However, a higher level of engagement, such as including a community member consultant on the project team and compensating them for their work, would have required a greater commitment to TD research at the proposal stage.

Another challenge related to community-engaged research is how assumptions and uncertainties are communicated (Schmidt and Pröpper, 2017). In a paper for a disciplinary audience, one can make assumptions that allow a problem or question to be simplified without being overly concerned about how those assumptions are communicated. For example, this project assumed, for all practical purposes, that the effects of multiple contaminants in fish tissue are not synergistic. In an academic paper, readers will recognize that this is an assumption made to simplify the analysis. However, in presenting to a community affected by such contamination, one cannot lightly assume away such concerns. The co-PI who translated atmospheric concentrations into fish tissue concentrations also wrestled with how best to communicate that a wide range of fish tissue concentrations were possible owing to variations in watersheds and aquatic ecosystems.

The atmospheric modelers, in generating data to address a question of interest to a non-academic community, also had to wrestle with similar issues. Strictly speaking, simulated futures are not always meant to be predictive. Often, they are used to generate hypotheses about the effect of different factors on whatever is being modeled, with the goal being to better understand the dynamics of that particular piece of nature. The use of a model for forecasting always comes with assumptions, and not all are easy to communicate. In this case, we eventually made an accommodation that simplified the need to communicate assumptions. We started out by asking how long (in terms of "generations") would be required to achieve the goal of safe fish, but even that low level of precision (generations) turned out to be problematic. Ultimately, we ended up asking whether the world could meet the goal of safe fish in 50 years (under the different scenarios), which substantially reduced the level of uncertainty that had to be communicated.

Finally, an important outcome of TD research is the role that it plays in building relationships (Harris and Lyon, 2013). Within disciplines, relationship-building processes usually occur through institutional mechanisms such as disciplinary conferences and in the reviewing and publishing of journal articles. Building equitable relationships among investigators in diverse disciplines and between investigators and community partners requires other mechanisms, with participation in TD projects being one of those mechanisms. Indeed, the TD aspect of this project would have been difficult to execute without relationships established by one of the social science researchers in a previous project. Furthermore, one of the important outcomes of this project was that it led a subset of the project team and community partners into productive new collaborations.

In particular, at the closing workshop, after a researcher discussed the importance of local, landscape-scale factors on fish tissue concentrations, a participant asked if there were ways in which tribal communities might use information about the local area to their benefit. The research agreed that a project to produce this type of knowledge, specific to the local area, would be beneficial. For example, the age and type of fish affects contamination levels as does the location where that fish is harvested. The type of fish matters because fish higher up the food chain accumulate more contaminants than those below it. Similarly, all things being equal, older fish have had more time to accumulate contaminants than younger fish. Where fish are harvested matters because the ratio of land-to-water in a given watershed (with more land increasing the amount of mercury being captured), the type of land (with wetlands facilitating methylation of more mercury) and the specifics of the aquatic ecosystem all affect the level of contamination. Given that the concentration of mercury in circulation will remain high enough for multiple generations of fish consumers to be concerned about health risks, producing this type of knowledge could have significant value.

However, it is important that the production of knowledge about local landscapes, knowledge that can be used to reduce exposure to contaminants, is co-produced with the affected community. Otherwise, the framing of the research and the translation of results into guidance would reflect the choices of the researchers rather than those of the affected community. Such a project, made possible by the relationships established in this project, is now being proposed.

Conclusion

This chapter examined an interdisciplinary research project that included space for incorporating stakeholder and decision-maker participation in research design, resulting in the co-production of knowledge of interest to both the researchers and project partners. Steps that facilitated this research included: (a) involving all potential investigators in the preparation of the project proposal; (b) proposing a budget that valued research in all disciplines; and (c) including space in the project to include a TD research component. The TD research question pursued in this project emerged out of a workshop held with project partners soon after the project began. Intentional efforts taken to facilitate equitable dialog and flatten the power dynamics contributed to project partners significantly influencing the themes that emerged in the workshop, which led to the question "when will it be safe to consume as much fish as desired?"

A variety of challenges emerged in the framing and execution of the project, which were magnified by the TD aspects of the research. Examples of challenges at the proposal stage were the need to reconcile different visions of how to examine the "dynamics of the human system" and minor points of miscommunication that complicated the initial discussions and diverted from substantive issues. During execution of the project, issues revolved around the funding available to support the participation of community partners, communicating simplifying assumptions and issues of uncertainty to non-academics, and working within institutional structures that are not necessarily designed with TD research in mind.

Challenges aside, pursuing the TD component of this research not only directed the efforts of researchers toward a question of interest to community partners but also resulted in an area of new research. In particular, the project highlighted the importance of producing knowledge about specific watersheds and finding ways to use that knowledge to adjust practices and reduce exposure to contamination. Addressing the question of when it will be safe to consume as much fish as desired helped to establish the relationships needed to conduct this future research in a meaningful fashion.

Acknowledgments

This project was made possible by US National Science Foundation Award ICER-1313755 (2013–2018).

10 Lessons from the transdisciplinary, international BIOPIRE project

Jennifer L. Dunn, Jessie L. Knowlton, Robert M. Handler, Erin C. Pischke, Kathleen E. Halvorsen, M. Azahara Mesa-Jurado, Theresa L. Selfa, David J. Flaspohler, Julian Licata, Ena E. Mata-Zayas, Rodrigo Medeiros, Cassandra Moseley, Erik A. Nielsen, Valentin D. Picasso Risso, Julio C. Sacramento-Rivero, Tatiana de Souza, Cesar J. Vazquez Navarrete and Nathan Basiliko

Introduction

This chapter tells the story of the BIOPIRE project, a transdisciplinary, multicountry, multiyear examination of the socioecological consequences of bioenergy development. We first introduce the BIOPIRE project and give the history of the formation of the large project team. We then discuss the barriers encountered by this transdisciplinary and international team during the project and the strategies employed to resolve them. Our aim in conveying the experiences with BIOPIRE is to allow environmental managers and researchers to learn from our processes of team development, including mistakes we made and various strategies we tried along the way, to be able to engage in transdisciplinary environmental science for managing socioecological systems.

Building the BIOPIRE team

BIOPIRE was a National Science Foundation-supported project involving a transdisciplinary group of scientists and industrial, governmental and NGO partners investigating the sustainability of bioenergy development across the Americas. The team included scientists and partners from six study countries: Argentina, Brazil, Canada, Mexico, Uruguay and the US. The roots of this project team were established years ago when a small group of engineering scientists came together to create several environmental sustainability initiatives at Michigan Technological University (MTU). They believed that such initiatives needed to be interdisciplinary, involving groups of social, natural and engineering scientists. This group of engineers realized that efforts to solve sustainability problems often failed when they lacked corresponding social and ecological science components and perspectives. As a result, they invited social and natural scientists from across MTU to collaborate on sustainability research. While much of the work was fundamentally interdisciplinary, the engineering scientists' longstanding linkages with various private sector companies brought industrial partners into the efforts at multiple levels.

The group ultimately garnered a US National Science Foundation Integrative Research and Education Traineeship (IGERT) grant with Southern University that combined public policy and engineering components. They also created the MTU Sustainable Futures Institute (SFI) and Sustainability Graduate Certificate.

After the creation of SFI, several of the group members continued to collaborate, pursuing multiple grants focused on transdisciplinary research. In the early 2000s the SFI applied for but did not receive an NSF Material Use: Science, Engineering, and Society (MUSES) grant focused on cellulosic ethanol from woody biomass. Instead, the group was granted a smaller planning grant of US$100,000 to collect preliminary data and revise their initial proposal. This grant set the precedent for future grants that the team collaborated on by creating an organizational structure with weekly team meetings. The weekly team meetings allowed the members to become more deeply integrated and led to improved understanding of the individuals and their work.

Following the planning grant-funded work, the team revised their original proposal and was successful in procuring a large (US$1.7 million) MUSES grant to expand their work together over five years. Weekly meetings and presentations helped foster relationships and expand shared knowledge of the project. For example, chemical engineers learned about plant community biomes and soils and ecologists learned about pyrolysis and transportation optimization. This greatly aided the group in developing more integrated project outputs, such as interdisciplinary publications and proposals. The team developed and co-authored an edited volume that had its roots in the project and included a number of authors from other US institutions (see Solomon and Luzadis, 2008).

As the MUSES project ended, several of the core IGERT and MUSES team members continued to work together and identified a funding opportunity in the new NSF Research Coordination Network (RCN) program. This program focuses on funding groups that work to expand and develop scientific networks around a theme, rather than fund empirical research. The group decided to pursue an RCN proposal around bioenergy projects across the Americas and yet again created a proposal team across universities, research laboratories and industrial entities within the US and across North and South America. The SFI devoted staff support to identifying potential partners from Argentina, Brazil, Canada and Mexico; team members contacted colleagues across the five countries who might be valuable members of the proposal team and future network. The team successfully procured a four-year US$750,000 grant mostly dedicated to supporting the travel of individuals from the six countries to yearly meetings rotating between member countries and two conferences on the topic of bioenergy impacts on socioecological systems. This interdisciplinary, international group also included industrial, governmental and NGO partners. At this point,

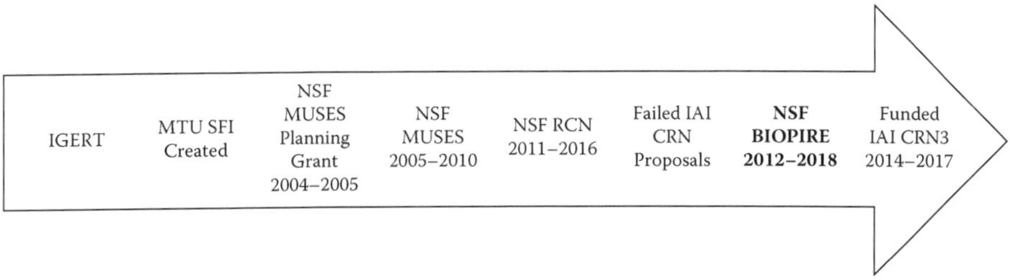

Figure 10.1 Timeline of projects leading to BIOPIRE

the group of collaborators had become not just interdisciplinary but also international and transdisciplinary. A timeline of projects leading up to BIOPIRE can be found in Figure 10.1.

The BIOPIRE Project

Within the first year of the RCN project, a new NSF Partnerships in International Research and Education (PIRE) call for sustainability-related proposals was issued. A subset of individuals from the MUSES grant were part of this NSF PIRE (BIOPIRE) proposal: two social scientists, two natural scientists and two engineering scientists. The group identified and invited individuals from the RCN network and other prior collaborations from Argentina, Brazil, Mexico and the US to collaborate on the BIOPIRE proposal drawing for a total of 32 scientists from universities and governments across the four countries with strong non-governmental organization (NGO) and industrial partnerships. They began the work to develop a proposal for the parallel Inter-American Institute for Global Change Research Coordinated Research Network (IAI CRN3) program that could provide substantial funds to all the partner countries (NSF strictly limits its funds to people at US organizations), but ultimately some international partners were unable to complete the needed paperwork. After two more proposals and the addition of partners from Canada and Uruguay, the team received a CRN3 grant for about US$200,000 with most of the funds going to non-US partners.

The BIOPIRE proposal was funded at US$4.8 million for five years and began in October 2012. It was extended an extra year in 2017 and will end in 2018. The project was structured around four bioenergy case studies shared across the team, one in each partner country, including eucalyptus in Argentina, oil palm in Mexico and Brazil, and Northern hardwood forests in the USA. Once the IAI CRN3 grant was received, the team was able to leverage these funds to add case studies and research in Canada and Uruguay.

BIOPIRE's main research question focused on understanding the socioecological impacts of bioenergy development, using various types of models to integrate them, and making policy and sustainability-metrics recommendations to maximize positive bioenergy outcomes and minimize negative impacts. Over the course of the project, the group grew as additional students, scientists and other social actor representatives (NGO, industrial, governmental) joined the project.

The project and management structure were designed to facilitate communication and transdisciplinary coordination. Developing technical subteams (i.e., socioeconomic, metrics, ecosystem; Table 10.1) and country team leaders required extra coordination and communication, both of which are essential to ensuring a successful project. Developing subteams also allowed multiple people to assume positions of responsibility within the project, which increased the level of engagement across the project team.

The socioeconomic/policy subteam consisted of sociologists, economists and policy scientists. The other two subteams were the ecosystem subteam and the metrics subteam. The ecosystem subteam consisted of natural scientists (i.e., avian ecologists, forest ecologists, soil ecologists, hydrologists, etc.) and the metrics subteam was made up mostly of engineering scientists (i.e., transportation engineers, chemical engineers, agronomic engineers, etc.). The questions and research methods of each subteam are listed in Table 10.1.

Table 10.1 BIOPIRE subteams

Subteam	Research question(s)	Research methods or tools used	Total team member numbers (2018)
Socioeconomic/ policy	How will biofuel or bioenergy development affect socioeconomic systems? How will policy address biofuel-related socioecological impacts?	Interviews, surveys and document analysis	Researchers: 22 Students: 30
Ecosystem	How will biofuel or bioenergy development affect ecological systems?	Soil sampling and modeling; sap flow measurements, watershed modeling, biodiversity assessment (birds and pollinators)	Researchers: 36 Students: 16
Metrics	What sustainability indicators and metrics best assess biofuel sustainability across highly variable Pan American socioecological systems?	Transportation logistics modeling, life cycle analysis and integrated system sustainability modeling	Researchers: 18 Students: 12

The BIOPIRE project lasted for six years. Roughly 130 individuals from six countries and over 50 organizations participated to ultimately study six bioenergy development cases. An NGO, Conservation International Brazil, had formal representation on the team. The group collaborated with communities and industry in formal and informal ways, garnering access to industrial feedstock cultivation sites for data collection and to communities for interviews and surveys. The team ultimately procured an IAI CRN3, two USAID PEER and one NSF International Research Experience for Undergraduates grants, totaling over US$600,000.

Strategies for success of a transdisciplinary international research project

Early in the planning stages of the BIOPIRE project, organizers were already thinking critically about the potential challenges associated with such an ambitious, complex project. For example, how can a project team develop healthy and productive working relationships among all of the scientists, engineers and local experts living in different countries, with different technical backgrounds, who are used to communicating in different vocabularies and languages? It was a challenging task, but several project team members had previous experience working in multidisciplinary, multinational project settings. Based on previous experiences with good and bad project outcomes, the team developed the project structure and management strategy designed to optimize the strengths of the group and avoid or reduce obstacles to achieving project goals. For example, the creation of both country and disciplinary subteams (Table 10.1), each with an experienced leader who could communicate in several languages, partitioned the large and complex project into more manageable segments with clear leadership and accountability. Below we summarize several other strategies that were fundamental to the success of the BIOPIRE project.

Building on previous working relationships

The BIOPIRE project was an ambitious effort, with a large network of scientists, engineers and other partners spread across multiple countries. The reality of such a large effort is that even with the most careful planning and management strategies in place, this project was likely to struggle if not built on successful professional relationships between several project team members. Trust, commitment and communication are key components of success when conducting multidisciplinary and transdisciplinary research (NAS, 2005; O'Rourke et al., 2014; Thompson, 2009). Of these three, trust may take the longest to develop. Although the entire project team had not worked together before, several linkages existed between a core of project team members who had worked together on smaller research efforts in the same discipline, across disciplines or across countries. The success of the BIOPIRE project was based on the project team's ability to weave this network of smaller connections into a larger, stronger web of researchers who were more quickly able to gain each other's trust and acceptance when working to address complex scientific problems in the face of multiple barriers (i.e., communication, budget, safety, cultural differences, integration across disciplines and time constraints).

Promoting effective communication

In such a large project network, it is often possible to lose sight of other aspects of the overall project, in terms of how the pieces of the project rely on each other and how they all ultimately work together to satisfy important project outcomes. To combat this tendency, developing a robust system of regular constructive communication is key (Brown et al., 2015).

The project team held a series of monthly meetings and each technical subteam used regular phone or video conference calls to provide updates on the technical aspects of the work plans developed by each project team as it was carried out in each country. Country leaders were in charge of organizing regular meetings and information exchange between all team members conducting work in that country. This ensured that logistical details and information exchange between team members were facilitated. For instance, if fieldwork for socioeconomic interviews and biodiversity assessments were scheduled to occur in the same season, the country leader ensured that the researchers were aware of each other's plans, which could facilitate coordination and sharing of in-country resources like lodging whenever possible. Country leaders would meet as a group to make sure work plans developing in each country were communicated widely.

Whole-team video conference calls were also scheduled at regular intervals, often every month during periods of the year when fieldwork was less intense. These whole-team calls were a chance to make introductions and keep in touch with a large project team, to provide guidance on upcoming project items of interest to the entire team, and to provide opportunities for various subgroups to share their work plans and study results with the larger team. Coordinating over several time zones was not easy but planning ahead by several months allowed most members to join in the meetings.

Yearly meetings (see Table 10.2) were developed at the same time and location as yearly RCN meetings, rotating between the countries; since many of the same

Table 10.2 BIOPIRE annual meetings

Annual meeting date	Place
May 2013	Buenos Aires, Argentina
July 2014	Belém, Brazil
June 2015	Houghton, USA
May 2016	Villahermosa, Mexico
May 2017	Eugene, USA

people attended both, the projects were able to leverage substantial travel funding to bring 50–60 people from five to six countries to attend each one of the meetings. This approach allowed the entire team to take tours of relevant field sites that were associated with the project and ensured that our international team members felt a sense of ownership and equal representation within the project team. Annual in-person meetings were scheduled to last for roughly one week and were critical venues for the types of detailed, thoughtful transdisciplinary and creative exchanges that are often difficult to coordinate over the phone or internet. These venues also offered us a chance to socialize and interact with the entire project team, which made it much easier to maintain a working relationship after a sense of community engagement and collegiality was developed.

In the context of supporting regular and useful communication in our virtual and in-person meetings, it was vital to identify potential barriers to communication and work to overcome them throughout the project. Language barriers are often present in international teams no matter where they conduct their research (Barrett and Cason, 1997; Pischke et al., 2017; Ross, 1984). Language barriers were perhaps the most significant issue to address on the project and exist in multiple areas. The most obvious is communication challenges between foreign languages, and this was an issue for the BIOPIRE project, with at least three native languages spoken (English, Spanish and Portuguese) amongst project team members. While English was the most commonly spoken language among the project team members, efforts were made to enhance the experience of non-native English speakers, particularly graduate and undergraduate students. At several in-person events, translation services were offered for those who were more comfortable speaking or listening in Spanish or Portuguese. At the outset of the project, native English speakers were given a series of best practices to facilitate better communication during meetings or presentations. Even simple things like speaking more slowly and clearly than you would for an audience of English speakers could benefit team members who were familiar with but not fluent in English. Several team members with English as their native language also had years of prior training in Spanish, which helped to facilitate communication across countries, especially when conducting fieldwork. However, deficits in the levels of Spanish or Portuguese language skills of some English-speaking researchers posed some challenges for the team's research. In these cases it was invaluable to have the help of local, native speakers, particularly in areas with unique dialects (Pischke et al., 2017).

Subtler but equally problematic language barriers also existed between scientific disciplines, and this required more diligence to identify and overcome. When conducting transdisciplinary work, having a common understanding of disciplinary vocabulary can be critical in ensuring that the entire team has a clear vision of the research plan and agenda (Brown et al., 2015; Morse et al., 2007). Taking the time to fully understand what seemingly common terms like "control group," "resilience" or "system" mean in the context of different disciplines or to chart out what the data collected by each team would ultimately consist of in terms of scope, qualitative/quantitative characteristics and detail was crucial to forming a common understanding of the research that would be taking place and how it could be used effectively in transdisciplinary settings. The context differences of key terms across disciplines were initially identified in monthly meetings and then discussed in more depth during annual meetings when all of the researchers were able to meet in person and apply the terms in connection with field site visits. The ongoing discussions helped the researchers to come to an agreement on how to best integrate concepts when planning future data collection and publications.

Incorporating local expertise

With a project spanning several research areas across several countries, it was critical to have local experts included in the development and execution of our research plans for each case study. Given that the project team included scientists based in each of the study countries often with prior experience working in the case study areas, their involvement was critical. In addition to this important baseline level of local expertise, the team tried to deepen our working relationships with local experts in all project areas. This included involving local NGOs and government agencies in the planning and execution of fieldwork, engaging with local press outlets to disseminate and publicize our work and meeting with community leaders to encourage community cooperation and engagement in data collection.

This ultimately resulted in turning the BIOPIRE project into a transdisciplinary team project in some of the country cases. These relationships were critical to developing a thorough understanding of the social, ecological and technical context surrounding the bioenergy development issues being studied by the team, and to ultimately conduct an effective research program in each case. By incorporating local expertise, the researchers were able to gain trust and, in some cases, increase participation/cooperation from the local communities, which ultimately led to a more complete understanding of the socioecological impacts of bioenergy in each case study.

Promoting visible and achievable goals or end products

It is important for all team members to have a clear understanding of the ultimate goals of the project and how their work contributes to a larger mission in addition to their personal goals (Brown et al., 2015). If researchers understand their personal contribution to the project, it will help them be more accountable in the development of the ultimate successes of the project.

One tangible end goal that researchers were encouraged to achieve was publishing interdisciplinary articles involving authors from multiple locations within the project. To prevent miscommunication and loss of trust among researchers, research team members began discussing expectations about authorship early on in the project. This strategy has helped co-authors to successfully work together to publish their research findings from the project. On a broader level, this demonstrates the power of working through foreseen problems ahead of time to set clear guidelines amongst group members, whether it be on authorship, research tasks or group coordination for meetings. Setting guidelines ahead of time can reduce miscommunication and lead to better inclusion amongst team members because they have a better understanding of their role and expectations of others.

Transferring knowledge and expertise

During the course of the project, the team hosted several workshops and professional development seminars and taught several courses related to transdisciplinary teamwork. Two of the courses involved several graduate students from different institutions and disciplinary backgrounds, focusing on grant writing and development. The students were tasked with writing an interdisciplinary grant, teaching them the value of collaboration and the skills necessary to create strong research networks (as described in Knowlton et al., 2014). Another course, titled "Biofuels in Pan-America" hosted several guest lecturers from different institutions and organizations across the Americas to discuss bioenergy development as it related to their disciplines and organizations. This course required that students from different disciplines write a paper about bioenergy development in the Americas incorporating information from their diverse disciplinary perspectives. Last, by hosting the workshops and courses, the senior members of the research team were able to train the other members of the team in the skills necessary to make this transdisciplinary project a success.

In addition to courses, several members on the project have held professional development seminars related to transdisciplinary research, grant writing and publishing. Each of these forms of outreach has contributed to sharing expertise and knowledge and they ultimately are valuable tools for training other researchers on transdisciplinary collaboration. Not only have these opportunities provided an avenue for this team of researchers, but indirectly and directly they have helped them build their professional networks, creating new transdisciplinary collaborations and strengthening their skill sets.

Unexpected problems and barriers

Any research project as broad in scope and scale and involving such a large and diverse team of researchers as the BIOPIRE project is bound to face a number of challenges. The team faced challenges not only inherent to working across multiple disciplines in social sciences, natural sciences and engineering, but also related to conducting research in six different countries. Some of these challenges, or barriers, such as problems with integration across disciplines and additional time commitments required to complete work, were anticipated by the team leadership and strategies such as those mentioned above (coordination, communication, etc.) were implemented to lessen the impact of these barriers. Other problems, however, were not anticipated and had to be addressed as they occurred over the six-year lifetime of the BIOPIRE. In this section, we outline the barriers that were both anticipated and unanticipated, which we hope will be useful for lessening the impact of these barriers in future, similar large-scale projects.

Based on observations from the BIOPIRE leadership and an anonymous survey that was administered to the BIOPIRE team, we identified 11 general categories of challenges that emerged during the life of the project: budget and money, bureaucracy, communication, consistency and coordination, danger and safety, different cultural traditions, integration, language, fieldwork logistics, personnel and relationships, and time commitment (Pischke et al., 2017). Some of these challenges stem from the transdisciplinary nature of the project, while others relate mainly to the international scope of the research and still others stem from the combination of the two. Barriers related mainly to the international scope of BIOPIRE included budget and money, which referred to constraints on transferring, accessing or converting currency between countries; bureaucracy, which referred mostly to difficulty in procuring insurance, permits or visas to work abroad and difficulty gaining permission to work in rural areas or on private lands; danger and safety, which referred to uncertainties about the safety of students and faculty working in both rural and urban settings; and navigating different cultures and languages (Pischke et al., 2017). The rest of the barriers mentioned related mainly to the interdisciplinary nature of BIOPIRE or the combination of the interdisciplinary and international setting.

Integration of disciplinary views on questions, experimental design, data collection, analysis and synthesis of findings in interdisciplinary research teams is usually one of the greatest challenges researchers engaged in interdisciplinary work face (Barrett and Cason, 1997; Gardner, 2013; Knowlton et al., 2014; Halvorsen et al., 2016; Morse et al., 2007; Palmer et al., 2016; Romero-Lankao et al., 2013; Strober, 2006), and this was certainly true for the BIOPIRE team. While the project leadership had anticipated this challenge from the beginning and took steps to lessen its impact (see the section "Strategies for success of a transdisciplinary international research project"), some specific barriers to integration did arise.

For example, some participants felt that there was a lack of integration across disciplines with data collection sites and methodology, in part because the social and natural scientists had different timelines and spatial scales for their fieldwork (Pischke et al., 2017). In one case, social and natural scientists shared housing, which was beneficial for building relationships, but proved at times to be more challenging for the team members as they had varying distances to travel to field sites and different schedules. Others identified integration of data as a difficult barrier and pointed to the need to identify software or other specific methodology capable of integrating data from multiple disciplines even before data collection began, which has also been mentioned by other researchers (Barlow et al., 2011; Morse et al., 2007). In addition, there was considerable confusion about what kinds of data some subgroups could provide to other subgroups. For example, some modeling scientists wanted particular social data that could not be realistically collected given time or resources or could not be prioritized given the agreed-upon research questions. Finally, some BIOPIRE researchers seemed to end up staying within the comfort and familiarity of their own disciplinary questions, rather than trying to work on the more complex interdisciplinary questions (Pischke et al., 2017).

Owing to the broad geographical scope of BIOPIRE – encompassing six different countries across the Americas – logistics was one of the main challenges faced by the team, but this barrier also related to the logistics required to integrate the experimental design and fieldwork of multiple disciplines. Multiple field seasons in each country had to be coordinated, including when, where and how to share resources across disciplinary researchers. These logistical challenges included securing permits and dealing with cumbersome bureaucracy, finding local contacts, obtaining housing and transportation for all team members, traveling long distances on rough roads, and seasonal concerns such as who would be available to be interviewed or surveyed or what biophysical measurements could be taken while researchers were in the field (Pischke et al., 2017). In addition, because this research involved human subjects, permissions to conduct this research had to be secured from all home institutions and coordinated through a single research compliance office in the US to ensure compliance with US federal regulations. Not only was this time intensive, but it also required substantial education of team members about the US rules around human subjects' research.

Any large team of people attempting to work together must contend with problems surrounding personal relationships. While for the most part members of the BIOPIRE team got along amazingly well, a few problems did arise. Some participants were concerned that they were not being compensated or recognized for their time, as has been found in other large research groups (National Research Council, 2008; Palmer et al., 2016). Other conflicts were due to differences in personality types or differing expectations about roles, authorship, timelines or what would be provided (e.g., monetary and field help), as has been found elsewhere (Romero-Lankao et al., 2013). Difficulty of communication among BIOPIRE members was also viewed as a barrier at times, for reasons other than the different native languages of the participants.

Miscommunication arose relating to the focus and objectives of the research, fieldwork plans and basic disciplinary concepts. There was also difficulty by some participants in understanding the societal context or history of the field sites abroad, and some misunderstanding of researchers' objectives by local community members and collaborators at the field sites (Pischke et al., 2017). The miscommunications that arose in this project demonstrate the necessity for clear communication at two levels: internal team communication and communication to the greater public (i.e., policy makers, local community members, and other scientists; Gardner et al., 2013; Strober, 2006).

The extra time that it takes to conduct transdisciplinary, international research is a recognized barrier to this type of research (e.g., Morse et al., 2007; Ross, 1984), although many scientists do not fully anticipate just how much extra time will be required when conducting this type of work. In BIOPIRE, some participants felt frustrated with the seemingly slow progress in preparing for and conducting the transdisciplinary research abroad as well as the large time commitment required after the fieldwork to combine disciplinary data and write interdisciplinary papers (Pischke et al., 2017). Some of the graduate students on the project found it difficult to plan to spend weeks doing fieldwork abroad while being full-time students with many other responsibilities, including coursework and family commitments. Other students were caught up in disagreements among advisors and team members over methods that further slowed their progress even as they were eventually worked out. Despite the challenges that arise from large international, transdisciplinary research projects, the team has been successful in producing disciplinary and interdisciplinary publications aimed at understanding the impacts of bioenergy production across the Americas.

Lastly, while the project was labeled as transdisciplinary owing to the incorporation of governmental and non-governmental organizations such as Conservation International in Brazil, the project was not "deeply" transdisciplinary. The reason we make this argument is to acknowledge the challenge that the research group faced in incorporating other social actors in the research process. In several of the country cases these actors served as collaborators in making connections with the local communities to conduct interviews and surveys and identify sites for ecological studies; however, they were not involved in data collection and analysis. While these team members' involvement in the project was limited, they did provide valuable connections, field sites and other resources essential to project success. The transdisciplinary nature of the project could have been improved by bringing outside organizations into the project sooner to help with data collection and producing tangible recommendations that they could provide back to the communities that were studied.

BIOPIRE's contribution to the literature

At the end of the BIOPIRE project's planned timeline, the research team has, individually and in interdisciplinary groups, published journal articles and book chapters in a number of different venues. These publications and the group's ongoing work to return to the communities and report/educate about our results are beneficial for environmental managers to see how researchers can engage with local communities and inform policy actors about research implications for future management decisions. Out of eight publications relating to interdisciplinary, socioeconomic and policy aspects of the project, they contained 36 total keywords, 17 of them unique, which illustrates the breadth of the research topics addressed by the BIOPIRE team.

The publications span the years 2014–2017, with more publications in preparation for the coming years. Thirty-three co-authors, some of whom were included as co-authors on multiple publications, were involved in the preparation, data collection and writing of the articles. Co-authors included undergraduate and graduate students, university professors and representatives from NGOs. Researchers/co-authors represent each of the nationalities of the PIRE case study countries and include members from NGOs. The publications, presentations at conferences and meetings with local communities in the case studies provided the researchers with the opportunity to discuss implications of their findings and how they can be applied to inform environmental management and policy.

Findings from the articles show the multidimensional and wide-ranging types of inquiries pursued. Each of the articles focuses on a social, ecological or technological component of bioenergy development or the integration between components, and provides recommendations for environmental management and policy to reduce the negative impacts of bioenergy development. The team also wrote two books published by Mexican UADY Press, one short piece with sections translated into Spanish and Mayan for Yucatecan community members who participated in the project and a second, broader work addressed to the general public aiming to illustrate the many multidisciplinary issues that arise when analyzing the sustainability of a bioenergy case study. Several team members also published a special issue of the journal *Environmental Management* out of their work on the RCN and BIOPIRE projects. The group has a Facebook group and two websites, which allows team members to keep in touch easily, share potential new research ideas and recruit new collaborators from both within and outside of academia. Team members continue to work together on new publications, projects and proposals.

The team has also given numerous public presentations at conferences, organizations, universities and community meetings and over 20 undergraduate and graduate students have graduated across the six countries. It has supported over 250 international trips by team members to annual meetings, conferences and field sites. These outcomes focus on disciplinary as well as transdisciplinary research and demonstrate the need to think in terms of socioecological systems or coupled systems when developing environmental management strategies and policies for bioenergy systems across the Americas.

Conclusion

The BIOPIRE team, with diverse scientific backgrounds, employed multiple research methods to collect and analyze data that provides the scientific and non-scientific communities with a better understanding of the impacts of bioenergy systems across North and South America. During the research process, the team identified key strategies for interdisciplinary collaboration. The team used venues such as workshops, courses and professional development seminars to share this expertise and train the next generation of researchers to overcome current interdisciplinary constraints. Critical to the success of this team was sustained dialogue at multiple levels from generalized project management to very detailed field research planning, data collection instrument development, and analysis and writing. Structured but flexible venues and communication strategies that engaged people broadly but focused on getting the key people into the dialogues at the right time were crucial. In addition, shifting quickly from one communication approach to another when the first was not working helped reduce wheel-spinning. Finally, engaging as many people as possible in sustained dialogue was important, but so was moving forward even when people did not all participate in any given conversation to ensure the team continued to move forward in a timely manner.

Despite the challenges that inevitably arise with large transdisciplinary research projects that are broad in scope and scale, we believe that it is worthwhile to conduct this type of work. Not only is it necessary for tackling the wicked, interconnected environmental and societal problems, but also team members found the process to be extremely rewarding both personally and professionally. Team members shared knowledge across disciplines, created and strengthened existing relationships, and gained a better understanding of the socioecological systems they study by immersing themselves in transdisciplinary research. This research project demonstrates the importance of recognizing environmental management issues as socioecological problems and that studying them requires interdisciplinary or transdisciplinary teamwork.

In summary, building a transdisciplinary team based around a core group of researchers with existing relationships, creating a hierarchical team structure with multiple "leaders" who can help coordinate research questions and methods and provide points of accountability, and fostering a flexible, fun, open and inclusive environment for all members of the team help to ensure the ultimate success of large and complex projects like BIOPIRE.

Acknowledgments

This work was supported by the National Science Foundation's Partnerships in International Research and Education Program grant IIA no. 1243444 and Research Coordination Network Program grant CBET no. 1140152, as well as the Inter-American Institute for Global Change Research's CRN3105 grant.

11 Applying transdisciplinary research to enhance low-to-moderate income households' access to community solar

Brad Barnett, Emily W. Prehoda, Abhilash Kantamneni, Richelle L. Winkler and Chelsea Schelly

Introduction

As communities around the world search for strategies to reduce their dependence on fossil fuels, solar electric technology is emerging at the forefront of the transition to clean and sustainable energy sources (International Renewable Energy Agency, 2017). Solar technology is an economically viable option for electricity production at multiple scales, including residential-, community- and utility-scale installations (Branker et al., 2011; Bazilian et al. 2013; Solar Energy Industries Association, 2017), even in some rural, northern climate communities such as Michigan's Upper Peninsula (Kantamneni et al., 2016). In the first three quarters of 2017, solar accounted for nearly a quarter of all new generating capacity in the US – the second highest energy source behind natural gas (Solar Energy Industries Association, 2017). Still, adoption of solar technology at the household level faces a number of social, economic and technical barriers including high upfront installation and equipment costs (Hirshberg and Schoen, 1974), poor installation site conditions (Mills and Schleich, 2009), technology maintenance concerns (Rai et al., 2016) and inadequate community outreach and engagement (Margolis and Zuboy, 2006).

Community solar, defined as a solar energy installation whose electricity is shared by more than one household (Coughlin et al., 2010), is a relatively new innovation designed to provide solar PV for households that have traditionally lacked technical, financial or social access (Funkhouser et al., 2015). Traditional community solar programs seek to overcome these barriers by taking advantage of economies of scale and optimal siting locations and by leveraging community outreach efforts that tap into peer-to-peer marketing. Since 2015, the number of community solar programs operated by utilities in the US has increased from 68 to 228, growing from a total of 88 MW of installed capacity to 734 MW (Smart Electric Power Alliance, 2018).

More recently, community solar has been promoted as a tool to assist low-to-moderate income (LMI) households in accessing the economic benefits of solar

PV technology (Paulos, 2017). LMI households, defined as individuals or families whose household income does not exceed 115% of the median income for the area when adjusted for family size, face additional barriers to traditional residential solar PV adoption owing to lower credit scores inhibiting access to financing, an inability to capitalize on federal and state tax incentives, and higher rates of living in multi-family rental properties which can prohibit tenants from installing solar or negate economic motivation through split incentives (Paulos, 2017). Despite its promise to enhance access to solar, community solar programs have generally failed to achieve high rates of LMI participation (Interstate Renewable Energy Council, 2016).

Environmental managers seeking to develop a community solar project optimized for LMI participation must achieve the buy-in of a diverse array of stakeholders whose motivations to sanction and participate in a project often vary (e.g., climate change mitigation, energy independence, economic development, energy poverty alleviation). This creates a lack of uniform problem definition among participating parties, making program design optimization difficult if not impossible to reach (Brown et al., 2010). Using a transdisciplinary (TD) research approach helps to address these challenges by harnessing the scientific expertise of multiple academic disciplines to develop practical, socially acceptable solutions while generating transferable knowledge (Cash et al., 2003).

This chapter reflects on the process of applying a TD research process to design a viable community solar program using an on-going case study in a remote rural community in Michigan's Upper Peninsula. The goals of the TD team, comprising university scientists and local public policy practitioners, are to address barriers to community solar adoption among low-to-moderate-income residents. With this chapter, we aim to demonstrate both the successes and challenges of incorporating a TD project approach so that other teams, focused on any number of environmental problems, may benefit from our experiences. We also hope to describe a process that other communities or research teams might adapt in their own efforts to build successful community solar programs. While focusing on a single case may limit the generalizability of the study's findings, it provides the opportunity to explore in-depth the real-life challenges faced by a community and develop paths for future research (Hodkinson and Hodkinson, 2001).

The rest of the chapter is organized as follows. First, a brief overview of relevant literature on household level solar adoption is presented. Then, we examine the local context for solar adoption, describing the necessity for a TD team and a TD approach to studying, designing and implementing a community solar project for LMI families in L'Anse, Michigan. Subsequently, challenges confronted by the team in operationalizing the TD approach and strategies used to overcome them are described. We conclude the chapter by identifying key findings and discussing their place within the existing literature.

Challenges to residential solar PV adoption

While installing residential solar PV offers both economic and environmental benefits (Borenstein, 2017; Kalogirou, 2004), adoption rates are limited by technical, economic and social factors. The intermittency of solar energy and limited solar radiation in some geographic locations are potential barriers to solar technology (Sovacool, 2009; Zahran et al., 2008). Inadequate battery storage technology necessary to store intermittent solar resources is also referenced as a primary technological hurdle, but this is quickly changing as storage technology becomes more efficient and cheaper (Pearce, 2009). Housing stock characteristics can also prevent solar adoption as many homes cannot support the additional weight of solar arrays on the roof, do not have space for ground-mounted systems or receive insufficient sunlight due to shading (Mills and Schleich, 2009). High upfront costs and inadequate access to financing can further prevent solar adoption (Interstate Renewable Energy Council, 2016; Rai et al., 2016). However, many barriers to solar adoption are neither technical nor economic (Margolis and Zuboy, 2006; Schelly, 2014; Sovacool, 2009). Factors such as limited consumer awareness, inadequate community outreach and engagement, limited or inhibiting policy support, inadequate workforce skill and training, and lack of adequate codes, standards, interconnection and net-metering guidelines can create additional barriers to solar technology adoption (Margolis and Zuboy, 2006; Schelly et al., 2017).

The literature shows that solar adoption increases with rising electricity costs (Kwan, 2012) and implementation of policies like tax credits (Durham et al., 1988; Sener and Fthenakis, 2014), local grants (Lobel and Perakis, 2011), solar-specific provisions in renewable portfolio standards (Sarzynski et al., 2012) and third-party ownership. At a residential scale, rooftop solar adoption is strongly influenced by cultural factors like political affiliation (Kwan, 2012), environmental concerns (Chen, 2014) and personal interest in technical innovation and energy systems (Schelly, 2014).

Some researchers have shown that while such cultural and technoeconomic factors are necessary precursors for solar adoption, their effects may be magnified and accentuated by community networks and peer-to-peer communication (Schelly, 2014; Rai et al., 2016). Drawing from social network theory and diffusion of innovation theories, researchers have demonstrated that social factors like community-based social marketing schemes and networked knowledge-sharing mechanisms (Viardot, 2013; Noll et al., 2014; Rogers, 2010; Schelly, 2014), peer effects (Bollinger and Gillingham, 2012; Graziano and Gillingham, 2015; Rai et al., 2016) and assistance from local champions (Simpson, 2018) expedite the diffusion of solar energy technologies.

L'Anse case study context

By all accounts, the village of L'Anse, Michigan is an unlikely location for a community solar program. It is a remote rural location with relatively little solar radiation, low average income and education levels, and average electricity prices, located in a state without policies or programs that explicitly promote or subsidize community solar programs. These characteristics suggest that solar development in L'Anse will be more expensive than in other markets and that L'Anse lacks a customer base with enough purchasing power to absorb these higher costs. However, L'Anse is an interesting case to review, because projects that overcome these challenges will be replicable in other communities that are likely to face fewer obstacles.

The village, with an estimated population of approximately 1900 residents, is located in Michigan's Upper Peninsula on the shoreline of Lake Superior, approximately 100 miles away from the Canadian border. The village economy is dominated by the service industry with a small number of metal and equipment manufacturers that serve as major employers. An abundance of natural amenities including coastal areas, forestland, lakes and rivers, waterfalls, trails and parks attract outdoor enthusiasts and tourists. The median household income for L'Anse is US$39,194 compared with the national median of US$55,322, and approximately 66% of L'Anse households meet the US Department of Housing's LMI definition (US Census Bureau, 2012–2016). An estimated 15% of children live below the poverty line (US Census Bureau, 2012–2016). It is estimated that at least 43% of households in the village of L'Anse (417 of 975 in total) are below the State of Michigan's US Department of Housing and Urban Development "Low Income Limit". All told, this suggests that the majority of L'Anse residents would struggle to afford the upfront costs of solar PV technology and probably face challenges securing debt financing for such a project.

While environmental and technical feasibility alone cannot predict residential adoption of solar PV (Schelly, 2010; Kwan, 2012), adequate solar resources are necessary to generate power. L'Anse is known for its cold, snowy winters and long, sunny and mild summer days. In January, the average high temperature is only 20°F, and L'Anse receives 216 inches of snowfall per year. According to the National Renewable Energy Laboratory's PVWatts Solar Calculator, L'Anse receives an average of 4.40 kWh/m^2/day in solar radiation. In comparison, Phoenix, Arizona receives an estimated average of 6.57 kWh/m^2/day, or 49.7% more solar energy than L'Anse. The village's potential energy peaks in July and August (5.66 kWh/m^2/day) and it receives the least amount of solar energy in November (2.83 kWh/m^2/day), reflecting a substantial seasonal swing in solar resources.

L'Anse operates a municipal electric utility that serves village residents. Owning the utility means that the village has flexibility to construct a community solar project for its members if local leaders deem the project to be in the best interests of its customers. This helps to mitigate some institutional challenges to solar project development pertaining to permitting requirements, interconnection, site control and zoning that increase project "soft" costs – non-hardware-related expenses.

The village utility obtains its power from WPPI Energy, a not-for-profit regional power company based in Sun Prairie, Wisconsin. Member organizations like the village of L'Anse enter into long-term power supply agreements with WPPI Energy, which funds WPPI Energy's investment in power generation, transmission and wholesale power purchases. Thanks to the savings generated by the collective economies of scale, WPPI Energy is able to offer its members lower-cost power than the local utilities could purchase individually. This results in a much lower cost per kilowatt hour for L'Anse utility customers (approximately US$0.13/kWh) compared with nearby regional investor-owned utilities (US$0.22–0.26/kWh). The village also receives technical assistance from WPPI staff to support local utility operations such as energy optimization programs, grants and low-cost financing for local energy projects, and support for billing software. The unique partnership between the municipal utility and WPPI energy indicates the importance of regulatory and policy context that allows L'Anse to access these benefits, which can help to reduce the cost of developing a community solar project and increase the economic incentives for households to participate in such a program.

Despite its northern location, wintery climate, small population and low household median income, the village decided to explore the feasibility of offering a community solar program. The decision came on the heels of the village's installation of an 11 kW solar array in late 2016 to help offset its water treatment plant's electricity costs. The water treatment plant project was well received by the community and the village anticipates that the investment will result in savings for local taxpayers over time. Village leaders thought that a community solar project could help residents and businesses achieve similar results while increasing the community's access to renewable energy resources.

Assembling a transdisciplinary research team

To determine the feasibility of a community solar program and identify strategies to increase LMI households' access to community solar benefits, the village partnered with a nearby research university (Michigan Technological University), the non-profit power company that provides the village with electricity (WPPI Energy) and a regional planning and technical assistance agency (the Western Upper Peninsula Planning and Development Region). The partnership resulted in the formation of the Upper Peninsula Solar Technical Assistance & Resource Team (UPSTART), whose membership comprises academic researchers with expertise in sociology, energy policy, engineering and energy law, in addition to representatives from the local government, the utility, and the regional planning agency. This TD team was tasked with (a) conducting a site solar analysis and developing an engineering design for a community solar array to assess the project's technical and economic feasibility, and (b) executing a mix of qualitative interviews, community meetings and a community survey to identify the social feasibility of the project, including both support for and sociocultural barriers to the project. By designing a research program grounded in a TD approach, the team sought to assess the feasibility of a community solar program in L'Anse and develop viable strategies to address barriers to household level participation.

Transdisciplinary research methods to explore community solar feasibility

Projects that only assess technical and economic feasibility can often overlook the adverse social impacts that an energy development project can have on the surrounding community. Previous studies indicate that renewable energy projects that fail to account for the interests and concerns of affected communities risk project delays, higher project costs and ultimately project cancellations (Wüstenhagen et al., 2007). Social feasibility studies can help environmental managers, project developers and community leaders to better understand how to address community energy needs and the types of projects that communities want. Including a social feasibility study can influence a project's design by identifying key features and preferences (e.g., energy sources) and identify concerns early on so that they can be addressed in the project design phase. Social feasibility studies can also help to create accessible and digestible project information and help managers work with community members to identify key stakeholders, ask project significant questions and determine what themes should be considered during project design. Despite the benefits of conducting social feasibility studies, community leaders and environmental managers may not possess the skills or resources to successfully complete an assessment. However, utilizing a TD research approach can help to mitigate these challenges through collaborative efforts with institutions with more robust research resources.

In the case of the L'Anse community solar project, the research team conceptualized social feasibility with two separate but mutually reinforcing components. First, the project would be considered socially feasible if the study indicated that the majority of stakeholders and key community leaders expressed general support for the community solar project. Second, the project would be considered socially feasible if enough community members were willing to participate in the community solar program and support the cost of building and maintaining the solar array. Wüstenhagen et al. (2007) described this as "market" acceptance, a form of social feasibility, whereby consumers who purchase a good or service indicate general support. In order to design a program to achieve these aims, the research team needed to understand more nuanced information about how to work with a community with varied interests and attitudes pertaining to solar technology and energy more generally.

The researchers decided to use an exploratory social science research design that incorporated the use of qualitative interviews, community meetings and a community survey in order to explore a socially feasible community solar program for L'Anse. Given that very little research has been conducted on the topic, particularly in rural communities, qualitative interviews provided insight into potential participation drivers unknown to the research team. Interview questions and interviewee selection were both developed with input from non-academic research team members in order to provide local context and ensure that important community stakeholder representatives' views were incorporated in the study. The interviews were meant to examine how residents and business owners feel about a community solar project in their community, what problems/obstacles/hurdles might come up if the village pursues a community solar project, and what cultural, economic, social or institutional factors could impact the success of a project.

Three community meetings were also held to conduct discussions regarding the potential community solar project. Two were designed to solicit feedback from the general public, and a third was hosted in partnership with the local chamber of commerce to specifically engage local business leaders. The purpose of these meetings was to share preliminary information about the proposed community solar project, to gain insight and understanding into how L'Anse area community members felt about the possibility of beginning a community solar project in their village, and to learn more about potential opportunities and obstacles for designing a project that meets community interests. This gave community members an opportunity to learn about the project and share feedback about potential program options (e.g., upfront versus pay-as-you go models), overall program costs and potential participation barriers. A key aim of the community meetings was to incorporate a broad set of community members into the decision-making process in meaningful ways from the outset.

Finally, a community survey was distributed to all village of L'Anse utility customers – potential community solar participants if a program were developed (n = 925 residential customers and 111 commercial businesses). The survey sought to determine residents' and business owners' interest in participating in a community solar program, obtain feedback from residents on perceived barriers to participating in a community solar program, provide residents with a medium by which to voice concerns and be involved in the decision-making process and help the village develop a business model to evaluate the economic feasibility of a community solar program in L'Anse. The survey used the insights uncovered through the previous interviews and first community meeting with the general public to develop questions to measure variables hypothesized to influence individual participation in a community solar program.

Owing to its partnership with the village, the research team was able to insert the survey in the utility customers' monthly electric bill. This reduced the cost of survey implementation since the research team did not have to pay for postage or envelopes. Also, it presumably helped boost response rates as households are more likely to open utility bills than letters perceived as junk mail (Dillman et al., 2014). Respondents were also offered a US$5 gift certificate for completing the survey in order to enhance participation. Local officials suggested using "Baraga County Gift Checks", a program offered by the local convention and visitors bureau, for the survey gift certificates. These checks were redeemable at any business in the county. This was viewed as a way to emphasize the importance of keeping money in the community, a key theme of community solar. A response incentive strategy was seen as an effective way of encouraging higher response rates, particularly from individuals who did support community solar and were less likely to complete the survey. Following the initial distribution, team members traveled to L'Anse to canvas neighborhoods and provide a follow-up distribution of the survey to residents. This method was used to help increase the response rate of the survey in order to insure the survey sample was representative of the L'Anse population.

Analysis of the data generated from the survey research activities described above is ongoing. However, approximately 161 residential customer and 13 commercial customer responses were received, resulting in response rates of 17.4 and 11.7%, respectively. These low response rates suggest that results should be interpreted with caution given that the sample probably disproportionately represents households and businesses with a strong interest in the community solar program. However, when combined with the additional forms of social science data collection, the survey results provide some insight into potential challenges and opportunities for community solar in L'Anse. The next section describes some preliminary findings that reveal the benefits and challenges of conducting TD research to support the village's pursuit of community solar.

Addressing sociotechnical challenges in community solar through transdisciplinary research

One of the key tenets of TD research is that it is informed by real-world conditions and contexts owing to the involvement of local practitioners as team members. In the case of UPSTART and the L'Anse community solar program, the early involvement of the village manager and WPPI Energy staff helped to provide context that shaped the team's research questions and research design. First, researchers were told that any community solar program needed to be rate-neutral, whereby non-participating utility customers' rates did not increase owing to the solar program. This goal was given owing to concerns that many community members would object to having their rates increased to support a program they did not choose to participate in. Second, program participants could only be L'Anse utility customers. This made designing an economically feasible program more challenging because the research team had fewer potential participants to support the program. Third, any potential solar array would be constructed at a nearby, under development, industrial park. The site was selected because it was already owned by the village and near electrical transmission infrastructure. It was also previously identified in the county's economic development strategy as a source for green power development to entice environmentally conscious industrial park tenants. This helped to avoid potential project siting concerns such as zoning conflicts and public objections and reduce the project cost if it were developed. Finally, local practitioner involvement gave the team initial insight into the social science research design through feedback on questionnaires and surveys, identified key informants to interview, provided access to space for hosting community meetings and provided local insight throughout the process as to how to design meetings and the survey process to encourage participation.

In order to evaluate the technical potential and challenges of the community solar project, the research team included faculty and student members with expertise in electrical engineering and renewable energy systems design. Technical challenges are often cited as a challenge to solar PV development. However, it is important to note that these technical limitations, which are often a social construct, are rectifiable given advancements in storage and energy grid technology and appropriate policy environments (Sovacool, 2009). To determine the power generation potential for a village community solar program, UPSTART team members from the Michigan Technological University Keweenaw Research Center conducted a solar PV efficiency assessment at the industrial park designated by the village as a potential location for the community solar array. The solar potential assessment data was used to determine the total power output potential of a community solar array, and ultimately, the amount of credits individuals would receive if they chose to participate in the community solar program. The Keweenaw Research Center team members also designed a solar PV module system within the size and location of the potential installation site for the village. This process identified the types and quantity of equipment, and estimated total equipment and construction costs. These costs, in addition to the solar power output data, were used to inform the financial models applied to estimate the individual economic costs and benefits for participation in the community solar program.

Social science UPSTART members were tasked with addressing the challenge of LMI household access to solar and understanding the economic and social opportunities and constraints of community solar. One of the primary barriers to residential- and community-scale solar programs is the typically high upfront cost of participation. This is particularly true for LMI households. In most community solar programs, participants are required to pay a fixed cost per panel or portion of a panel (often referred to as a "share") in return for the value of the energy produced from the panel(s) over the life of the program. Like many communities in the region and rural communities throughout the US, L'Anse faces challenging sociodemographic and economic conditions that make larger investments difficult or impossible to achieve for most residents. In the case of L'Anse, the cost per share was estimated to be approximately US$500 before any tax credits or additional financial supports were taken into consideration. Securing financing (e.g., loans) for these purchases can be a challenge for LMI households because of limited or poor credit history. This can prevent families from securing short-term financing to help pay for larger purchases.

Recognizing that entry price would be too high for many residents and businesses, UPSTART team members targeted a number of strategies to reduce the upfront cost. First, they worked with the village utility to explore the feasibility of offering on-bill financing, where the cost of participating could be added to the customer's monthly electric bill, reduced according to the value of the energy generated from his or her panel(s). This is referred to as "pay as you go" financing. By doing this, participants would not be required to come up with a large upfront payment. This strategy helps to eliminate the need for outside financing and removes the upfront cost barrier.

A second approach was to design a rate structure so that program participants weren't required to purchase full panels. Recognizing that many residents and businesses would probably not seek to obtain all their energy through the community solar program, the UPSTART team recommended that residents be offered the option of partial panels. Under this rate, the cost of panels would be cut in half or in quarters, with the credits subdivided accordingly. By doing this, community members would have a lower upfront price to entry while still receiving a financial benefit (albeit lower).

At the time of the study, the primary federal-level policy affecting solar development in L'Anse involved a 30% renewable energy tax credit (US Government Publishing Office, 2011). This tax credit is one of the best mechanisms available to reduce the overall cost of solar project development. The credit can be applied to residential-, commercial- and utility-scale solar projects. The US International Trade Commission (ITC) can help reduce the project developer's tax liabilities, thus making the project more profitable or enabling the cost savings to be passed along to community solar program participants to reduce the upfront panel purchase price. For commercial-scale projects, system owners, developers and/or financiers are able to capitalize on the ITC. An important point of consideration regarding the ITC is that only individuals or organizations with federal tax liabilities can directly take advantage of the tax credit. Given that the village of L'Anse is a public entity which does not pay taxes to the federal government, the village could not directly apply the ITC to the project (US Internal Revenue Service, 2018).

UPSTART recognized that the ITC was critical to reducing the program entry cost to LMI households; however, the team lacked expertise in tax law. To fill the gap, the team recruited additional assistance in legal expertise to identify strategies to incorporate the ITC. One option identified by the team focused on a temporary "developer-owned" ownership structure. Under this arrangement, the developer would build the solar array for the village and own the system for a period of time so that the company could take advantage of ITC's value. Allowing the developer to temporarily own the system would also let the company take advantage of accelerated depreciation expenses (another tax advantage). These cost savings would then be passed along to the village, and ultimately to program participants, resulting in lower upfront costs.

Social feasibility: moving beyond technical and economic feasibility

UPSTART's public outreach revealed a mix of general community support for the village's pursuit of community solar while identifying a number of early concerns expressed by potential participants. Conveyed through the results of UPSTART's mix of interviews, focusgroups, and survey responses and encapsulated in a report produced by students in Michigan Technological University's autumn 2017 Community Solar Applications course, the community expressed support for the village of L'Anse moving forward with a community solar project. Most participants were excited about the potential project and saw it as a positive development for the community. Statements were made thanking the village for its pursuit of renewable electricity sources, environmental stewardship and innovation. Many community members liked the idea of L'Anse "being at the forefront" of renewable energy power generation, tapping into a sense of community pride. Energy independence also appeared to be a salient theme as residents liked the idea that power would be generated and consumed locally. The "community" part of community solar resonated with people who saw this as a potential opportunity for the community to come together to meet common aims, promote community pride and act for the greater good for the community. Finally, community members indicated a high level of trust in their local government and electric utility officials to assess and design the project to best meet the community's needs.

Some residents were concerned with the project's long-term viability and wanted a guarantee that participants would not be left with stranded costs if the village could not find a "buyer" for the solar project's power. Other residents were concerned that the cost of the project would be distributed to all of the village's utility customers, not just those who chose to participate in the program. To address these concerns in the design of the community solar program, it was critical to have UPSTART members from the village administration and WPPI Energy engaged at the beginning and throughout the process. The importance of engaging community stakeholders in every stage of the energy transition process is also discussed earlier in Chapter Seven. WPPI Energy agreed to serve as the primary purchaser for the village's solar project – committing to purchasing the power for the life of the project. This helps to ensure that participants would receive monetary returns for their investment while also signaling that village taxpayers would not be paying for the participants' credits. WPPI Energy also proposed a rate-neutral credit value, which prevented the project's cost from being shifted to non-participants. Under this structure, program participants receive credits valued at less than retail electricity rates, but higher than the wholesale price of electricity. While this increases the time required for participants to recapture their investment, it also helps avoid a potential political challenge for the village administration given concerns about increasing costs for non-participants.

Despite the community's general support of the village pursuing community solar, many expressed concern that the region lacked adequate solar resources owing to the region's annual snowfall and long winters. UPSTART team members attempted to address this concern during the community meetings by demonstrating the village's previous experience with incorporating solar at its water treatment facility. The team provided an overview of the energy generated to date by the village's water treatment plant solar array to demonstrate that power was produced during the winter months (albeit not as much as during the summer). Members from UPSTART representing the local government and WPPI Energy explained how the water treatment facility solar project helped save taxpayers money by reducing operating expenses, which helped validate the economic and technical feasibility of a larger community solar project. Combining the technical expertise of Michigan Technological University with the community's high level of trust in the village electric utility may have helped to alleviate some community members' concerns pertaining to solar performance in the region.

Participants in the community discussions, particularly business owners, expressed a strong desire for short payback periods where the value of the solar credits surpassed the amount invested to participate in the program. Preliminary feedback from the community survey suggested that community residents expected annual rates of return ranging from 7 to 25%. Local business owners expressed the belief that payback periods greater than three to five years were poor investments. Another common economic critique from both residents and business owners was that electricity prices in the village were low, particularly compared with the regional averages. Some did not see the point of participating in the program given their already low electricity bills.

While this feedback indicated the importance of economic performance for an individual's own participation in a potential community solar program, UPSTART's research uncovered that many community members were interested in community solar for its community and environmental benefits, beyond its potential as an economic investment. Community members viewed the program as an opportunity to help community institutions such as the local schools, churches and human service organizations reduce their operating expenses. Community members favored program design options that allowed residents and businesses to "donate" panels to these organizations. By reframing community solar participation in the context of supporting these institutions, many of which serve LMI households, the individual economic payback period considerations may be less important to community members. Community members wanted to see the project developed by locals, with the jobs and economic benefits staying local. Community members liked the idea of keeping the community solar ownership at a local level, despite the potential for ultimately higher participation costs, which speaks to empowering the community as well as having a voice in the decision-making process.

Another concern expressed by the community was the issue of transferability. Community members, both younger and older residents, worried that they might move out of the village or not live long enough to reap the full benefits of participating in the community solar program. This is a major consideration for populations living in rental and multifamily housing, since they are more likely to move (Phinney, 2013). Participants expressed an interest in wanting to sell or donate the right to these panels if their residential status changed or if a share-owner passed away. This speaks again to the concept of stranded costs. To mitigate transferability concerns, UPSTART recommended that panel ownership be interchangeable so that participants have the ability to sell or donate the rights to the panel credits as necessary.

Conclusions

One of the powerful benefits of TD research is the ability to harness the scientific resources of academic research institutions to address real-world problems. As this in-progress study demonstrates, enhancing access to the benefits of renewable energy through a community solar program requires developers to overcome a mix of social, economic and technical hurdles. These challenges can be even more difficult when developing projects in rural low-income communities. Consistent with findings from previous work on residential solar adoption, the UPSTART team confronted socioeconomic circumstances, policy limitations and environmental conditions that presented roadblocks to community participation; however, creative community partnerships and public participation, driven by TD research design, have proved to be invaluable tools to assist with energy transition management. By utilizing a TD approach, the research team gained access to real-world context that helped form socially acceptable program design features to enhance community members' participation in the community solar program. The TD approach also helped the research team communicate technical concepts to the community, which facilitated community understanding and potential program participation. Finally, the collaboration has helped village officials obtain a US$45,000 grant from the Michigan Department of Agriculture and Rural Development to reduce upfront cost barriers if a project is developed. This demonstrates that TD research can help to attract additional resources to address real-world challenges.

This study is an early look into the specific use of community solar as a sociotechnical innovation to surmount the challenges of solar technology adoption, which has traditionally occurred at either the residential or the utility scale. While community solar programs help to mitigate many of the technical challenges for residents and local businesses, they do not necessarily eliminate the economic and social impediments to solar adoption. Access to capital, long payback periods and low energy costs can still deter participation. This is exacerbated in communities with a higher proportion of LMI households. Utilizing a TD research approach, our current study suggests that individuals may also consider community-scale criteria when considering participation, such as keeping energy generation in the community, the opportunity for community-level decision making and to benefit local non-profit organizations, and community pride that stems from innovation and leadership. The work offers additional support to previous findings that suggest that trusted technical experts, such as institutions of higher learning and local leaders, can assist in sociotechnical transitions like renewable energy adoption (Rai et al., 2016). This may be particularly true in communities with higher levels of distrust of outsider entities and when dealing with technically complex topics. At the time of writing and based on the study summarized here, the community sees potential for developing a community solar system and is currently seeking bids from solar developers in order to further evaluate possibilities. Regardless, this case study using a TD approach demonstrates that integrating expertise in engineering, sociology and energy policy with local knowledge and leadership can overcome many social, economic and technical challenges and facilitate support for sustainable energy transitions.

12 In search of common ground: energy justice perspectives in global fossil fuel extraction

Roman V. Sidortsov, Raphael J. Heffron, Tedd Moya Mose, Chelsea Schelly and Bethel Tarekegne

Introduction

On April 20, 2010, high-pressure methane built up in an exploratory well of the British Petroleum (BP)-operated Macondo Prospect in the Gulf of Mexico. The gas expanded through the riser to the rig and exploded, severely damaging and ultimately sinking it. What ensued is regarded as the one of the most devastating accidents in the history of energy development in the US. The accident left 11 crewmembers dead and 17 injured and led to a 4.9 million barrel oil spill, one of the largest in the world, which in turn caused massive environmental, public health and economic damage to the Gulf of Mexico region (USCG, 2011). The spill has had profound short- and long-term impacts on the region's 8332 species as well as their habitat (Biello, 2010). BP agreed to pay US$8.8 billion for natural resource injuries arising out of the spill, the largest civil settlement ever reached (National Oceanic and Atmospheric Administration, 2016). According to several studies conducted by the US Department of Health and Human Services, the National Institute for Occupational Safety and Health and Louisiana Department of Health, exposure to chemicals in the aftermath of the spill and the cleanup led to negative health consequences among rescue workers and residents of the impacted areas, including children (Louisiana Department of Health, 2010; Schmidt, 2011). The losses to the tourism industry were estimated at US$22.7 billion through 2013 (Tourism Economics, 2011) and losses arguably persist; for the fishing industry, losses are estimated to be US$8.7 billion by 2020 (Sumaila et al., 2012).

The National Commission on the BP Deepwater Horizon Oil Spill and Offshore Drilling described the complexity of the damage as "unknown impacts shaped by the Gulf region's distinctive cultures, institutions, and geography – and by economic forces resulting from the unique coexistence of energy resources, bountiful fisheries and wildlife, and coastal tourism" (National Commission, 2011: xiii). This complexity led to conflicting responses among key actors in the affected region to Interior Secretary Ken Salazar's decision to impose a six-month moratorium on deepwater drilling activities (US Department of the Interior, 2010). Whereas the decision received enthusiastic bipartisan support in Florida, it came under sharp bipartisan attack in Louisiana (Sasser, 2010). The likely explanation is that Florida is among the world's top tourist destinations, providing annually over a million jobs in this industry (Florida Government, 2017). In contrast, the offshore oil and gas industry reins supreme in Louisiana, directly and indirectly providing 315,000 jobs, or 17% of all jobs in the state (Sasser, 2010).

The Deepwater Horizon oil spill exemplifies the challenges involved in fossil fuel extraction where sizes, scopes, timelines and scales of environmental, social, economic and political considerations form an environmental management equivalent of the Gordian Knot. The conventional approach to resolving such challenges – applying statistical averages and valuations derived from an actuary table – has largely failed to account for these complexities to find an ethically sound common ground (Sovacool, et al., 2014).

In this chapter, we introduce energy justice, an emerging approach capable of tackling such complex energy problems. Energy justice is a term that has been used in practice (i.e., in non-academic work, such as in the commercial and public sectors) far longer than in academic research, albeit to a very limited degree. Two non-governmental organizations (NGOs), Energy Justice Network in the US and Centre for Sustainable Energy in the UK, have used the term since 1999 and at least 2009, respectively. There is another later reference to its use in 2011 by the Chief Executive of National Energy Action (UK), a charity whose focus is on ending fuel poverty, who referred to it in the context of the UK energy sector only (see Hall, 2013).

The term energy justice was first used in academic research literature in 2010 in an article entitled "Energy justice and sustainable development" (Guruswamy, 2010). However, the article focuses more on the latter than the former. This is similar to a 2013 article entitled "Energy justice and ethical consumption: comparison, synthesis and lesson drawing", in which the author elaborates on ethical consumption while noting the lack of an accepted definition of the concept (Hall, 2013). The 2013 book entitled *Energy Justice in a Changing Climate* largely relates energy justice to climate change issues – which is a rather limited perspective (Bickerstaff et al., 2013).

The next wave of academic scholarship on energy justice explored the core pillars of the concept. Sovacool and Dworkin (2014), Heffron and McCauley (2014), Guruswamy (2016), Jenkins et al. (2016) and many others premise the concept on the application of the different forms of justice that are integral to energy system operations. Jones et al. (2015), as well as Schelly et al. (2017) and others, take a less straightforward approach. They decipher the conceptual foundation through reconciliation of insights from applicable justice theories, giving explicit consideration to the unique characteristics of energy as a good.

Thus, as the concept of energy justice has emerged, two approaches have come to dominate, one that considers energy systems using existing understandings of forms of justice, and one that centers energy service provision as the primary justice consideration. To differentiate between these two approaches, we call them, respectively, the "system" and "foundational" approaches. In doing so, we do not intend to elevate one over another as being easier to apply within energy systems or grounded in a more fundamental analysis. Rather, we highlight two different pathways that scholars take to defining energy justice in order to demonstrate how these conceptual tools work for unpacking the energy justice implications of fossil fuel extraction.

Thus, the overarching objective of this chapter is two-fold. First, the chapter explores two energy justice approaches. Second, it explores the potential for finding common ground in understanding the justice implications of fossil fuel extraction. To meet this objective, we begin with untangling the perspectives of the parties involved in and affected by fossil fuel extraction. We pay particular attention to the perspective that often gets overlooked in the academic literature, that of the fossil fuel industry, by examining corporate statements from the world's three largest oil and gas companies (Gensler, 2017). We continue with examining the fundamental ethical challenge of fossil fuel extraction through the lenses of the system and foundational approaches to energy justice. We conclude with the assessment of the results of our analysis and with remarks regarding reconciliation of the two approaches. The purpose of the chapter is to demonstrate the importance of grappling with issues of justice in any instance of environmental management decision making, to show that there are diverse perspectives that offer tools for doing so specifically in the realm of energy systems management, and to illustrate the use of an important research tool by considering how controversial subjects like fossil fuel-based energy systems can be evaluated using different approaches to energy justice.

The ethics of fossil fuel extraction

We start our search for common ethical ground with an examination of how fossil fuel companies see themselves and their impact. As the ensuing discussion indicates, there is little mystery regarding the principal objective pursued by most if not all companies operating in the fossil fuel sector – to generate profit. This is embedded in the legal structures pursuant to which they are organized – for-profit corporations, companies and partnerships. These entities aim to benefit their employees and owners by extracting and selling oil, natural gas and coal and/or by providing goods and services required for exploration, extraction, transportation and processing of fossil fuels. The end result of these activities is contribution to fulfillment of human needs and wants – mobility, productivity, lighting, heating and cooling among others. In addition, generating profit is subject to conditions designed to mitigate negative environmental and socioeconomic impacts arising throughout the fossil fuel cycle, from prospecting to combustion and from construction to decommissioning.

PetroChina, the world's third largest oil and gas company, describes itself as "the largest oil and gas producer and distributor, playing a dominant role in the oil and gas industry in China. It is not only one of the companies with the biggest sales revenue in China, but also one of the largest oil companies in the world" (PetroChina, 2017a).The company defines its mission as follows: "PetroChina is committed to accelerating the transformation of economic growth, improving the self-innovation capacity, establishing long-efficient [sic] mechanism of safety, environmental protection and energy conservation and creating a harmonious enterprise, in order to transform itself to an international energy company with strong competitiveness" (PetroChina, 2017a). In the introductory letter to PetroChina's 2017 Interim Sustainability Report, its Chairman of the Board notes the foci of the company's effort to manage negative impacts on the society and environment: (a) safety, environmental protection, and green development; (b) support of public welfare and corporate citizenship excellence; and (c) legal compliance and company-wide integrity. Yet the letter to the sustainability report begins by assuring the shareholders that the company mustered an appropriate response to the recent plunge in oil prices (PetroChina, 2017b).

According to Royal Dutch Shell, oil and gas will continue to be critical resources for meeting the "energy needs of society . . . for many decades to come" (Shell Global, 2017a). The company, therefore, defines its principal role in extracting and delivering these energy sources profitably whilst "maintaining a strong and growing long-term position in the competitive environments in which we operate" (Shell Global, 2017a). Royal Dutch Shell sees affordability of the energy that it provides, social responsibility and environmentally sound approaches as important conditions for fulfilling its role. Correspondingly, Shell declares its intention to be a good neighbor, work closely with communities and contribute to economic development in the countries in which it operates, whilst acknowledging the energy access, education and healthcare nexus (Shell Global, 2017b). On the environment side, the company notes their commitment to "cause no harm to people, and help the world move towards a lower-carbon future", improving air quality and protecting biodiversity and water resources (Shell Global, 2017a).

Exxon Mobil delivers perhaps the most straightforward description of its identity. It emphasizes its core objective – "to help meet the world's growing energy needs" – while touting its size, scale and scope as "the largest publicly traded international oil and gas company", "industry-leading inventory of resources" and "the world's largest integrated refiners, marketers of petroleum products and chemical manufacturers" (ExxonMobil, 2017a). In a similar laconic fashion, it lists its two guiding principles, striving to "achieve superior financial and operating results" and "adhering to high ethical standards" (ExxonMobil, 2017b). The company connects "high ethical standards" to compliance with international and national laws of the countries in which it operates, including US anti-corruption and anti-trust laws (ExxonMobil, 2017c). ExxonMobil notes that although it is not a party to the United Nations Global Compact, the world's largest corporate sustainability initiative, the Compact's core values form the foundation of the company's Standards of Business Conduct (United Nations General Assembly, 2017; ExxonMobil, 2017d). ExxonMobil sees environmental management, biodiversity and ecosystem services, air emissions, environmental drilling initiatives, freshwater management and decommissioning as key areas of its environmental performance (ExxonMobil, 2017d). The company also states its commitment to managing climate change risks in the annual corporate citizenship reports (ExxonMobil, 2016). In addition, ExxonMobil's corporate social responsibility areas include indigenous people, cultural heritage and diversity, human rights, women's rights and economic development (ExxonMobil, 2017e).

The voices objecting to fossil fuel extraction solely on the basis that the companies aim to benefit their owners and employees are few and far between. In our overwhelmingly capitalist world, even state-owned companies are expected to be economically efficient and well run. This ethical cornerstone is further bolstered by the fact that fossil fuel companies employ millions of people worldwide who occupy the entire length of the socioeconomic ladder. Some of these jobs provide much needed employment in the areas lacking options for fulfilling economic activities. Some of these jobs provide further societal benefits in the form of scientific and technological discoveries that are applicable beyond the fossil fuel sector.

However, fossil fuel companies and parties affected by extractive activities often disagree regarding the other two ethical cornerstones of fossil fuel extraction – the necessity for fossil fuels to provide energy services and the sufficiency of conditions mitigating the environmental and socioeconomic impacts thereof. For example, rapidly improving efficiencies and plummeting prices of wind, solar and automotive battery technologies call into question the necessity of new oil, natural gas and coal development to meet lighting, cooking, cooling, heating and personal mobility needs (US Energy Information Administration, 2018; International Energy Agency, 2017: 14). In addition, although fossil fuel companies might have improved their environmental performance and found ways to partially mitigate social impacts, they are yet to eliminate oil spills, solve the problem of climate refugees, prevent oil-driven military conflicts and address many other ills associated with extraction of oil, natural gas and coal (Sovacool et al., 2014).

The conventional utilitarian approach to balancing the ethical considerations of fossil fuel extraction reduces human suffering, societal decline and environmental degradation to statistical averages. These are often assessed against ostensible economic benefits of extraction without regard to actual communities, families and persons, making a search for common ground a difficult affair (Sovacool et al., 2014). Yet the emerging concept of energy justice offers a path forward as a conceptual foundation for transdisciplinary work in environmental management decision making, as we explore in the ensuing sections.

The system approach to energy justice

The energy sector is no more or less deserving of preferential legal treatment than any other sector of the economy. It should be subject to the same national and international laws. The system approach to energy justice centers on the forms of justice that are integral to energy sector operations. Proponents of this approach focus on the insights from different justice theories and their application in the context of production, transportation, processing and use of energy. In this sense, the approach is streamlined and systematic as it aims to address an energy justice problem largely with an already existing arsenal of conceptual tools. Over time, distributive, procedural, recognition, cosmopolitan and restorative justice have emerged as five key forms of the system approach to energy justice.

McCauley et al. (2013) define energy justice as having three central tenets (they refer to them as a *triumvirate of tenets*) – distribution, procedural and recognition justice. Sovacool and Dworkin (2014) and Sovacool et al. (2016) draw on a larger pool of justice theories and premise their definition on eight core principles. These include: availability, affordability, due process, transparency and accountability, sustainability, intra-generational equity, inter-generational equity and responsibility.

These two definitions of energy justice have led to further advancement of the system approach. Heffron and McCauley (2014) explore how the concept applies across the energy life-cycle. Heffron and McCauley (2017) also add restorative and cosmopolitan justice to the framework depicted in Figure 12.1. The energy system approach as outlined in Figure 12.1 aims to be an interdisciplinary tool that could be used by all

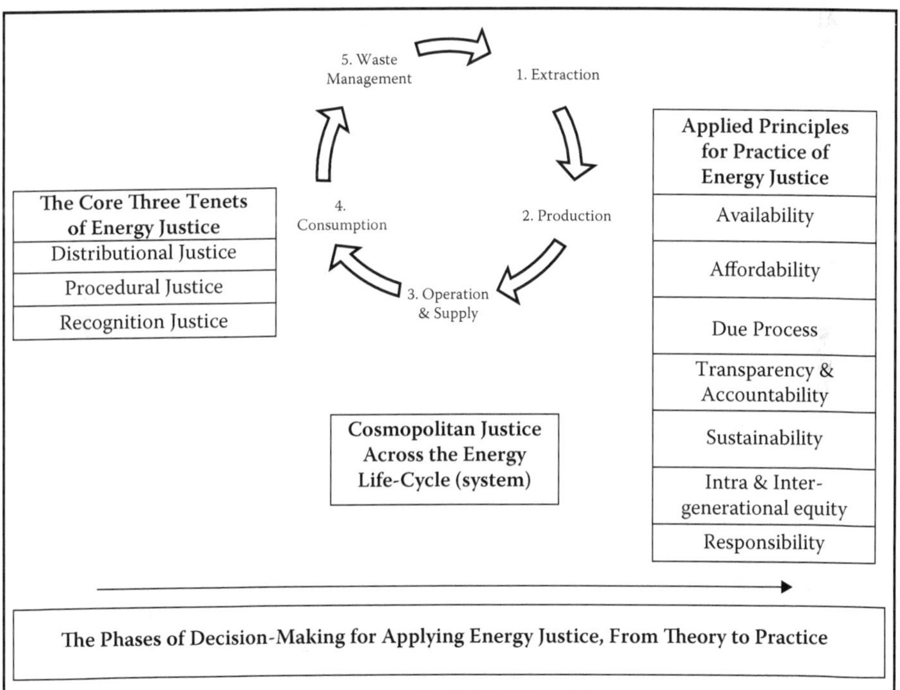

Figure 12.1 Energy justice conceptual framework (developed from Heffron and McCauley (2017))

energy researchers and also policy makers. In aiming to achieve change in the energy sector, there is a need for researchers to unite and co-develop their work (such as we are doing here!) but also a fundamental aim has to be to connect with stakeholders from across the energy sector. The energy system approach explicitly focuses on the energy life-cycle so as to ensure that there is increased understanding around how a decision that is made in one part of the energy sector is influenced by and influences other aspects of the energy life-cycle. Too many decisions in the energy sector in the past have been made in isolation and there is a need for more interdisciplinary research in energy scholarship (Heffron and McCauley, 2017).

In looking at the systems framework, this approach begins with examining the core tenets of energy justice (distribution, procedural and recognition justice) to see if they are present. It then broadens the scope to see where the issue fits within the energy life-cycle. Then the systems approach asks how to apply energy justice in practice and looks for how the problem, issue and/or challenge they are researching can be addressed (or not) by the principles. The application of restorative justice at each phase aims to ensure energy justice is functional in practice.

The foundational approach to energy justice

The foundational approach to energy justice is premised on two cornerstones. First, it recognizes the unique characteristics of energy as a good. Second, it establishes a theoretical foundation by connecting insights from applicable justice theories with these unique characteristics. The result of this exercise is the definition of energy justice through two principles, prohibitive and affirmative, which we explain in more detail below.

Sovacool et al. (2014) first introduced this "energy-centric" approach to the concept of energy justice, which we describe as foundational, in *Energy Security, Equality, and Justice*. The foundational approach has yet to garner the same acclaim as the system approach, although there have been a few attempts to develop it. For example, Sidortsov and Sovacool (2015) apply the approach to energy development in the Arctic and Banerjee et al. (2017) employ the approach to evaluate the ethical implications of renewable energy development.

Sovacool and his co-authors begin developing their approach with identifying three key forms of justice: distributive, procedural and cosmopolitan (Jones et al., 2015). The next step of their analysis is constructing a foundation for the two principles through which they define energy justice, prohibitive and affirmative. Sovacool et al. (2014), Sidortsov and Jones work through four assumptions (as depicted in Figure 12.2) to lay out the foundational approach. In doing so they also enrich the available analytical arsenal for applying the principles. This includes (but is not limited to) identifying the origin of a response to energy injustice, contextualization of obligations prompted by energy injustice, and perhaps most importantly, determining the nature of basic goods (Jones et al., 2015).

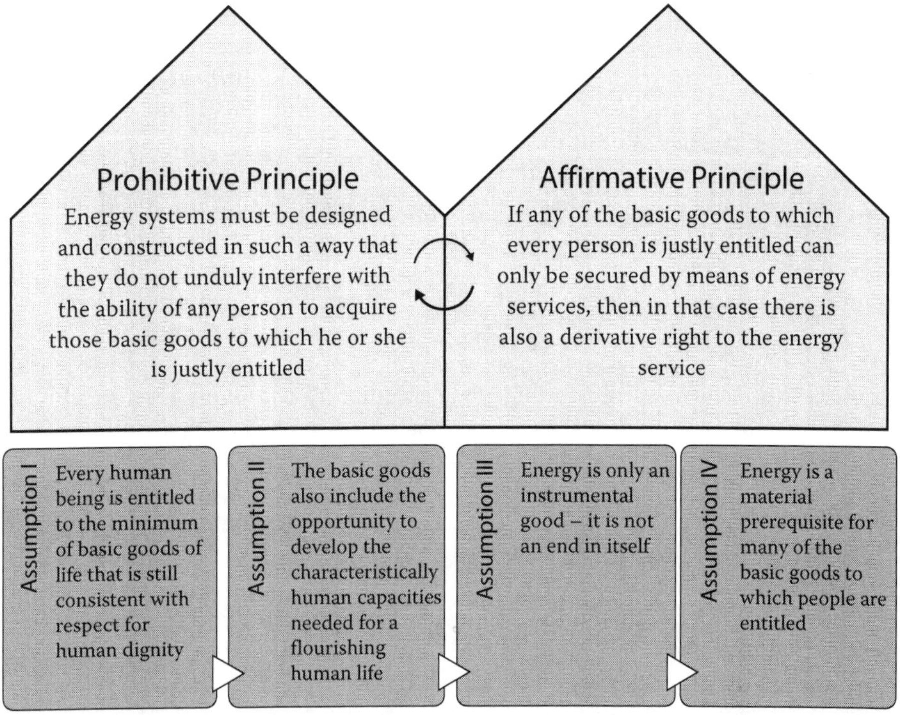

Figure 12.2 Assumptions and principles of energy justice (adapted from Sovacool et al. (2014))

The centerpiece of the analysis to which Sovacool and his co-authors come back repeatedly is recognition of the unique role that energy plays in the global economy and modern society – that it is in fact a prerequisite to many other goods, including basic ones. Thus, energy exhibits instrumental domination of the ends it is supposed to serve. Meanwhile, energy is not an end in itself. Rather as Jones et al. (2015: 160) put it, "the use of energy must be determined by the human ends it serves (rather than these ends being distorted to fit the technical imperatives of the energy system), and these ends must be consistent with respect for the equal dignity of human beings".

To explore how the foundational approach tackles the "Gordian Knot" presented in the first section of this chapter, it is worth restating the prohibitive principle: "energy systems must be designed and constructed in such a way that they do not unduly interfere with the ability of any person to acquire those basic goods to which he or she is justly entitled" (Jones et al., 2015: 162). This inevitably pins the fossil fuel industry's argument about the benefits of wealth and job creation against the environmental, social, economic, cultural and politically known (impacts) and unknown (risks) burdens of fossil fuel development. At a glance, this exercise appears to be similar to cost–benefit analysis. However, this is where the similarities end, as the prohibitive principle requires distributive justice in terms of spatial, temporal, sociopolitical and economic fairness premised on the socially defined range of inequality in benefits and burdens (Sovacool et al., 2014). The next step is identifying the minimum basic goods with which fossil fuel extraction does or might interfere, as well as determining the degree of such interference. What constitutes the minimum of basic good requires further analysis. The minimum needs to be consistent with respect for human dignity and must include opportunities for the development of human capacities needed for flourishing human life; this means that the list of basic goods extends beyond "vital interests" – shelter, clothing, nutrition, bodily integrity and so on (Jones et al., 2015: 152). Thus, the minimum of basic goods includes social, political, economic and cultural structures and processes like community, participation in the political process and traditional economic activities. This part of the analysis is contextual. For example, considerations of interference with the livelihood of an indigenous community occupying traditional lands should arguably diverge from considerations of interference with a community of vacationing tourists that regularly flock to the same beach.

The ethical cornerstone suggesting the necessity of fossil fuel extraction to meet "world's growing energy needs" serves as a potential counter-argument to the prohibitive principle analysis. As noted in the first section, in absolute terms, this argument suffers from the logical flaw of confusing necessity with sufficiency. Yet because the global energy system is built largely around fossil fuels, currently, at least some of the world's energy needs can only be met via fossil fuel extraction. The affirmative principle brings further clarification regarding the extent of the fossil fuel mandate. The affirmative principle states: "if any of the basic goods to which every person is justly entitled can only be secured by means of energy services, then in that case there is also a derivative right to the energy service" (Jones et al., 2015: 165). Accordingly, the counter-argument works only to the extent that the aforementioned shelter, bodily integrity, community, traditional economic activities and other basic goods can only be obtained through fossil fuels. For example, if the only way to perform a surgery is to keep a backup diesel generator going, diesel fuel and crude oil production are necessary. However, the counter argument starts falling apart once the world transitions away from the status quo and in our examples diesel generators are replaced with batteries or biodiesel becomes more available. The counter argument suffers further by taking into account historic fossil price volatility and interruptions and limitations of physical supply of fossil fuels; these considerations only become possible in the context of the foundational approach to energy justice.

Conclusion

Issues of social justice arguably arise only in the context of real or perceived resource scarcity and when there are "institutions designed to allocate scarce things" (Wenz, 1988: 7). In the context of fossil fuel extraction, resource scarcity is two-fold. First is the scarcity of the extracted fossil fuel. Coal, oil and natural gas are finite resources and the most accessible and pure deposits have been depleted significantly. Second is the scarcity of other resources that fossil fuel extraction creates. Coal mining and hydrocarbon production take a devastating toll on water and air quality, contribute to climate change and negatively impact agricultural lands and forests (Sovacool et al., 2014). Thus, ideas of justice extend to the context of energy through the concept of energy justice. However, scholars have offered diverse conceptualizations of energy justice, as reviewed above.

From both the system and the foundational views of energy justice, resource accessibility is an issue. According to the system approach, justice requires accessibility and lack of accessibility means a lack of justice. The foundational approach states that if energy is necessary for people to survive and flourish, energy justice requires that access to energy be maintained. The approaches differ in how they tackle the issue, with one arguing that justice is defined by access, while the other argues that access is just because energy is requisite. They both imply that because at present the global energy system is largely premised on fossil fuels, extraction of fossil fuels can contribute to ensuring energy justice.

Yet neither approach ends with the energy access issue or assumes that the global energy system is static. The approaches highlight different areas of injustice based on their relative emphases, and recognizing these differences in application to fossil fuels also indicates the differences in the approaches more generally. The system approach emphasizes key questions and areas of consideration for pursuing energy justice related to both process and outcome, asking how, within a given energy system or regime, risks and benefits are distributed and how users are able to participate (or not) in decision making. These principles allow for consideration of environmental harms and lack of participatory TD processes in energy policy making. The foundational approach expands beyond consideration of existing regimes to raise a more fundamental question: if energy services are necessary, do current energy regimes that are dependent on fossil fuel resources violate the affirmative principle by restricting the ability of users to access energy outside the context of fossil fuel dependence? In other words, does the locked-in nature of existing energy infrastructures based on fossil fuel resources violate a right to access energy by limiting the choices of users regarding the origin of primary and end-use energy?

Any attempt to engage in management decision making regarding energy systems requires grappling with questions of justice and energy systems inevitably involve complex decisions and disproportionately distributed environmental burdens. Acknowledging that fossil fuel extraction under certain circumstances contributes to justice by providing access to a socially necessary good allows the conversation to move beyond an oversimplified binary of good/bad when it comes to assessing energy resources for sustainable futures. Interrogating the diverse perspectives on energy justice also highlights that conceptual nuance does involve substantive difference in terms of emphasis. Therefore, the system approach might be more suitable for dissecting an energy problem with a well-defined justice issue, a deficient decision-making process, for example. The foundational approach might work better for setting parameters for achieving optimal socially just outcomes by providing necessary and equitable access to the energy services without violating the ability of current or future energy users to do the same. Thus, the differences between the two approaches should not define them. Rather, it should be their collective contribution to building the common ground for an equitable, secure and just future.

13 Understanding household conservation, climate change and the food–energy–water nexus from a transdisciplinary perspective

David Watkins, Rachael Shwom, Chelsea Schelly, Datu B. Agusdinata, Kristin Floress and Kathleen E. Halvorsen

Research context

Global atmospheric carbon dioxide levels are not likely to return to below 400 ppm in a current human lifetime (Kahn, 2016), which probably ensures a global temperature increase of 2°C relative to pre-industrial times and represents a critical challenge to global sustainability. Attempts to address climate change through policy are often ineffective in shaping organizational practice (Wright and Nyberg, 2017), and systems of production are often recalcitrant to change (Gould et al., 2004). Thus, formal policy change or changes focused on production systems have yet to produce a workable option for mitigating the impacts of greenhouse gases on the global environment and its ability to sustain human life.

Households in societies marked by economic affluence are a key source of greenhouse gas emissions via both direct and indirect resource consumption sourced primarily from fossil fuels. For example, accounting for direct and indirect energy usage, US households consume 80% of all energy, with corresponding amounts of associated carbon dioxide emissions (Bin and Dowlatabadi, 2005). The direct energy consumption of US households is estimated to be 23% of total energy consumption, with 77% attributable to indirect energy use (Jones and Kammen, 2011). Further, estimates suggest that voluntary actions could reduce direct household emissions from US residential energy use by 20%, which would reduce overall US greenhouse gas emissions by 7.4% (Dietz et al., 2009). Estimates of household contributions to curtailing the greenhouse gas emissions associated with residential usage are not confined to the US or limited to direct energy use; for example, one study of food consumption in Stockholm estimates that dietary changes could reduce indirect energy use by 30% (Carlsson-Kanyama et al., 2005).

The greenhouse gas intensity of households located within national contexts of economic affluence highlights the opportunity for household actions to reduce GHG emissions (Shwom and Lorenzen, 2012). However, understanding and seeking to change consumption behaviors within a household context is an inevitably wicked problem, as it involves a complex matrix of resource sectors (including direct energy consumption and the indirect impacts associated with water use and food production, as well as food waste), locked-in infrastructures (Unruh, 2000, 2002) and systems of provision (Spaargaren, 2003, 2011), all operating across multiple geographical and geopolitical scales and intersecting with the complexities of household decision making, which is itself not particularly well understood. Thus, effective environmental management decisions that maximize household-driven reductions in greenhouse gas emissions require the integration of interdisciplinary knowledge across the domains of natural and engineering sciences as well as social and behavioral sciences. Interdisciplinary teams that successfully integrate multiple forms of expertise from outside the academic research context, representing the possibilities for truly transdisciplinary (TD) research in environmental management, are arguably necessary for addressing the kinds of complex, wicked problems faced by environmental managers and decision makers today and in the foreseeable future (Brown et al., 2010).

This chapter describes the efforts of a multi-institutional team to develop a TD research program focusing on the challenge of reducing household food, energy and water consumption for the primary purpose of mitigating greenhouse gas emissions. An initial workshop and workshop report (Watkins et al., 2016) helped to clarify the research objectives and approach, leading to a full project proposal and subsequent funding from the US National Science Foundation (NSF). Activities in the first year of the five-year research project are outlined and some challenges that have arisen are discussed, along with recommended strategies for TD research teams. This chapter is complemented by Chapter 14, which describes the process of creating and testing a role-playing game that is one component of the five-year project.

Developing a research agenda

This project arose in response to the NSF's call for Interactions of Food Systems with Water and Energy Systems (FEW) workshops in February 2015 (Watkins, 2016). NSF sought to sponsor workshops that would ultimately shape an NSF call for large proposals to be issued in 2016. The funder ultimately issued the request for proposals before the workshop reports were due because of its internal imperatives. However, one or more NSF program officers attended each funded workshop and reported back on workshop findings, giving the agency early insight into outcomes of the workshops.

The lead author of this chapter, a civil/environmental engineer specializing in water resources systems modeling, convened a group of collaborators to discuss pursuing a workshop grant. The initial group included several environmental engineers and one social scientist. The lead author and the social scientist have an extensive history of collaboration with each other, including on a long-term, international and TD NSF Partnerships International in Research and Education project described in Chapter 10.

Proposals had a quick turnaround time with a due date at the end of March 2015 and limited funding availability of a maximum of US$100,000, primarily to support participant travel to a workshop focused on the particular topic or area of interest developed in the workshop proposal. The group therefore began meeting weekly at the beginning of February to identify and narrow down workshop topics. Given the nature of the group with a number of individuals focusing on water quantity or quality, there was significant interest in the water component of FEW, and somewhat less for the others, although it was recognized that there are close linkages from water to energy and food. Discussions over time narrowed down a focus on food, energy and water conservation to reduce greenhouse gas emissions. This focus interested several of the initial participants, but not all were interested or felt that they could contribute (e.g., engineers interested in waste recovery or water/energy production), and some individuals therefore left the group. This represents an important practical lesson for research on complex environmental issues: not everyone will have the interest or expertise necessary to contribute and building the team most capable of successfully completing the research should be based on both individual expertise and experience working on interdisciplinary teams. Further, camaraderie is often an important factor in successful team research.

With a clearer focus, the team was ready to begin adding members to a larger organizing committee that would develop the proposal and be responsible for developing and running the initial workshop. Individuals were added iteratively, as the lead author and initial social scientist led the process of identifying additional social, natural and engineering scientists to add to the organizing committee. Although the organizing committee did not include individuals from other sectors outside of science, invitees and workshop participants came from other sectors. The Co-principal Investigators and organizing committee finalized and submitted the proposal, which was funded by early summer. This allowed the team to move forward with planning the workshop.

The workshop organizing committee comprised eight individuals, including multiple social, natural and engineering scientists. Although the group had limited time to prepare, they were ultimately able to organize a multiday workshop in late October 2015 at Michigan Technological University. There were 50 attendees, all based in the US except for one Canadian and one Dutch participant. Attendees were mostly a mix of social, natural and engineering scientists and students, although participants also included representatives from government and local, national and international NGOs.

Prior to the workshop, participants were requested to complete a set of preparation activities. The first recommended activity was to read a paper by Brown et al. (2015) on ways to promote interdisciplinary research and catalyze collaboration across disciplines. FEW organizers utilized the authors' principles of developing a shared mission, encouraging researchers to look beyond their own discipline, and fostering constructive dialogue to engage workshop participants (Brown et al., 2015).

In order to prompt dialogue, workshop participants were also requested to prepare and submit annotated bibliographies including at least three key references related to the workshop and their own research interests. Finally, participants were asked to sketch mental models of the FEW system, two of which are shown in Figure 13.1. The bibliographies and mental models were made available to all workshop participants prior to their arrival.

Following a welcoming reception on the evening of the first day, technical workshop activities were conducted over two days, with the first day focusing on defining the problem and reviewing the current state of knowledge and the second day focusing on solutions and research priorities. Each day included overview presentations by selected participants, breakout sessions with reports to the full group and synthesis discussions by the full group. A closing session was devoted to developing an outline for the workshop report and identifying volunteers for completing writing assignments. In addition, group meals and an outing to a nearby state park were planned as team-building experiences. After the workshop, participants were asked to complete an online evaluation of the workshop and express their specific interests with respect to a full proposal. The interest statements were made available to all participants, and they were used by at least two different groups to develop full proposal teams.

The workshop report (Watkins et al., 2016) consisted of three main sections: an introduction characterizing FEW systems and their interrelationships with the climate system; a section on cross-cutting research themes; and a section outlining seven specific research priorities. In identifying strategies to mitigate climate change, the team recognized that successful strategies would ultimately be multi-objective, since in addition to reducing greenhouse gas emissions, they should also improve food, energy and water security and avoid unintended consequences such as ecosystem degradation or adverse impacts on individual production sectors. The strategies must also be designed under great uncertainty, since some important system interactions are poorly understood and future conditions are unknown. These considerations led to a focus primarily on FEW conservation strategies, along with opportunities to improve understanding of FEW systems across their life cycle (i.e., production, consumption, disposal, recovery and reuse).

Three cross-cutting themes were highlighted as being important to any FEW Nexus research project. First, studies must address multiple scales and levels of analysis. The boundary conditions in production and consumption systems can be defined in myriad ways, but all are composed of multiple subsystems, and all interact with other systems within a larger context. Second, studies must consider feedbacks between production and consumption activities and between technical and social systems. In studies involving systems modeling, this requires integrating biophysical factors with models of human decision making. Third, it is important for studies to address governance, including the analysis of how policies and institutions can either impede or facilitate transitions to more sustainable FEW provisioning systems.

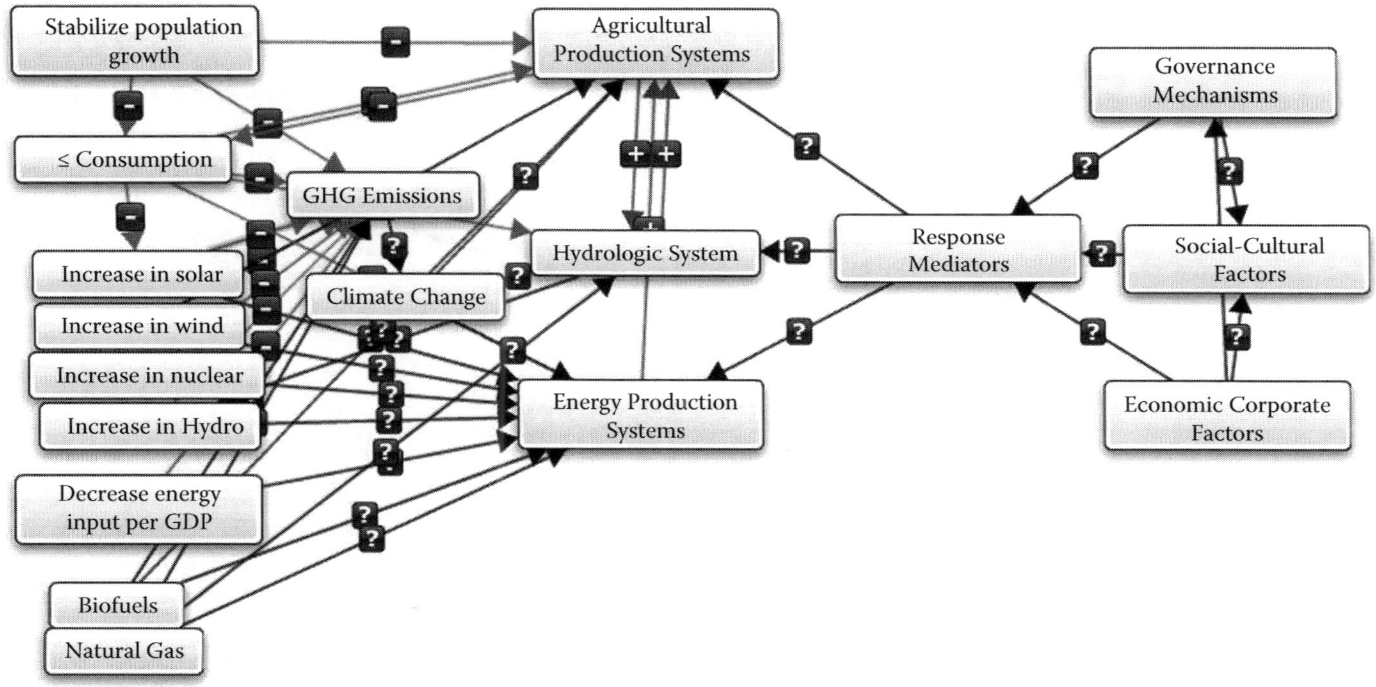

(a)

Note: (a) Model by R. Shwom, a social scientist, focusing on renewable energy development and human responses; and (b) model by D. B. Agusdinata, an engineering scientist, with more focus on the linkages between food, energy and water production systems.

Figure 13.1 Mental models of the food–energy–water system

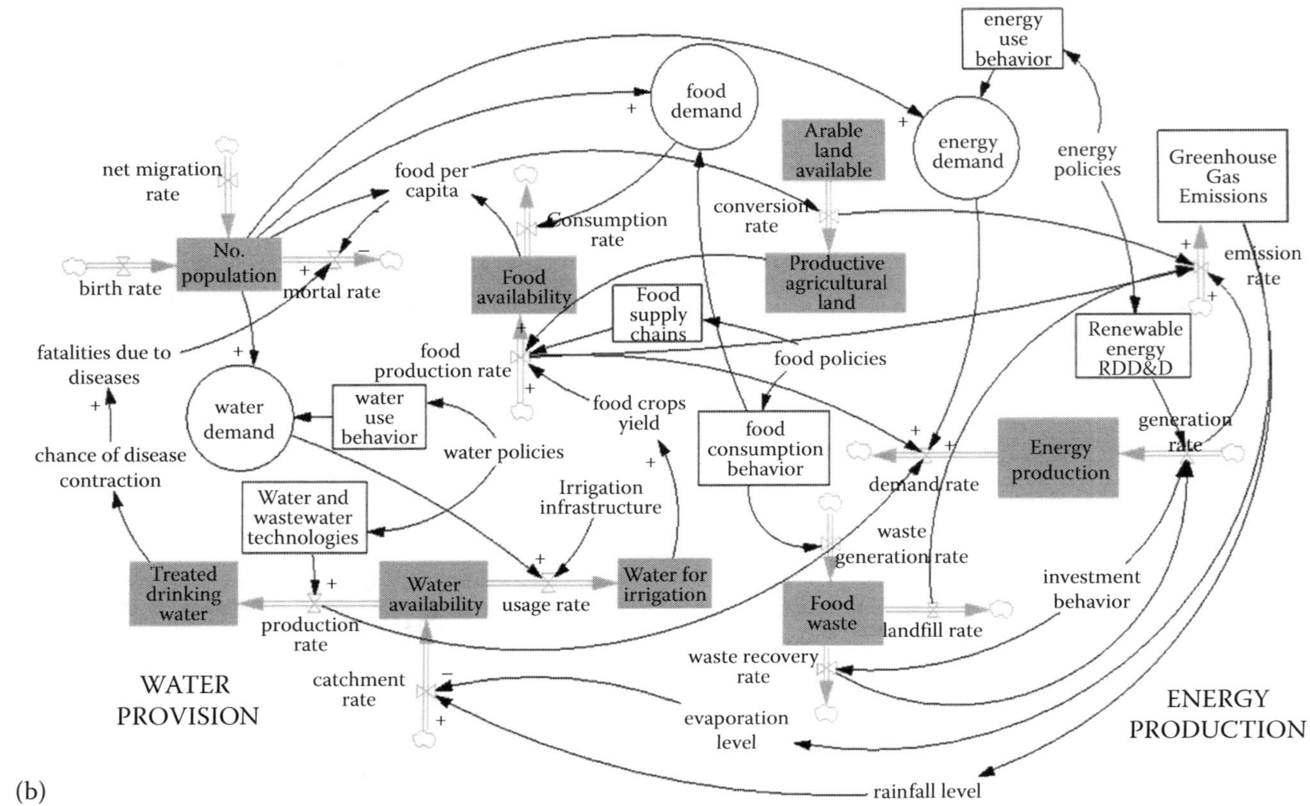

(b)

Figure 13.1 (Continued)

The seven research priority areas outlined in the report were greater in number than initially expected, which stemmed from the diversity of research interests and expertise among the workshop participants. However, the research areas were interrelated in several important ways. First, because climate change is expected to have the most severe impacts on developing countries, despite being caused mainly by industrialized countries, there is a need to conduct comparative studies that provide insights into different development pathways. Related to this is the issue of lock-in, particularly how affluent societies have institutionalized aspects of FEW production and consumption systems. A predominant development pathway has been the extensification of FEW systems – using an increasing amount of land for production – which presents land use intensification as a potential conservation strategy in need of further study. One priority research area was integrated, "closed-loop" engineered systems (e.g., food waste reduction and recovery systems, optimized bioenergy systems and zero-discharge water resource recovery systems), which in turn requires consideration of technological lock-in and other associated priority research areas – consumer-producer linkages and decentralization of production. Finally, given the complex interactions among biophysical factors and human decision making at multiple scales and levels, improving data and systems analysis tools was identified as the seventh research priority.

An overall conclusion from the workshop was that mitigating climate change while improving FEW security and avoiding other adverse ecosystem impacts will require divergence from current trends, along with significant socioenvironmental research to address important knowledge gaps and create new opportunities for system integration and FEW provisioning. Perhaps even more challenging will be implementing governance structures and policies that aid in the transition to more sustainable development pathways. However, this goal is also an imperative for society, one that can motivate the interdisciplinary and international collaboration necessary to achieve it. The workshop was considered a valuable step in building an interdisciplinary research community united by this common goal, which provides another insight into the challenges and practices of interdisciplinary research on complex environmental management issues: time devoted to discussing the context and the problems with knowledgeable and interested experts can be of critical importance for future project success, as dialogue during meetings, workshops, conferences and other events can help refine or rethink the scope of the problems and the possibilities for addressing them.

Developing the research proposal

Following submission of the workshop report, the team again faced a tight timeline, with full research proposals due in March 2016. Fortunately, the momentum of the workshop and report writing allowed the team to regroup quickly for the full proposal. The proposal team initially consisted of the Principal Investigator and co-Principal Investigators of the workshop proposal, along with five other participants. This group decided to invite five other colleagues to round out the expertise of the proposal team, including a social psychologist, a natural resource economist, an energy policy analyst, a climate scientist and a computer scientist. Letters of collaboration were also obtained from four researchers conducting related research in the Netherlands.

Early discussions by the team confirmed the central theme of the proposal – the potential for household-level decisions related to food, energy and water consumption to mitigate climate change. This focus not only built on the expertise and interests of the team members but was also strategic in that the other FEW workshops held around the country focused mostly on supply-side issues of the FEW Nexus, leaving an opportunity to develop a niche in the area of demand-side management. The team decided that the project would use a mixed methodology social science approach to test behavioral change theories, specifically feedback, messaging and social norms approaches to reducing resource use. Several critical details remained to be determined, however, including how to recruit study participants, what specific social science methodologies to use, how to track FEW resource use and measure or model its direct and indirect impacts on climate, and how to provide timely feedback to study participants.

To work out these details, the team determined that it would be efficient to divide into two subteams based on disciplinary expertise. A socioeconomic subteam would focus on the first two questions, and an engineering and natural science subteam would focus on the third and fourth questions. Both subteams would consult with the computer scientist as needed. This divided approach to proposal writing appeared to be working well as sections of the proposal were initially drafted. However, it soon became apparent that the two subteams were diverging in their conceptual views of the project, and more dialogue between subteams was needed. Aligning proposed tasks with the project personnel, budget and timeline was another practical issue that required further discussion. An interesting observation was that, at one point, each subteam was essentially considering the work of the other subteam to be the primary focus of the project. Specifically, the socioeconomic subteam was viewing their primary role as providing human behavioral and decision-making inputs to a complex systems model, while the engineering and natural science subteam was considering their role to be providing impact measurements and models to support the work of the socioeconomic subteam.

In hindsight, the deference of each subteam to the role of the other may have been critical to integrating the tasks in the final research plan. Had the opposite occurred – each subteam viewing their own role as central to the project – there may have been intractable differences of opinion that would have hindered research integration, or at least produced some hurt feelings that could potentially affect future collaboration. In the end, the team decided on an iterative research plan, whereby staged social science methods would both support and be informed by systems models (including LCA, or life cycle assessment models) of the direct and indirect impacts of household FEW consumption. The social science data collection began with qualitative, in-depth interviews with residents to explore their perceptions

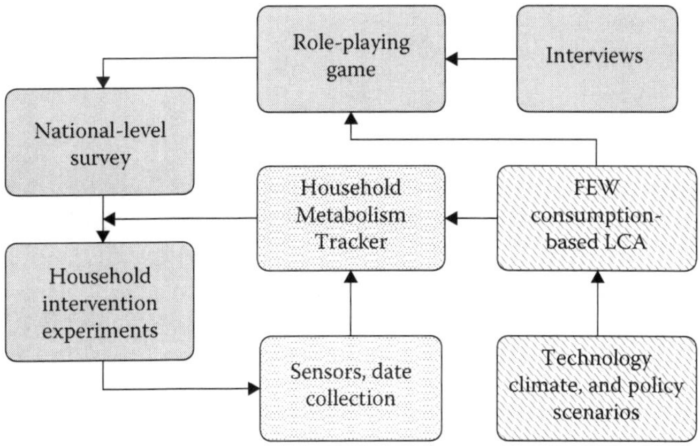

Note: The schematic shows multiple stages of feedback between the sub-teams: socioeconomic (solid), computer science (dotted) and engineering and natural sciences (hatched).

Figure 13.2 Schematic of research task integration

of food, energy and water consumption, followed by a role-playing game (RPG) administered to college students to begin testing potential messages and their resulting behavior changes, a national survey to further refine those messages, and finally, implementation at the household level of feedback on consumption patterns. The systems models would also be developed in stages, with preliminary impact models used in the role-playing game and more refined models used in the household interventions. The overall integration of research activities is shown in Figure 13.2.

Carrying out the research plan

The team learned of the proposal's success a few months after submission and work began in October 2016. Progress was slow at first, as there was a need to recruit graduate students and help them get up to speed on the project. By the summer of 2017, several new students had joined the team and were contributing to project activities, including conducting the preliminary interviews, developing the RPG, and assembling the first version of impact assessment models. Both the preliminary interviews and the RPG were designed to collect information critical to the design of the national-level survey and the household interventions, while the RPG also served to integrate the project subteams early in the project.

A total of 43 preliminary interviews were conducted with households in the study area. The team initially planned to conduct 15–25 interviews, but recruitment went better than expected, and time and human resources allowed for additional interviews to be conducted. The interviews provided insights into how behavior is affected by individual characteristics (e.g., values, beliefs, knowledge), social norms and household dynamics and characteristics. The interviews also sought to increase understanding of how local provisioning systems and regional resources provide a context for household decision making.

As with the interviews, a goal of the RPG approach is to uncover insights regarding household FEW consumption behaviors, but it also allows for testing different potential options for behavior change in a safe but realistic environment. Thus, the RPG serves as a cost-effective way to provide insights before the (more costly) full-scale interventions are deployed. In the first year of the project, the RPG development subteam worked closely with the rest of the project team to obtain their input on various aspects of the activity. A detailed description of the RPG is provided in Chapter 14.

Early in the project, the RPG development subteam worked with the engineering and natural science subteam to develop a decision impacts model and define technology and climate scenarios. Various impact models and indicators were considered to assess the impact of household decisions, including measures of the quality and availability of FEW resources and different life cycle impacts. Given the time and resources available, the team decided to focus on greenhouse gas emission impacts resulting from a set of five to 10 decision alternatives in each of the food, energy and water sectors, leading to a set of approximately 25 total decision alternatives. These include alternative diets and a number of existing and future technologies in the energy and water sectors. Examples of existing energy technologies are solar panels and LED light bulbs, and water technologies include low-flow faucets and showerheads. Future technologies under consideration include waterless washing machines and household gray water treatment facilities. In addition to decision alternatives and impact indicators, plausible climate scenarios were defined, with a focus on extreme weather impacts (i.e., drought, storms, and heat waves). As part of the plot, players will be given information about changes in the probability of occurrence of such events as the decision sequence progresses.

The socioeconomic subteam is responsible for specifying interventions that will be tested using the RPG. The intervention measures focus on "norming" by providing information about players' relative greenhouse gas emissions and the impacts of those emissions across the FEW Nexus. This information is incorporated in the indicators and through messages that appear in the graphical user interface. Some specific requirements for conducting experiments to collect data were also set, one primary requirement being that only one variable is changed at a time in order to see the effect of a specific intervention. Intervention experiments also require a control group, i.e., players who do not receive any intervention information during a game round. The RPG and socioeconomic subteams have co-developed the protocol for the game to allow for a consistent playing experience.

The RPG was play-tested during the project first annual meeting in October 2017. The entire team had hands-on experience playing the game, and during debriefing, team members provided some valuable feedback. This feedback ranged from improvements to the graphical user interface to ways to make the game more realistic (e.g., adding options of going on a vacation and dining out). During the course of our research, the game will be played by college students, city officials, utility staff and the general public. Data collected from game players, including pre- and post-game assessment surveys, will be used in the design of the national-level survey and the household intervention experiments. Thus, the RPG is viewed as an innovative approach to combine information and expertise from multiple disciplines in the study of a complex environmental management issue.

In addition to the in-person annual meetings, virtual subteam meetings are held monthly, or more often as needed, and whole-team virtual meetings are held quarterly. Communication occurs frequently via an email list, and an on-line repository is maintained for meeting summaries, status updates and research products. Visits to collaborating institutions are encouraged and have proven fruitful, especially a March 2017 visit by five project personnel to collaborating universities in the Netherlands that are doing similar work. Student exchanges and joint supervision of graduate theses and dissertations are also being planned to strengthen collaboration across institutions. For communicating with the public, a project Facebook page and Twitter handle were set up, and a project website is under development.

Moving into Year Two of the project, focus shifted to the development and implementation of the national-level survey and recruitment of households for the intervention experiments. The survey will be conducted online with 1200 randomly selected US homeowners in single-family dwellings. The household intervention experiments will be conducted in approximately 200 homes in the communities of Prairie Crossing and Gurnee, Illinois. Prairie Crossing is a conservation community located in Grayslake, Illinois, which neighbors Gurnee. The community was designed to promote low-impact development, including the preservation of open land and the use of public transit. To some extent, participating households in nearby Gurnee will serve as a control group in that they are expected to be a more representative cross-section of suburban US households in terms of their knowledge of and motivation towards environmental conservation. Since the intervention experiments will involve the installation of home energy and water meters, as well as significant effort by participants (e.g., tracking food purchases) over an extended period, financial incentives will be provided to participants during the project, and they will be able to keep all installed technologies if they choose.

Challenges and strategies for transdisciplinary teams

Working collaboratively across disciplines, as well as working beyond academic disciplines in order to include professionals and community members with insight into particular dimensions of community identities and barriers to change, is an essential element of any environmental management project seeking to understand residential resource use and reduce its impacts. Yet the challenges associated with this form of TD collaboration span intellectual and practical concerns, including different disciplinary ontologies, vocabularies and methodological priorities, as well as the hurdles of scheduling and communication across large teams. In this project, the research team was developed in stages, starting with a TD workshop, followed by collaboration on a workshop report that identified research priorities, and finally the development of a research focus in a full proposal. Throughout the process, researchers were encouraged to look beyond their own discipline, with strategies for cross-disciplinary dialogue including providing ample time for brainstorming and discussion, along with the development and sharing of annotated bibliographies and mental models. The authors of this chapter believe that the group was highly successful in developing a shared mission – addressing the problem of climate change through a focus on food, energy and water conservation – although some attrition occurred, as it inevitably does, owing to some workshop participants seeking to focus more on engineering and technology-based approaches. Moving forward, the research team recognizes the need to consider the professional cultures of different disciplines (e.g., expectations for tenure and promotion, such as which research products are the most highly valued), in order to ensure the success of both the team and the individuals making up the team.

Along with the challenges of engaging researchers across disciplines, there are also challenges associated with engaging community members in residential household research, as homeowners are busy people with their own priorities, just like the rest of us. As most Americans are overworked, overspent, and overscheduled (Schor, 2008), engaging homeowners in research on household consumption can be challenging. In order to develop a sample of households that represents the diversity of homeowner experiences, positions and perspectives, the research team is explicitly exploring a range of sampling methods as well as recruitment messages, given that some homeowners may be motivated to participate in a study of resource consumption, while others may be primarily interested in the technical tools provided to them to track household expenditures on consumption, and still others may be motivated by direct financial incentives to participate. Oakes et al. (2009) found that the characteristics of random and convenience samples were quite similar, and that non-random methods garnered more participation from lower-income women of color. The literature on participant recruitment, though, is largely grounded in health-related studies (e.g., Sullivan-Bolyai et al., 2007), and there are few studies in environmental management research that require the longer-term commitment needed for our project.

As is the case with any social science research involving human subjects, participants may be willing to be involved with research for a multitude of reasons, and these reasons are likely to correlate with how they will respond to the research or behave in a number of real-life decision-making contexts. If, for example, we want to study environmentally consequential behaviors, and we advertise as such, a biased sample of those who are concerned about the environmental consequences of their behavior are likely to participate. Thus, in order to apply the scientific method to understanding behavioral change for the purposes of improving environmental management, it is important to recruit a diverse sample of participants with a range of motivations for participating.

For these reasons, it is critical to have community partners who are interested in and engaged with the work, and who have perhaps already done work to change the environmental impacts of residential life. Developing these partnerships may require university scientists or environmental decision makers to reach out to local organizations involved in related issues prior to engaging in the research itself. In this project, the research team is collaborating with two community partners – Liberty Prairie Foundation and the Openlands – who will help to provide access to residential communities organized around reducing the environmental impacts of household resource consumption and patterns of residential life. The Liberty Prairie Foundation, whose headquarters is located within Prairie Crossing, develops and supports enterprises for local food systems and natural landscapes. Through the Openlands' Conserve Lake County Conservation@Home program, residents are encouraged to adopt ecologically friendly gardening practices at their homes, schools and workplaces, including providing wildlife and native plant habitat, capturing rainwater and minimizing the use of chemicals. The research team is using these organizations and their participating communities as both collaborators and inspiration for understanding the constraints homeowners face and the possibilities for change. While these partners are not representative of the general population, and thus studying their decision making and behaviors may not provide generalizable knowledge relevant to other communities, they are important collaborators for understanding the lived contexts in which decisions are made and the possibilities for change across household, infrastructural and institutional scales.

Conclusion

Household resource consumption and its direct and indirect impacts on climate is a "wicked problem" (Lazarus, 2008; Levin et al., 2012), intersecting multiscalar and multidimensional facets and constraints. It is an issue that simply cannot be addressed via a single disciplinary lens. Accordingly, a TD team, including community-based organizations and government scientists along with academic researchers, is developing new models for assessing climate impacts of household consumption and will apply them in a mixed-methodology study to test feedback, messaging and social norms approaches to reducing resource use. An innovative role-playing game is being used to collect information and gain insights into behavior change prior to the actual household interventions. Game development and testing have been a focus of cross-disciplinary collaboration early in the project, and the mixed-methodology approach provides a framework for further integration, as well as iteration, in the research plan. In collaboration with community organizations, the research team is currently working to engage individual homeowners in a cohort study, and the research team will evaluate to what extent direct incentives, opportunities for households to reduce expenses and the common cause of climate change mitigation provide motivation to participate.

Acknowledgments

This material is based upon work supported by the National Science Foundation Innovations at the Nexus of Food, Energy and Water Systems Program under grant numbers 1541816 and 1639342. Any opinions, findings and conclusions or recommendations expressed in this material are those of the authors and do not necessarily reflect the views of the National Science Foundation.

14 A role-playing game development for supporting interventions to reduce household greenhouse gas emissions: transdisciplinary pathways and challenges

Datu B. Agusdinata, Muhammad A. Hanif, Heide K. Lukosch and Excel Ortega

Introduction: the research context, problem, and approach

Households consume considerable food, energy and water (FEW) resources. As a result, the direct and indirect greenhouse gas (GHG) emissions generated by the household sector is significant. For example, US households consume 80% of total direct and indirect energy used and are responsible for a similar share of CO_2 emissions (Bin and Dowlatabadi, 2005). Food consumption contributes 10–14% of total anthropogenic GHG emissions (Pradhan et al., 2013). Nearly 5% of total US GHG emissions come from the water sector (Rothausen and Conway, 2011). The GHG intensity of US households presents an opportunity for households to contribute significantly to GHG emissions reductions by reducing their FEW consumption (Wilkinson et al., 2009).

To inform effective interventions to reduce household GHG emissions, researchers need to deal with the challenge of knowledge production, and specifically to grapple with questions regarding what knowledge is needed and where the knowledge comes from. To address this challenge, we used a transdisciplinary (TD) approach to bring social actors from outside science, including industry, government and community members, into the research process. Through such inclusion, a TD approach can potentially facilitate integrating the best available knowledge, reconciling values and preferences, and building support for resultant problem and solution definitions and choices.

In addition to TD approaches, we employed a gaming approach that provides another promising mechanism for knowledge co-production (Smeds, 1997). Role-playing games (RPG) in particular can offer an environment where behavior can be immediately observed, allowing for experimentation in a safe situation, and enabling knowledge transfer through reflection or so-called debriefing after the actual gameplay (Mayer et al., 2005a; Wenzler et al., 1995; Kriz, 2003). Gaming can also potentially overcome traditional barriers when it comes to knowledge co-production and transfer between scientists and practitioners. This chapter describes in more detail one part of the larger FEW TD research project described in Chapter 13.

Our RPG was designed to identify intervention factors (e.g., messages, policies, cultural commitments) that could help households to manage their FEW consumption practices. The RPG assisted both the researchers and players with exploring solution-oriented behavioral interventions and developing potential strategies to make household FEW consumption more sustainable. Technological and behavioral interventions were modeled in the simulated gaming environment. This RPG environment provided a platform for players to understand the environmental impacts of their actions. The game was developed so that the costs, savings and carbon reductions associated with game players' choices would be understandable to the general public. This learning helped the researchers and players to prioritize interventions.

In TD projects scientists tend to be mostly concerned about the credibility of the research (i.e., whether the methodology is valid and reliable; Cash et al., 2003). In contrast, practitioners are more concerned about project impact (i.e., whether the outcomes have some practical relevance). By adopting a TD approach to game development, we integrated both scientific and practice-driven values and goals.

This chapter introduces our gaming approach in the context of influencing household FEW consumption and discusses our experience developing an RPG using a TD approach. First, we provide an overview of the state-of-the-art of gaming approaches relevant to our research. Second, we describe the interdisciplinary process of the game development. Third, we reflect on what we have learned and discuss the challenges and benefits of adopting the TD approach in the game development process.

State of the art of games for awareness and behavioral change

Games have potential to influence awareness of environmental issues. They provide an engaging experimental environment for studying strategic behavior in complex systems (Duke and Geurts, 2004). For example, the game Infrastratego, as discussed by Kuit et al. (2005), was used to illustrate aspects of the liberalization of the energy market. They examined patterns of strategic behavior in a liberalized Dutch electricity market and aimed at evaluating the effectiveness of two main energy policies using a game. Zhou et al. (2013) described how their "Climate Game" could be used in water management and spatial planning. The game simulated realistic water management and spatial planning options and enabled players to develop new policies and actions. The authors showed that the game presented immediate feedback on the implications of different policy options representing the real system in such a way that stakeholders were able to respond to the possible outcomes of various policies.

In another project, Mayer et al. (2005b) show that the combined use of a decision-support tool and a gaming procedure can lead to an increased shared understanding of problems and potential solutions in the field of sustainable urban renewal. They were able to show that games can be a powerful tool to support collaborative stakeholder decision making. Another study on water management gaming showed that the use of the game helped stakeholders to better understand and communicate water management uncertainties, which was a first step toward improved water-related decision making (Van Pelt et al., 2015).

The games mentioned were all mainly used for awareness development and as decision-support tools. Other studies emphasize the effectiveness of games as a behavioral change tool, generally referred to as "persuasive games". These types of games are intended to alter people's behaviors through gameplay (Stanley et al., 2010). Technologies that aim at changing people's behavior make use of insights from many scientific fields including psychology, sociology and economics. This assumes that changing the behavior of a player in a certain and intentional way is possible. In this sense, games may be powerful persuasion tools (Bogost, 2007). The simulated realities within games can give players the freedom to fail, experiment and interpret outcomes without the cost or risk of real-world actions (Klopfer et al., 2009). Games then are a promising approach to encouraging behavioral change.

Game type: role-playing games

We further highlight how a particular type of game, RPGs, can be used to try to change behavior. RPGs make use of the concept of role-taking, as introduced in the sense of a cognitive activity by George Herbert Mead (Mead, 1934; Mead and Miller, 1982). In game terms, this mechanism is understood as "perspective-taking", enabling an individual to take another person's point of view (Peng et al., 2010). For example, an immersive role-playing experience can give participants in a community meeting a strong feeling of connection to the real context and a deep understanding of the issue at play (Gordon and Schirra, 2011).

RPGs can further help players to identify with new roles and behaviors (Peng et al., 2010). In our case, players might already have an idea about what behavior would be expected in a more environmentally friendly household and tend to make decisions that relate to this interpretation. They can thus step into a role that they would normally not "play", and take actions accordingly. Game feedback can then be used to confirm these choices and illustrate the consequences in a safe, experiential environment. Identification with the role in the game helps the player to understand and adapt to feedback. In the game discussed in this chapter, roles are used to represent the dynamics of household decisions on FEW resources and to enable a better understanding of the consequences of such decisions.

Table 14.1 Relevant disciplines and sectors related to household greenhouse gas emissions

Scientific disciplines	Sectors
• Systems engineering • Economics • Cognitive science/psychology • Computer science	• Utility companies: electricity, water and gas • City government

Transdisciplinarity and household emissions RPG development

Our initial core team involved in household emissions RPG development consisted of a systems engineer, a sustainability scientist and a computer scientist. To form a larger transdisciplinary team, we identified key scientific disciplines and sectors relevant to the problem of household GHG emissions, as shown in Table 14.1. These individuals from diverse disciplines and sectors formed the full group with which we worked and periodically consulted during the development and testing of our RPG.

During the development of the RPG, we reached out to different scientists and social actors to get their inputs and feedback. We knew that it was important to include a psychologist or cognitive scientist to contribute to the understanding of how humans think, learn and influence each other (Grogan and Meijer, 2017). This field could also help with our understanding of how actors act in relation to each other and to their environment. Including an economist helped us design and research the RPG player choices.

Systems engineering

Understanding complex systems such as the FEW nexus involves several challenges, as such systems comprise a large number of interrelated actors, with multiple relationships between them as well as different values and interests involved (De Bruijn and Herder, 2009). Systems engineering uses methods such as simulation, modeling and gaming to change the system into a preferred state. In our study, systems engineering used a transdisciplinary approach to gaming to understand the interactions among actors and their behaviors.

In the development phase, we set up weekly meetings with the core team to ensure that feedback from different disciplines was integrated into the RPG design. These meetings were also meant to figure out which sections of the game needed further expert input. Once those needs were identified, appointments were then set with those experts. They were given briefings about the goal and vision of the game and current development stage, and then asked for their input. These expert interviews were done a number of times during the development of the RPG.

Economics

Insights from the field of economics are useful for guiding the valuation of decision utility within the game. A discussion with an economist on decision motives helped us to understand the so-called "warm-glow" phenomenon. This refers to an experience where people obtain satisfaction from philanthropic activities such as charity, recycling, voting and volunteering owing to the feeling of having done the right thing. This approach provides an alternative to the assumption that humans are only motivated by self-interest. However, the alternative altruistic values involve more complex motivations that may be driven by a sense of civic duty, protection of self-image and prevention of public shame or private guilt. We approached another economist to further understand the concept and discuss its implications to the rules of the game. The expert also helped us to match monetary values with climate scenarios and behavioral choices. One key aspect emphasized by these economists was the need to make sure that all of the rules of the games were easy to understand and clear to the players.

From the game theory discipline point of view, Bolton (2002) argues that game theory can provide lessons for constructing RPGs. Modern game theory is about the study of motives, particularly in conflict situations. In our application, we met with game theory experts a few times to construct a payoff matrix that tied one player decision to the decisions of other players. For example, if one single player decides to reduce her carbon footprint while the rest do not, then collectively all the players will suffer the same consequences (e.g., higher resource prices owing to drought).

Cognitive science

The interactions with scientists in the Department of Psychology at the University of Groningen in the Netherlands brought key insights during the development of our RPG. In particular, we learned how important it was to factor in players' motives into their decisions and behaviors. The well-being of humans improves when they are engaged in behaviors that benefit the environment (e.g., charity and carbon offset; Venhoeven et al., 2016). Environmentally friendly behaviors result in a more positive self-image ("feel good"). As more people see themselves as pro-environment, they will engage in more environmentally friendly behaviors that will lead to a self-reinforcing dynamics.

These insights led to several modifications in the game design. First, they helped us choose which environmentally friendly behaviors to include in the game (in the context of the game, this type of behavior increases "wonder"). Second, they led us to incorporate a feel-good factor into the aggregate measure of players' payoff.

Computer science

The development of the RPG ideas into a usable, testable product was the responsibility of our computer scientist and software developer. Over time, the game was shaped through team discussions of proposed ideas and assessment of their feasibility and effectiveness. Furthermore, designs stemming from flowcharts, discussions and documents were prototyped, tested and revised quickly in order to improve upon or change initial ideas.

Apart from the input from the computer scientist on our core team, we talked with additional computer experts who gave us valuable feedback about enhancing the gaming experience by working on the visuals, placement of the dialogue box and information presentation in such a way that it could be easily understood by a general audience. This allowed for rapid iterations that proved or disproved assumptions from those theories. Gaming experts were consulted to ensure that the fundamentals of an RPG game were included. They gave us insights into the elements that keep player focus and attention during gameplay. This helped us to make our RPG fun for players.

Sectors

Our analysis revealed that several sectors were essential to understanding the problem of household GHG emissions. It was therefore very important for us to get their feedback during RPG development. We briefly discuss each sector and describe the roles they played in game creation.

Utility companies

Utility companies provide gas, water and electricity to households. These companies interact directly with customers and can therefore influence consumption behaviors. We worked with people at various utility companies to understand the kinds of programs and messages they use to influence customer consumption. We then incorporated some of these practices into our RPG as reference points for what has been tried out and as leverage points for our behavioral interventions.

City government

Interactions with our local City of Phoenix government revealed some relevant information for RPG development. Working with city sustainability officers helped us learn that the city incorporates household resource conservation into their sustainability strategic planning, particularly with regard to water and solid waste. This helped us choose between potential behavioral options (e.g., installing low flow faucets and shower heads) based on what the city was already doing. It also helped us understand how to communicate these choices as clearly as possible to game players. City officials are interested in insights from the RPG that can in turn help them improve their homeowner information and education programs. In the future, we hope that our RPG can provide a platform for cities like Phoenix to test the effectiveness of various FEW conservation policies before putting them into practice.

Reflection on transdisciplinary challenges and benefits

The development of our RPG took place through transdisciplinary teamwork with interdisciplinary scientists and diverse social actors. This was particularly important in the early game conceptualization phase as it provided a blueprint for subsequent phases. Employing a systems engineering perspective, we put considerable effort into defining the system of interest related to the goal of the game. Our transdisciplinary team helped us with this conceptualization. Based on our system definition, we then considered features of game elements in a systematic way. Constant feedback from team members helped us better understand issues with our planned RPG early on and provided ample time to address them in development.

The process of designing an RPG was iterative as it went through conceptualization, prototyping and a play-testing stage. In such a process, the TD nature of our RPG development team was critical. Interactions among the disciplines involved included behavioral psychology (on the effect of games), economics (on the valuation of decision utilities), engineering (on technology scenarios and life cycle impacts) and computer science (on game features).

During the early development, social scientists – who use games as a tool for research – were consulted. They gave valuable insights into the different types of games that can be used for learning and research. They told us about the best practices and the necessary skills to develop an RPG. They also provided relevant examples of games that have been used for research. Game prototypes were shown to transdisciplinary experts for their feedback at different stages of development. The feedback helped us to identify the areas we need to focus on.

Furthermore, the feedback also led to an initial prototype that was then discussed with an economist to understand how we can assign monetary values to certain actions and resources. The modeling and gaming scientist explained different submodules of the game that are needed to make it a coherent educational RPG. We consulted with the game theory experts to better use the concept of payoffs in the game. The climate scientist gave us feedback to better integrate the concepts of carbon trade and climate scenarios in the RPG. Life cycle analysis experts helped to calculate the carbon reductions and expenditures because of the actions/tasks available in the game. Computer scientists guided us about the strengths of a simulated game, thus enabling us to better design the game. More generally, our development of the RPG highlights some challenges surrounding transdisciplinary RPG development and strategies for dealing with them (Table 14.2).

Table 14.2 Challenges to the TD research in the RPG setup with an outline of strategies and benefits

TD principle	Challenges and realization	Strategies and benefits
Collaborative problem framing and building a collaborative research team	• Need to maintain contact and commitment • Interactions occurred on an ad-hoc basis • Reconcile and integrate different actors' perspectives	• Initial study to understand the problem • Create a team structure that enables participation
Co-creation of solution-oriented and transferable knowledge through collaborative research	• Efficiently and effectively involve people from different fields • Development of a solution-oriented strategy within a scheduled time frame	• Initialize actions first to stimulate research
Integrating and applying the co-created knowledge	• Iterative RPG modeling and playtesting to ensure that the goal of the study is met • Tracking the scientific and social impacts	• Comparative studies to derive generalizable results

Collaborative problem framing and building a collaborative research team

We benefited from interacting and getting input from experts from across different disciplines including behavioral psychology, economics, engineering, climatology, social science and computer science. Integration of these disciplines added perspectives in the way we looked at the complex interactions between technology, behavior, climate impacts and policies. Some of the interactions were formal and regular (i.e., within the research project team). Others were more informal and ad-hoc.

We faced the challenge of communicating effectively across different subteams given the highly technical expertise of these different groups. We dealt with this challenge through frequent communication across the subteams. Since some subteams were not deeply involved in making game design decisions, they were not always aware of key decisions about the game. Consequently, we had to update economists and game theory experts via email and informal meetings. This helped us to obtain their input in time to integrate it in the game development. The earlier the designers understood which questions to ask and how to get the most information in meetings, the better it was for the project. One simple strategy we used to coordinate RPG development across the group was to prioritize tasks, e.g., which task would affect the game most, and to finish the prioritized task first. Setting realistic deadlines for task completion enabled the subteams to better plan and coordinate activities. We also conducted prototype play sessions with members of the various subteams. These sessions were the ones that provided us with the most constructive feedback.

Another challenge was the reconciliation of very different perspectives across disciplines and sectors. This challenge was tackled with open discussion, adapted agreements and reflexive meetings accompanying the TD research process. Some gaming concepts could only be explained across the group with the help of prototypes. Thus, regular RPG prototype testing helped us to better ensure that people across the team understood how the game was developing and how their feedback was affecting the game.

We also used flow charts, system diagrams and other visuals to help integrate our knowledge across the team. The development of the game was slow at the start but adding a structure to the development team helped us to move on with better pace. This structure helped us establish shared rights and responsibilities and a sense of ownership in the game, and allowed us to better coordinate work together.

Co-creation of solution-oriented and transferable knowledge through collaborative research

In our TD team, some experts were not constantly needed for their input. Some were only needed after certain elements of the project had been completed. The challenge in this regard was to effectively involve people from different fields in a timely manner. We faced this challenge at the start of the conceptualization phase. The gaming experts that we talked to at the start helped us to create a structure to involve scientists during the process of RPG development. Their interest and commitment were maintained by giving detailed updates at regular intervals about game development.

Another challenge was the development of a solution-oriented strategy within the scheduled timeframe. RPG elements are difficult to visualize, and sometimes certain elements may seem simple theoretically but they cannot be implemented/embedded in the RPG by the developer. Enthusiastic team members in our team sometimes took on more work than what they could finish in time. One strategy that helped us overcome this issue was to initialize actions first by the designers to stimulate research within the team and constantly update the prototype to play-test new elements.

Integrating and applying the co-created knowledge

Iterative RPG modeling and play-testing was required to ensure that the goal of the research project in developing an RPG that could test out behavioral interventions and assess impacts on player FEW choices was met. It was challenging to keep this in mind through RPG changes because we had to make sure that the changes we made during the development and the newly added modules in the gameplay did not change the rules of the game. Sometimes we had to change payoff matrices to ensure that the goal of the study was not compromised because of updates.

Feedback from players showed that the game had the potential to highlight different strategies to decrease the carbon footprint of households. We conducted post-game debriefing sessions to discuss these strategies along with the consequences of the measures taken. By doing so, the game helped players better understand the various routes to FEW conservation.

Winning game conditions served as important mechanisms for players to explore successful strategies of energy-saving behavior. The game motivated the players to think about different strategies in an engaging way. One limitation of the current version of the game is that only a limited number of variations of behavioral change and technological updates are offered. This limitation is being addressed in the future development and research of the game. In conclusion, using a TD team to develop the RPG helped us to create a powerful tool for understanding the potential of various policies in reducing FEW consumption. A diverse set of scientific disciplines allowed us to better craft a game that could help us understand how behavioral interventions might affect FEW-related behaviors. Including utility and public sector employees on our team allowed us to choose behavioral options with the greatest applicability to real-world contexts and to better ensure that our RPG would be useful to these sectors in their own testing of potential new programs and policies in the future.

Acknowledgments

This material is based upon work supported by the National Science Foundation Innovations at the Nexus of Food, Energy and Water Systems Program under grant numbers 1541816 and 1639342. Any opinions, findings and conclusions or recommendations expressed in this material are those of the authors and do not necessarily reflect the views of the National Science Foundation.

15 Community implementation of potable reuse of treated wastewater

Ali Mirchi, Josiah Heyman, George Tchobanoglous, Daisuke Minakata, Shane Walker, Maryam Samimi, R. Brian Guerrero, Diego Sanchez and Robert M. Handler

Introduction

Existing and emerging concerns about fresh water quantity and quality at local to global scales (Mirchi et al., 2014) and associated implications for reliability of water supply systems amplify the need for efficient use of available water resources. To address this need, many water utilities in the US and around the world are moving to portfolio-based management approaches that include diverse water supply sources to cope with increasingly variable and in many cases dwindling surface water supplies. Surface water supply uncertainty is often compounded with increasing demand owing to population growth as well as heightened temperatures and greater evapotranspiration (Mehran et al., 2017). As the demand increases on groundwater resources that buffer surface water shortages in water-scarce regions that practice conjunctive water resources management, potable reuse of treated wastewater (PRTW) is gaining more traction as an alternative to conserve valuable fresh water resources.

There are three main ways to reuse wastewater for drinking (Amoueyan et al., 2017): (a) de facto or unintended wastewater reuse within the hydrological cycle, which includes supplying drinking water from surface water and groundwater sources that may receive varying quantities of wastewater; (b) indirect potable reuse (IPR), which refers to passing highly treated wastewater blended with raw water through an environmental buffer (e.g., river, reservoir, and aquifer) and treating it again to drinking water standard prior to delivery to end users; and (c) direct potable reuse (DPR) of treated wastewater, which refers to directly adding highly treated and monitored wastewater into pipelines with or without blending with other treated water.

This chapter provides an overview of PRTW as a next-generation adaptation strategy to cope with fresh water shortage by augmenting water supply, highlighting the critical importance of effective community engagement in the process of urban water management decision making. PRTW, especially DPR, is expensive, technologically complex and invokes a wide variety of concerns, both objective (public health) and subjective (understandings and feelings about ingestion and use). Thus,

PRTW programs require a transdisciplinary approach to water resources development grounded in the collaboration between interdisciplinary scientists and engineers as well as the involvement of policy makers, water utilities and community members in order to develop joint understandings of water reuse problems and solutions. Public discussion of PRTW needs to engage better with long-term thinking about sustainable alternatives to "business-as-usual". The public needs to be well informed and meaningfully engaged in these decisions, on a topic that is demandingly technical and emotional at the same time. Real engagement challenges transdisciplinary (TD) skills that span scholarship, utility management and community understanding. As an illustration, this chapter offers an account of two PRTW plans in the cities of San Diego, California, and El Paso, Texas.

Overview of PRTW

Engineered treatment systems for PRTW are designed to provide safe and reliable drinking water by using multiple barriers of treatment processes to substantially reduce health risks, both acute (e.g., infection by viruses or protozoa) and chronic (e.g., cancer or disruption of hormone signaling; National Research Council, 2012). To achieve very high reliability of safe drinking water, treatment systems with multiple barriers of treatment processes are designed with (a) redundancy (i.e., the use of more treatment units in parallel or series than the minimum required), (b) robustness (i.e., the use of a variety of treatment processes to be able to remove a wide variety of contaminants) and (c) resilience (i.e., in case of a malfunction or failure, a system that does not allow unsafe water to reach the public) (Pecson et al., 2015).

To augment water supply through PRTW, the treated effluent from conventional wastewater treatment plants,[1] which is often returned to a river or lake, undergoes a number of advanced purification processes. Two major reclamation treatment systems have been implemented for PRTW. The first system[2] includes microfiltration (MF) for the removal of protozoa and bacteria, or ultrafiltration (UF) for the removal of protozoa, bacteria and viruses; reverse osmosis (RO) for the removal of dissolved solids (e.g., salinity, bulk organic compounds) and many chemical contaminants, and ultraviolet (UV) irradiation for disinfection or a UV-based advanced oxidation process (AOP) for the breakdown of trace organic chemicals (micropollutants). Alternatively, a second reclamation treatment system could include membrane filtration (MF or UF), ozonation for the breakdown and oxidation of organic compounds and activated carbon (AC) filtration, which uses bacteria to consume trace compounds remaining after ozonation. Ozone-based treatment has concerns about insufficient removal of salinity and total organic carbon, as well as the possible formation of byproduct chemicals such as bromate and NDMA (Hollender et al., 2009). The ozone with AC treatment system has been implemented as IPR in El Paso, Texas and Gwinnett County, Georgia (Gerrity et al., 2013). Without an environmental buffer, systems with a combination of treatment processes as described above have been used as DPR in Big Spring and Wichita Falls, Texas.

Economic cost and energy requirements are important factors that determine the selection of treatment processes for PRTW, which vary according to environmental setting (Tchobanoglous et al., 2015; Scruggs and Thomson, 2017). Cost is categorized into four parts: (a) treatment; (b) residuals management; (c) concentrate management if an RO-based process is used; and (d) conveyance and blending. The costs for treatment with and without RO are estimated at US$2.10–2.76 per thousand gallons (kgal) and US$1.23–2.15/kgal, respectively. To put these numbers into context, the estimated treatment cost for brackish groundwater desalination is US$1.23–2.45/kgal, whereas seawater desalination costs US$5.89–10.74/kgal. Furthermore, the estimated costs for residual management, concentrate management and conveyance and blending for RO-based wastewater reclamation processes are US$0.03–0.15, 0.21–2.38 and 0.31–3.07/kgal, respectively. The energy requirement for PRTW has been estimated at 3.25–4.00 kW h/kgal; a typical value with an average design flow of 10 million gallons per day (mgd) is 3.60 kW h/kgal (i.e., 0.95 kW h/m^3). This energy requirement can be compared with that for brackish water desalination (3.10–6.20 kW h/kgal) and ocean desalination (9.50–14.75 kW h/kgal) (Tchobanoglous et al., 2015). RO-based wastewater reclamation requires additional costs and energy requirement not only for treatment but also for concentrate management, which provides additional concern about the environmental impact of disposal.

There are a growing number of examples around the world where direct or indirect recycling of treated wastewater for drinking purposes is practiced (Table 15.1). Perhaps the best example is the international space station where a water recovery and management system consisting of a urine processor assembly and a water processor assembly treats urine collected from the crew to drinking standard (Kayatin et al., 2016). Singapore established its first NEWater treatment plant in May 2000 after about 30 years of investigating IPR as an option to handle water shortages. Currently, five NEWater plants meet 40% of water demand in Singapore (i.e., over 5 million residents) by treating about 223,200 Olympic-size swimming pools of water annually. The PRTW's share is planned to increase to 55% by 2060 (Chew et al., 2011). The New Goreangab plant in Namibia has been providing high-quality drinking water for nearly 350,000 residents in the City of Windhoek. The DPR plant was opened in 2002, more than three decades after successful implementation of IPR at the Old Goreangab water treatment plant, mainly used for supplying irrigation water for sport fields and a golf course (Lahnsteiner and Lempert, 2007). In the US, Texas is the only state that has fully operational DPR projects, namely the Colorado River Municipal Water District project at Big Spring, TX, where disinfected tertiary effluent from wastewater treatment is reclaimed using MF, RO and UV-AOP with hydrogen peroxide. Likewise, DPR is used in Wichita Falls, TX as an emergency water supply. The Texas Commission on Environmental Quality developed permit requirements for these specific DPR projects to deal with prolonged droughts.

Importantly, successful implementation of PRTW depends on a definite public decision (since it is a large infrastructural investment) with a complicated mixture

Table 15.1 Examples of IPR and DPR facilities around the world

Type	Facility	Country/city	Technology	Capacity (mgd)	Reference
Indirect potable reuse	Changi Water Reclamation Plant	Singapore	Microfiltration/ultrafiltration, reverse osmosis, UV disinfection	50	Daigger (2008)
	Upper Occoquan Sewage Authority Water Reclamation Plant	US/ Centreville	Lime clarification, two-stage recarbonation, flow equalization, sand filtration, granular activated, carbon, ion exchange, post carbon filtration, chlorination		Upper Occoquan Service Authority (2017)
	Beenyup Advanced Water Recycling Plant	Australia/ Perth	Ultrafiltration, reverse osmosis, UV disinfection	10	Busetti et al. (2015)
	Fred Hervey Water Reclamation Plant	US/El Paso	Two-stage powdered activated carbon treatment, biological denitrification, lime softening, two-stage recarbonation, sand filtration, ozonation, biologically active carbon filtration, chlorination and storage	10–12	Sheng (2005)
	Torreele/ St-André Water Reclamation Plant	Belgium/ Veurne Region	Microfiltration, reverse osmosis, UV disinfection	1.32	Onyango et al. (2014)
Direct potable reuse	Big Spring Wastewater Treatment Plant	US/Big Spring	Microfiltration, reverse osmosis, UV disinfection, 20% treated wastewater blended with 80% raw water	2	Tchobanoglous et al. (2011)
	Cloudcroft Treatment Plant	US/ Cloudcroft	Membrane bioreactors, reverse osmosis and advanced oxidation, UV disinfection, 50% treated wastewater blended with 50% raw water	0.18	Tchobanoglous et al. (2011)
	River Road Wastewater Treatment Plant	US/ Wichita Falls	Coagulation, microfiltration, reverse osmosis	8-10	City of Wichita Falls (2017)
	New Goreangab Plant	Namibia/ Windhoek	Ozonation, enhanced coagulation, dissolved air flotation, biologically active carbon, granular active carbon adsorption, ultrafiltration and chlorination, up to 50% treated wastewater is blended with treated water	5.5	Lahnsteiner and Lempert (2007)

of psychological, socioeconomic, cultural, political and environmental factors. Po et al. (2003) offer an informative review of the social dimensions of PRTW. Public concerns about cleanliness include disgust or the "yuck" factor, making other types of water more favorable than treated wastewater when those choices are available. There likewise are concerns about the safety of drinking treated wastewater and risks to public health owing to the potential presence of trace amounts of harmful chemicals and pathogens. Interestingly, the source of raw sewage can influence the perception of the safety of recycled wastewater for drinking. Water users tend to think of wastewater produced on their property to be "less disgusting" than raw wastewater produced by others (Po et al., 2003). The acceptability of PRTW also depends on public trust in authorities and scientific investigations that endorse the technology (Kaercher et al., 2003). Furthermore, environmental awareness in terms of the need for efficient use of natural resources improves the technology's acceptability, although perceptions of environmental injustice (i.e., implementation of PRTW in economically disadvantaged areas) increase resistance. Finally, the cost of PRTW appears to pose a paradoxical challenge because users expect to pay less for water that they perceive to have lower quality while, in reality, it is more expensive to produce drinking water from wastewater than other readily available fresh water sources (Po et al., 2003). However, the cost of PRTW may be less than that of an alternative such as water imported from a distant water supply.

Implementation of PRTW

Currently, water reuse initiatives are underway in populous metropolitan areas that face water shortage in the US. Two example projects in San Diego, California, and El Paso, Texas, are presented in this section. These case studies illustrate the TD nature of PRTW programs, which require effective community engagement alongside techno-economically feasible design alternatives. In particular, the case studies demonstrate the need for and the challenges of meaningful democratic deliberation in developing water reuse projects, especially those related to potable reuse.

The water recycling program in San Diego, California, USA

The City of San Diego is currently working on a water recycling demonstration program known as "Pure Water San Diego" (PWSD). The PWSD recycling program is a multiyear phased project that, at buildout in 2035, will provide about 33% of the City's water needs. In the first phase of the PWSD program, purified water (30 mgd) will be added to a surface water reservoir called Miramar where it will mix with other water. Water from the Miramar reservoir will be treated in the Miramar Drinking Water Facility before being added to the City's water distribution system (Pure Water San Diego, 2017).

The PWSD program has evolved from activities that can be traced back to the late 1970s. In 1981, a small (25,000 gallon per day, gpd) aquaculture facility (Aqua I) was put into operation. In 1984, an expanded (180,000 gpd) pilot research facility (Aqua II) was implemented. In 1991, the 1.0 mgd Aqua III Water Hyacinth Water Reclamation Facility and Aqua 2000 Research Center were constructed in the San Pasqual. Using effluent from the aquaculture facility, advanced water treatment technologies and methods were studied until 2001, when the program was discontinued. The current PWSD program began in 2004, when the City Council authorized a study to evaluate options to maximize the use of recycled water. Completed in 2006, the Water Reuse Study was the first phase of the authorized study. The second phase involved the construction of a 1.0 mgd advanced water treatment demonstration project. The results of the demonstration program were adopted by the City Council in 2013. In 2014, the City Council approved the implementation of the program (City of San Diego, 2006).

Elements of the PWSD water recycling program

To minimize risk, the multiple barrier concept (National Research Council, 2012) has been applied in the development of the PWSD program. The six major components that make up the PWSD program for the production of purified water, each of which includes one or more management, operational and/or technical barrier(s), are: (a) source control within the wastewater collection system; (b) tertiary treatment at the North City Pure Water Facility (NCPWF); (c) advanced water treatment at the NCPWF; (d) a conveyance pipeline to Miramar Reservoir; (e) discharge of purified water to Miramar Reservoir which serves as an environmental buffer; and (f) water treatment at the Miramar Drinking Water Facility.

The characteristics of the NCPWF that differentiate it from other water reclamation plants include influent flow equalization, full nitrification/denitrification, effective deep-bed filters following secondary treatment and no sludge processing at this facility. All influent solids and excess biological solids are discharged to the City's Metro Biosolids Center, thus minimizing process impacts resulting from the unpredictable and high-strength constituent concentrations found in sludge processing return water flows. The advanced water treatment facility includes ozonation, biologically active carbon adsorption, microfiltration, reverse osmosis, advanced oxidation, stabilization and free chlorine addition. The conveyance system involves transport of the purified water with free chlorine and dechlorination before discharge to Miramar Reservoir. The discharge into Miramar Reservoir must meet dilution and retention criteria and all existing beneficial uses at the reservoir must be sustained (Pure Water San Diego, 2017).

To protect public health, the purified water must meet all State regulations and specific water quality standards of the Division of Drinking Water of the State Water Resources Control Board and any additional Regional Water Quality Control Board requirements. To date more than 28,000 water quality tests have been conducted at the City's demonstration Pure Water Facility. Based on the results of these tests, the purified water meets or exceeds all Division of Drinking

Water and Regional Water Quality Control Board requirements as well as all federal and state drinking water standards.

Public outreach to overcome polarization

In the early 1990s, many people, including the mayor of San Diego at the time, were opposed to the idea of using advanced treated wastewater to augment the City's drinking water supply. In 1995, the phrase "toilet-to-tap" was first coined and used in a debate over an IPR project in Los Angeles. The phrase was adopted immediately and used extensively in San Diego by those who were opposed to potable reuse. The San Diego Union-Tribune was relentless in their opposition to a potable reuse program. At this time, the frame of public decision making was polarized, which stalled meaningful discussion of complicated knowledge and considerations. A shift toward a more effective dialogue required an extensive outreach and engagement program.

Public support for purified water in San Diego has increased since the initial inception of the Pure Water Project. In 2004, approximately 23% of the public supported the project, and by 2015, almost three-quarters of the public was in favor of adding purified water to the City's drinking water supply (Probe Research Inc., 2015). During this period, the City implemented an outreach program including a variety of strategies, activities and informational materials to ensure community members understood what the Pure Water Project is. The outreach team found that focusing communication efforts on community leaders and stakeholder groups was an effective way to inform residents about the program.

The ongoing activities of the outreach team include: (a) development of outreach materials to inform the residents about the program and the science behind it; (b) participation in community events; (c) facility tours; (d) youth outreach programs; (e) Pure Water Day Open House; (f) social media and online engagement; (g) reaching out with all forms of media; and (h) sponsorship of an active speakers bureau. In addition, the outreach team sent e-newsletters and e-updates to more than 6000 stakeholders throughout the year; information booths have been placed at more than 180 community events; more than 14,000 people have toured the facility; tours, events and presentations designed for youth have reached thousands; more than 85,000 people have visited the website purewatersd.org; since 2010, more than 800 media events including articles, television spots, blogs and newsletters have been released; and 530 presentations have been made to more than 17,000 persons (Pure Water San Diego, 2017).

Based on the San Diego case, it is clear that a comprehensive and all-encompassing outreach program must be an integral part of planning for any potable reuse program. Project planning and outreach must go hand-in-hand from the inception of the proposed project. The outreach program must be even-handed, transparent and comprehensive as the public's perception or opinion of a project can change based on the information presented. The information presented should be: (a) free of technical jargon and acronyms; (b) easy to understand; and (c) of sufficient technical depth to engender trust. The point is not to persuade or maneuver the public for support, but to provide information to get past extreme frameworks (e.g., toilet-to-tap, which really is not the health issue that is crucially at stake) that paralyze decision making.[3] Even so, the parallel El Paso case (where similar informative efforts were made) suggests that widespread knowledge and engagement are hard to achieve.

Advanced water purification facility in El Paso, Texas, USA

El Paso Water (EPW), the utility that serves the entire City of El Paso, Texas, and some areas of the surrounding county (also named El Paso), plans to implement advanced purification on already treated wastewater and return up to 10 mgd to the drinking water distribution system. The DPR plan is expected to meet about 10% of El Paso's annual average total potable water demand (approximately 6% of peak daily demand) and is expected to be the nation's first direct-to-distribution DPR system (El Paso Water, 2018; Maseeh et al., 2015). The published start date in the state of Texas water plan for the first plant is 2020 (Texas Water Development Board, 2017), although the final go-ahead depends on cost relative to other supplies in EPW's long-term portfolio (e.g., inter-basin transfer/importation).

EPW faces a significant water supply challenge. The utility is located in an inland desert region, with competing demand for groundwater from Ciudad Juárez, Chihuahua, Mexico, another large city in immediate proximity, although across an international border, from a number of smaller municipalities and independent users in other parts of the region, and from irrigated agriculture in both the US and Mexico. Agriculture (the largest use sector) uses river water as the first supply source, but increasingly is drawing on groundwater. EPW has gradually acquired rights to river irrigation water to be treated and used as a municipal water source; in a full allocation year, treated surface water provides about half of EPW's annual drinking water supply. However, that supply is subject to "river drought" owing to climate change impacts on distant snowpack sources in the headwaters of the Rio Grande River in Colorado. Meanwhile, the Hueco Bolson, the aquifer from which EPW derives the most water, is gradually declining (Sheng, 2013) even with substantial efforts by EPW to introduce new water, such as IPR through injection wells and infiltration basins providing a total artificial recharge capacity of 1.2 billion gallons annually (4.7 million m^3). Another large aquifer, the Mesilla Bolson, is also at risk. In this context, EPW has a long-range planning approach, which includes successful conservation measures (129 gallons per capita per day, a low per capita urban water use figure by US standards; El Paso Water, 2016), increased river water rights, a large inland desalination plant, plans for importation of water from distant, non-basin sources, and DPR.

Elements of the advanced water purification facility

In 2015, EPW successfully conducted a one-year pilot study at the Roberto Bustamante Wastewater Treatment Plant (the largest in El Paso), which included: MF/UF for removal of suspended solids and pathogens; MF/RO for broad-spectrum removal of salinity and other dissolved chemicals; UV–peroxide AOP and granular active carbon adsorption for removal of very low concentrations of chemicals of emerging concern; and natural calcite media dissolution for stabilization of pH and alkalinity in the distribution system. The National Water Research Institute partnered with EPW to conduct a third-party expert panel review at multiple points throughout the pilot study to confirm that the pilot system reliably produced safe drinking water quality. The expert panel also discussed with EPW and consulting engineers the importance of public education and acceptance of the advanced purification process. In 2017, EPW proceeded with a preliminary design of a full-scale system, and commitment to construction could follow. At the time of this writing, the full-scale process is being designed to receive 10 mgd of treated (but unchlorinated) effluent from the Roberto Bustamante Wastewater Treatment Plant and to produce 7.5–7.8 mgd of product water with groundwater blending for a total blended product of up to 10 mgd.

Probing public knowledge

The El Paso case shows the challenges of engaging the public in important but also complex decisions. EPW carried out public information activities similar to those described above for San Diego, and in the middle of this campaign, conducted a random sample-based public opinion survey on DPR that suggested that 84% of respondents somewhat or strongly favored the technology. While interesting, this survey cannot be taken as adequate evidence about El Pasoans' collective attitude toward DPR. Rather, it fits closely the category of social marketing tool (Guerrero, 2016). First, the sequence of questions tested a series of persuasive justifications (and not objections) prior to asking the actual question about acceptance of DPR, so that respondents were prepped to answer positively. The survey then followed with three more persuasive statements and pushed the score to 95% favorable. Second, the survey allowed only for positive or negative opinions about DPR, and did not have an undecided or lack of information option. Yet those options might actually have represented the reality of incomplete information and engagement, as was indicated by two independent studies.

In order to understand the nuances of public perception, 32 community in-depth qualitative interviews were conducted in El Paso on consumer attitudes to a wide variety of water issues, including the utility's plans for DPR. This was after EPW's publicity push. The choice of interviewees was opportunistic, but was deliberately diversified as to demographic characteristics (age, education, gender, area of the city, language of survey, race–ethnicity). Only three of 32 interviewees had heard about the program. When engaged in discussion about the program, the large majority were supportive, especially because of sustainability considerations; this suggests that people could enter into a non-polarizing, deliberative process but widespread engagement had not yet taken hold (Sanchez Garcia, 2017).

Indirect evidence of the challenges for public engagement was provided by a study in which brief messages (typical of public information campaigns) left a large proportion of recipients undecided. Another study (Guerrero, 2016) involved conducting three classroom surveys at the University of Texas at El Paso,[4] one with a short positive lead-in, one with a short negative lead-in and one with a balanced presentation. The interesting result is not that the presentation affected the answers – which was expected – but that undecided was the most common response. Following the balanced presentation (n = 26), 46.2% chose undecided; following the negative presentation (n = 25), 44% chose undecided; and following the positive presentation (n = 30), 33.3% chose undecided, while 43.3% were positive.

Undecided is not the same as uninformed – indeed, the method of study for the survey research was first to provide brief but key items of information – but interestingly, it indicates a realistic feeling by members of the public that the decision was difficult and they did not know enough to commit. After all, the presentations just broached discussion of profound questions of sustainability, cost, health, ingestion of an intimate good (water) and so forth. This is challenging for those people involved in TD work seeking to inform and engage publics concerning PRTW. In this context, EPW has moved forward on the basis of internal planning and an insulated governance structure.

Governance considerations and DPR

While EPW is a public utility, it is relatively insulated from direct political control. EPW is governed by the Public Service Board: six members appointed by the El Paso City Council, and the El Paso Mayor as the seventh member. There are "seats" for different sectors, engineering, academic, business community, and so forth. When a seat is open they accept nominations or applications for that sector; EPW recommends one applicant to the board, but the board can choose any of the applicants. This structure results in a mostly closed loop of communication between the Board and the Utility. Furthermore, the officially public level of Board control (in reality, little known in the city except for interested parties) is layered on top of a relatively autonomous organization with markedly technocratic orientations toward planning, decision making and management. In making planning decisions (such as DPR), EPW also responds to another unit of bureaucratic governance, the three-member Texas Water Development Board appointed by the Governor. That entity has considerable influence over EPW both in receiving significant, detailed planning documents (including for DPR, cited above) and as a source of grants and loans, most recently US$2 billion in special water funding allocated by the Texas Legislature, following the approved 50 year plan (updated every five years). Finally, El Paso's Public Service Board has important real estate development functions, as it gradually releases a large stock of reserved land to developers (with funds going to the city), but such real estate processes require added long-term drinking water supplies and sanitation removal, helping to drive the long-term orientation of the EPW planning process.

If we conceive of the social dimension of PRTW as mainly concerning public attitudes, we may neglect another important social dimension: governance, institutions and inside politics. EPW genuinely attempted to inform the public about DPR; it conducted an energetic (if one-sided) information campaign. The process has not been secretive and it adheres to democratic norms. However, as with so many issues, it has been difficult to engage the public. No one has chosen to stir up controversy over DPR in El Paso, unlike San Diego. People accept that water is scarce in the region and trust EPW with their future. Meanwhile, the 50 year planning process tends to favor specialized technocratic knowledge, within which DPR has emerged as one solution in a diverse portfolio. Although panic has not happened in El Paso, the risk is that weak engagement will permit waves of panic to form, as reported in the San Diego case study.

Discussion

Meeting urban water demand is prioritized in many areas around the world where top-down water management schemes are in place, reducing the need for expediting the transition to closed-loop urban water systems through PRTW. Likewise, in many other areas where distribution of water is dictated by various strict water-rights schemes, the significantly greater economic value of water in the urban sector justifies trading of agricultural water rights (Dozier et al., 2017). However, wider implementation of PRTW in the future is likely owing to the compounding effects of continuous demand growth, climatic variability, declining groundwater tables and the difficulty of implementing less contentious water management alternatives because of cost and environmental considerations.

The science and technical design of PRTW have matured over the last half-century. Nonetheless, the technology is still on its way to broad adoption by population centers facing water shortages. Indeed, public policy dimensions of PRTW are emerging as crucial in how rapidly and extensively the technology is adopted as the purely technical side has matured. From a TD perspective, the key challenge is providing meaningful knowledge for democratic deliberation. In San Diego, for instance, the original water recycling plans were postponed until there was stronger trust in the science and evidence of acceptable levels of risk to public health. In El Paso, in contrast, a trusted but insulated institution is moving forward with plans for direct potable reuse amid weak public understanding and engagement.

Planned PRTW initiatives such as IPR in San Diego and DPR in El Paso teach us a number of lessons. Attitudes toward water – something we ingest into our bodies, our very being – inevitably will and should be sensitive. Public consideration will combine in complicated ways strong feelings and important objective knowledge about water treatment and health.[5] This in turn implies the need to communicate esoteric technologies to non-expert audiences. Additionally, water deliberations should include meaningful understanding of economics (such as cost impacts on poor ratepayers and communities as a whole) and long-run water sustainability in the face of urbanization, demand change and climate change. In addition to attitudes of the public, trustworthy and effective institutions and policy decision-making processes matter greatly. While insulated processes are at first convenient for experts, their "Achilles' heel" is the tendency to engender suspicion, polarization and conspiracy thinking. All of this can be overcome, but it is not easy.

Next-generation urban water management options such as PRTW will require TD research approaches founded on the social, economic and environmental pillars of sustainability. Environmental managers will always and in every issue face tradeoffs related to addressing public concerns as they arise, on the one hand, and on the other, redirect public dialogue to issues of concern raised by the technical and economic considerations of any project. To this end, it is necessary to increase public awareness and engage independent experts from pertinent scientific disciplines to facilitate informed democratic water management processes that address public concerns, to make decisions about proposed projects with consensus behind them, and to build confidence in those decisions. An important step is launching public outreach campaigns that educate consumers about the technical, socio-economic and environmental underpinnings of PRTW, encouraging the public to be involved and educating them to ask the most helpful and revealing questions during a constructive dialogue about adaptation planning in water-scarce regions.

Research on PRTW must include both the attitudinal and the political-process dimensions alongside technological inquiries. As population centers located in water-scarce regions consider PRTW, more systematic investigations are needed to understand the effects of governance and institutions on the public acceptance rate of this technology platform. Furthermore, research aimed at how to obtain more meaningful public information and engagement will be critical. An informed public will understand risk factors over a variety of time horizons and risk levels, recognizing the implications of "business as usual" supply-oriented water management for socioeconomic growth, resources sustainability and environmental integrity (Mirchi et al., 2014).

Conclusion

Around the world, PRTW is gaining traction as a feasible alternative source of water supply to alleviate concerns about urban water sustainability owing to increasing water demand and climate change-related water supply uncertainty, especially in water-scarce regions. In a quest to diversify their water supply portfolio, many water utilities are considering indirect or direct reuse of treated wastewater for drinking purposes. The technology has advanced significantly, reducing the risk of adverse human health effects based on the multibarrier concept. The interplay of multiple psychological, socioeconomic, cultural, political and environmental factors influences public acceptance of wastewater reuse projects, which is key for successful implementation of PRTW. This situation creates additional uncertainty for water utilities that have conventionally practiced top-down technocratic water management approaches. However, as the need for next-generation water management options such as PRTW continues to grow, it is timely for water utilities to implement TD research frameworks to prepare for major public debates and policy decisions outside existing community risk tolerance. Two important case studies in San Diego, California, and El Paso, Texas, illuminated the opportunities and challenges of PRTW as an urban water adaptation strategy. The case studies underscore the indispensable role of knowledge, trust in its scientific bases and the development of shared consensus about acceptable public health risks. Realistic assessments of public attitudes, as well as governance, institutions and political dynamics are critical social dimensions of community implementation of PRTW.

NOTES

1. Conventional wastewater treatment processes include: primary settling for removal of suspended solids (turbidity); secondary aeration, biological treatment and settling for removal of dissolved organic waste; disinfection for inactivating pathogens (microorganisms that cause infection); and sometimes tertiary treatment such as sand filtration for further removal of suspended particles.
2. This treatment system is defined as full advanced treatment by California Department of Public Health (California Department of Public Health, 2013) and has been implemented as IPR (by recharging the local groundwater) at the Orange County Water District in California, in Singapore and in Perth, Australia (Gerrity et al., 2013).
3. Also, San Diego has tempered earlier negativity about direct reuse by planning to use IPR, which adds a "touch of nature" by passing treated wastewater through an environmental buffer, a reservoir. This is currently done in the aquifer storage and recovery program in El Paso, more for technical than public opinion reasons, and that utility is now proposing to use DPR.
4. UTEP is an unselective commuter school with an almost entirely regionally originated student body. While younger and somewhat more educated than the wider community, and slightly more female, university-based surveys at UTEP are relatively representative in most regards (income, race–ethnicity, neighborhood, etc.).
5. For instance, in California, there is evidence of broad public concern about the presence of trace chemicals in treated wastewater (triggered by prevailing reports about chemicals of emerging concern) whereas pathogens have been neglected. Yet pathogens should be a serious question asked of DPR plans because of the immediate consequences to the public health.

References

Abrams, Philip (1988), 'Notes on the difficulty of studying the state', *Journal of Historical Sociology*, **1**(1), 58–89.

Adams, William M. (2014), 'The value of valuing nature', *Science*, **346**(6209), 549–551.

Agger, Peder (2002), 'Between Science and Policy – The experience of the Danish Nature Council', *The Journal of Transdisciplinary Environmental Studies*, **1**(1), 1–13.

Agrawal, Arun (2002), 'Common resources and institutional sustainability', in Elinor Ostrom, Thomas Dietz, Nives Dolšak, Paul C. Stern, Susan Stonich and Elke U. Weber (eds), *The Drama of the Commons*. Washington, DC: National Academy Press, pp. 41–85.

Agrawal, Arun and Clark C. Gibson (1999), 'Enchantment and disenchantment: The role of community in natural resource conservation', *World Development*, **27**(4), 629–649.

Alcantara, Armando, Salvador Malo and Mauricio Fortes (2011), 'Doctoral education in Mexico', in Maresi Nerad and Mimi Heggelund (eds), *Toward a Global PhD?: Forces And Forms in Doctoral Education Worldwide*. Seattle, WA: University of Washington Press, pp. 146–170.

Alonso-Yanez, Gabriela (2013), 'Mapping conservation on the ground: Situational analyses of a biosphere reserve in Mexico', PhD dissertation, British Columbia: Simon Fraser University, Faculty of Education.

Alonso-Yanez, Gabriela and Conny Davidsen (2014), 'Conservation science policies versus scientific practice: Evidence from a Mexican biosphere reserve', *Human Ecology Review*, **20**(2), 3–29.

Amoueyan, Erfaneh, Sajjad Ahmad, Joseph N. S. Eisenberg, Brian M. Pecson and Daniel Gerrity (2017), 'Quantifying pathogen risks associated with potable reuse: A risk assessment case study for Cryptosporidium', *Water Research*, **119**, 252–266.

Andersen, Hanne (2016), 'Collaboration, interdisciplinarity, and the epistemology of contemporary science', *Studies in History and Philosophy of Science*, **56**:1–10.

Anderson, William C. (2003), 'A history of environmental engineering in the United States', *Environmental and Water Resources History*, 1–12.

Ansell, Chris and Alison Gash (2008), 'Collaborative governance in theory and practice', *Journal of Public Administration Research and Theory*, **18**(4), 543–571.

Arnstein, Sherry R. (1969), 'A ladder of citizen participation', *Journal of the American Institute of Planners*, **35**(4), 216–224.

Aronoff, David M. and Barbara A. Bartkowiak (2012), 'A review of the website TeamScience.Net', *Clinical Medicine & Research*, **10**(1), 38–39.

Attwater, Roger, Sandy Booth and Alasdair Guthrie (2005), 'The role of contestable concepts in transdisciplinary management of water in the landscape', *Systems Research and Behavioral Science*, **22**(3), 185–192.

Babbie, Earl (1994), *The Sociological Spirit2: Critical Essays in a Critical Science*. Belmont: Wadsworth Press.

Bacon, Christopher M., Saneta DeVuono-Powell, Mary L. Frampton, Tony LoPresti and Camille Pannu (2013), 'Introduction to empowered partnerships: Community-based participatory action research for environmental justice', *Environmental Justice*, **6**(1), 1–8.

Baerwald, Thomas J., Penelope L. Firth and Sarah L. Ruth (2016), 'The dynamics of Coupled Natural and Human Systems Program at the U.S. National Science Foundation: Lessons learned in interdisciplinary funding program development and management', *Current Opinion in Environmental Sustainability*, **19**:123–133.

Bailey, Jennifer, Murat Van Ardelan, Klaudia L. Hernández, Humberto E. González, José Luis Iriarte, Lasse Mork Olsen, Hugo Salgado and Rachel Tiller (2015), 'Interdisciplinarity as an emergent property: The research project "CINTERA" and the study of marine eutrophication', *Sustainability*, **7**(7), 9118–9139.

Bailis, Robert and Jennifer Baka (2011), 'Constructing sustainable biofuels: Governance of the emerging biofuel economy', *Annals of the Association of American Geographers*, **101**(4), 827–838.

Balazs, Carolina L. and Rachel Morello-Frosch (2013), 'The three R's: How community based participatory research strengthens the rigor, relevance and reach of science', *Environmental Justice*, **6**(1), 9–16.

Balderas Torres, Arturo, Ricardo Ontiveros Enríquez, Margaret Skutsch and Jon C. Lovett (2013), 'Potential for climate change mitigation in degraded forests: A study from La Primavera, México', *Forests*, **4**(4), 1032–1054.

Ballard, Heidi L. and Jill M. Belsky (2010), 'Participatory action research and environmental learning: Implications for resilient forests and communities', in Marianne E. Krasny, Cecilia Lundholm and Ryan Plummer (eds), *Resilience in Social–Ecological Systems*. London: Routledge, pp. 152–168.

Bammer, Gabriele (2008), 'Enhancing research collaborations: Three key management challenges', *Research Policy*, **37**(5), 875–887.

Banerjee, Aparajita, Emily Prehoda, Roman Sidortsov and Chelsea Schelly (2017), 'Renewable, ethical? Assessing the energy justice potential of renewable electricity', *AIMS Energy*, **5**(5), 768–797.

Barlow, Jos, Robert M. Ewers, Liana Anderson, Luiz E. O. C. Aragao, Tim R. Baker, Emily Boyd, Ted R. Feldpausch, Emanuel Gloor, Anthony Hall, Yadvinder Malhi, William Milliken, Mark Mulligan, Luke Parry, Toby Pennington, Carlos A. Peres, Oliver L. Phillips, Rosa Maria Roman-Cuesta, Joseph A. Tobias and Toby A. Gardner (2011), 'Using learning networks to understand complex systems: A case study of biological, geophysical and social research in the Amazon', *Biological Reviews*, **86**(2), 457–474.

Barrett, Christopher B. and Jeffrey W. Cason (1997), *Overseas Research: A Practical Guide*, 1st edn. Baltimore, MD: Routledge.

Barwick, Melanie (2013), 'Knowledge translation planning template', The Hospital for Sick Children, http://www.sickkids.ca/pdfs/Learning/58366-58366-KT_Template.pdf, accessed 14 May 2018.

Battiste, Marie (2008), 'The struggle and renaissance of indigenous knowledge in Eurocentric education', in Maria Villegas, Sabina Rak Neugebauer, and Kerry R. Vengas (eds), *Indigenous knowledge and education: sites of struggle, strength, and survivance*. Harvard Education Review Reprint Series No. 44. Cambridge, MA: Harvard Education Press, pp. 85–92.

Bazilian, Morgan, Ijeoma Onyeji, Michael Liebreich, Ian MacGill, Jennifer Chase, Jigar Shah, Dolf Gielen, Doug Arent, Doug Landfear and Shi Zhengron (2013), 'Reconsidering the economics of photovoltaic power', *Renewable Energy*, **53**, 329–338.

Becker, Adam B., Barbara A. Israel, Jeanette Gustat, Angela G. Reyes and Alex J. Allen III (2005), 'Strategies and techniques for effective group process in community-based participatory research partnerships', in Barbara A. Israel, Eugenia Eng and Amy J. Schulz (eds), *Methods for Community-based Participatory Research for Health*, 2nd edn. San Francisco, CA: Jossey-Bass, pp. 52–72.

Belone, Lorenda, Julie E. Lucero, Bonnie Duran, Greg Tafoya, Elizabeth A. Baker, Domin Chan, Charlotte Chang, Ella Greene-Moton, Michelle A. Kelley and Nina Wallerstein (2016), 'Community-based Participatory Research Conceptual Model', *Qualitative Health Research*, **26**(1), 117–135.

Bennett, N. J., R. Roth, S. C. Klain, K. M. A. Chan, D. A. Clark, G. Cullman, G. Epstein, M. P. Nelson, R. Stedman, T. L. Teel, R. E. W. Thomas, C. Wyborn, D. Curran, A. Greenberg, J. Sandlos and D. Veríssimo (2017), 'Mainstreaming the social sciences in conservation', *Conservation Biology*, **31**(1), 56–66.

Berkes, Fikret (2009), 'Evolution of co-management: Role of knowledge generation, bridging organizations and social learning', *Journal of Environmental Management*, **90**(5), 1692–1702.

Berkes, Fikret, Carl Folke and Johan Colding (1998), *Linking Social and Ecological Systems: Management Practices and Social Mechanisms for Building Resilience*. Cambridge: Cambridge University Press.

Berkes, Fikret, Johan Colding and Carl Folke (2003), *Navigating Social–Ecological Systems: Building Resilience for Complexity and Change*. Cambridge: Cambridge University Press.

Bickerstaff, Karen, Gordon P. Walker and Harriet Bulkeley (2013), *Energy Justice in a Changing Climate: Social Equity and Low-carbon Energy*. London: Zed Books.

Biello, David (2010), 'The BP spill's growing toll on the sea life of the Gulf', Yale Environment 360, 9 June, https://web.archive.org/web/20100612181943/http://www.e360.yale.edu/content/feature.msp?id=2284, accessed 1 November 2017.

Bin, Shui and Hadi Dowlatabadi (2005), 'Consumer lifestyle approach to US energy use and the related CO_2 emissions', *Energy Policy*, **33**(2), 197–208.

Blaikie, Piers and Harold Brookfield (1987), *Land Degradation and Society*. London: Methuen.

Bogost, Ian (2007), *Persuasive Games: The Expressive Power of Videogames*. Cambridge, MA: MIT Press.

Bollinger, Bryan and Kenneth Gillingham (2012), 'Peer effects in the diffusion of solar photovoltaic panels', *Marketing Science*, **31**(6), 900–912.

Bolton, Gary E. (2002), 'Game theory's role in role-playing', *International Journal of Forecasting*, **18**(3), 353–358.

Bonney, Rick, Carin B. Cooper, Janis Dickinson, Steve Kelling, Tina Phillips, Kenneth V. Rosenberg and Jennifer Shirk (2009), 'Citizen science: A developing tool for expanding science knowledge and scientific literacy', *BioScience*, **59**(11), 977–984.

Borenstein, Severin (2017), 'Private net benefits of residential solar PV: The role of electricity tariffs, tax incentives, and rebates', *Journal of the Association of Environmental and Resource Economists*, **4**(S1), S85–S122.

Bornemann, Basil, Andreas Bernasconi, Olivier Ejderyan, Franziska Schmid, Patrick Wäger and Claudia Zingerli (2017), 'Research on natural resources: The quest for integration revisited', *GAIA*, **26**(1) 16–21.

Börner, Katy, Noshir Contractor, Holly J. Falk-Krzesinski, Stephen M. Fiore, Kara L. Hall, Joann Keyton, Bonnie Spring, Daniel Stokols, William Trochim and Brian Uzzi (2010), 'A multi-level systems perspective for the science of team science', *Science Translational Medicine*, **2**(49), 24–49.

Boyer, Robert H. W. (2016), 'Achieving one-planet living through transitions in social practice: A case study of Dancing Rabbit Ecovillage', *Sustainability: Science, Practice, and Policy*, **12**(1), 47–59.

Bradbury-Huang, Hilary (2010), 'What is good action research?', *Action Research*, **8**(1), 93–109.

Brandt, Patric, Anna Ernst, Fabienne Gralla, Christopher Luederitz, Daniel J. Lang, Jens Newig, Florian Reinert, David J. Abson and Henrik von Wehrden (2013), 'A review of transdisciplinary research in sustainability science', *Ecological Economics*, **92**, 1–15.

Branker, Kadra, M. J. M. Pathak and Joshua M. Pearce (2011), 'A review of solar photovoltaic levelized cost of electricity', *Renewable and Sustainable Energy Reviews*, **15**(9), 4470–4482.

Bremer, Leah L., Kathleen A. Farley and David Lopez-Carr (2014), 'What factors influence participation in payment for ecosystem services programs? An evaluation of Ecuador's SocioPáramo program', *Land Use Policy*, **36**, 122–133.

Bresman, Henrik and Mary Zellmer-Bruhn (2013), 'The structural context of team learning: Effects of organizational and team structure on internal and external learning', *Organization Science*, **24**(4), 1120–1139.

Briggs, Sue V. (2006), 'Integrating policy and science in natural resources: Why so difficult?', *Ecological Management and Restoration*, **7**, 37–39.

Brown, Rebekah R., Ana Deletic and Tony H. F. Wong (2015), 'How to catalyze collaboration: Turn the fraught flirtation between the social and biophysical sciences into fruitful partnerships with these five principles', *Nature*, **525**(7569), 315–318.

Brown, Valerie A., John Alfred Harris and Jacqueline Y. Russell (eds) (2010), *Tackling Wicked Problems through the Transdisciplinary Imagination*. London: Earthscan.

Brundtland, Gro Harlem (1987), 'Report of the world commission on environment and development: Our common future'. World Commission on Environment and Development, United Nations.

Brydon-Miller, Mary, Davydd Greenwood and Patricia Maguire (2003), 'Why action research?', *Action Research*, **11**(11), 9–28.

Buizer, Marleen, Bas Arts and Kasper Kok (2011), 'Governance, scale and the environment: The importance of recognizing knowledge claims in transdisciplinary arenas', *Ecology and Society,* **16**(1), 21–39.

Buizer, Marleen, Katinka Ruthrof, Susan A. Moore, Erik J. Veneklaas, Giles Hardy and Catherine Baudains (2015), 'A critical evaluation of interventions to progress transdisciplinary research', *Society & Natural Resources,* **28**(6), 670–681.

Busetti, Francesco, Matthias Ruff and Kathryn L. Linge (2015), 'Target screening of chemicals of concern in recycled water', *Environmental Science: Water Research & Technology,* **1**(5), 659–667.

California Department of Public Health (CDPH) (2013), 'Groundwater replenishment reuse draft regulations', California Department of Public Health, Sacramento, CA.

Campbell-Voytal, Kimberly (2010), 'Phases of "pre-engagement" capacity building: Discovery, exploration, and trial alliance', *Progress in Community Health Partnerships: Research, Education, and Action,* **4**(2), 155–162.

Cargo, Margaret and Shawna L. Mercer (2008), 'The value and challenges of participatory research: Strengthening its practice', *Annual Review of Public Health,* **29**(1), 325–350.

Carlsson-Kanyama, Annika, Rebecka Engström and Rixt Kok (2005), 'Indirect and direct energy requirements of city households in Sweden: Options for reduction, lessons for modeling', *Journal of Industrial Ecology,* **9**(1–2), 221–235.

Cash, David W., William C. Clark, Frank Alcock, Nancy M. Dickson, Noelle Eckley, David H. Guston, Jill Jäger and Ronald B. Mitchell (2003), 'Knowledge systems for sustainable development', *Proceedings of the National Academy of Sciences,* **100**(14), 8086–8091.

Castells, Manuel (2011), 'Humanitas: Professor Manuel Castells at the University of Cambridge, communication, power, and the state in the network society', University of Cambridge, https://www.youtube.com/watch?v=9-ubCGAV3iw., accessed 14 November 2017.

Castillo, Alicia and Victor M. Toledo (2000), 'Applying ecology in the Third World: The case of Mexico', *BioScience,* **50**(1), 66–76.

Chapin III, F. Stuart, Stephen R. Carpenter, Gary P. Kofinas, Carl Folke, Nick Abel, William C. Clark, Per Olsson, D. Mark Stafford Smith, Brian Walker, Oran R. Young, Fikret Berkes, Reinette Biggs, J. Morgan Grove, Rosamund L. Naylor, Evelyn Pinkerton, Will Steffen and Frederick J. Swanson (2010), 'Ecosystem stewardship: Sustainability strategies for a rapidly changing planet', *Trends in Ecology & Evolution,* **25**(4), 241–249.

Chen, Kee Kuo (2014), 'Assessing the effects of customer innovativeness, environmental value and ecological lifestyles on residential solar power systems install intention', *Energy Policy,* **67**, 951–961.

Cheng, Antony S. and Victoria E. Sturtevant (2012), 'A framework for assessing collaborative capacity in community-based public forest management', *Environmental Management,* **49**(3), 675–689.

Cheruvelil, Kendra S., Patricia A. Soranno, Kathleen C. Weathers, Paul C. Hanson, Simon J. Goring, Christopher T. Filstrup and Emily K. Read (2014), 'Creating and maintaining high-performing collaborative research teams: The importance of diversity and interpersonal skills', *Frontiers in Ecology and the Environment,* **12**(1), 31–38.

Chew, Michele Y. C., Chihiro Watanabe and Yuji Tou (2011), 'The challenges in Singapore NEWater development: Co-evolutionary development for innovation and industry evolution', *Technology in Society,* **33**(3–4), 200–211.

Christensen, Norman L., Ann M. Bartuska, James H. Brown, Stephen Carpenter, Carla D'Antonio, Rober Francis, Jerry F. Franklin, James A. MacMahon, Reed F. Noss, David J. Parsons, Charles H. Peterson, Monica G. Turner and Robert G. Woodmansee (1996), 'The report of the Ecological Society of America committee on the scientific basis for ecosystem management', *Ecological Applications,* **6**(3), pp. 665–691.

City of San Diego (2006), 'City of San Diego water reuse study, final draft report, attachment I', San Diego, CA.

City of Wichita Falls (2017), 'Wastewater treatment', City of Wichita Falls, http://www.wichitafallstx.gov/691/Wastewater-Treatment, accessed 31 December 2017.

Clark, William (1980), 'Witches, floods, and wonder drugs: Historical perspectives on risk management', in Richard Schwing and Walter Albers, Jr (eds), *Societal Risk Assessment: How Safe is Safe Enough?* New York: Plenum Press, pp. 287–318.

Cocklin, Chris, Naomi Mautner and Jacqui Dibden (2007), 'Public policy, private landholders: Perspectives on policy mechanisms for sustainable land management', *Journal of Environmental Management*, **85**(4), 986–998.

Cole, Daniel H. (2015), 'Advantages of a polycentric approach to climate change policy', *Nature Climate Change*, **5**(2), 114–118.

Collins, Scott L., Stephen R. Carpenter, Scott M. Swinton, Daniel E. Orenstein, Daniel L. Childers, Ted L. Gragson, Nancy B. Grimm, J. Morgan Grove, Sharon L. Harlan, Jason P. Kaye, Alan K. Knapp, Gary P. Kofinas, John J. Magnuson, William H. McDowell, John M. Melack, Laura A. Ogden, G. Philip Robertson, Melinda D. Smith and Ali C. Whitmer (2011), 'An integrated conceptual framework for long-term social–ecological research', *Frontiers in Ecology and the Environment*, **9**(6), 351–357.

Conrad, Cathy C. and Krista G. Hilchey (2011), 'A review of citizen science and community-based environmental monitoring: Issues and opportunities', *Environmental Monitoring and Assessment*, **176**(1–4), 273–291.

Conrad, Jobst (2002), 'Limitations to interdisciplinarity in oriented social science research', *The Journal of Transdisciplinary Environmental Studies* **1**(1), 1–15.

Cooke, Nancy J. and Margaret L. Hilton (eds) (2015), *Enhancing the Effectiveness of Team Science*. Washington, DC: National Academies Press.

Cornell, Sarah, Frans Berkhout, Willemijn Tuinstra, J. David Tàbara, Jill Jäger, Ilan Chabay, Bert de Wit, Richard Langlais, David Mills, Peter Moll, Ilona M. Otto, Arthur Petersen, Christian Pohl and Lorrae van Kerkhoff (2013), 'Opening up knowledge systems for better responses to global environmental change', *Environmental Science & Policy*, **28**, 60–70.

Cortner Hanna J. (2000), 'Making science relevant to environment policy', *Environmental Science and Policy*, **3**, 21–30.

Coughlin, Jason, Jennifer Grove, Linda Irvine, Janet F. Jacobs, Sarah Johnson Phillips, Leslie Moynihan and Joseph Wiedman (2010), 'A guide to community solar: Utility, private and non-profit project development', National Renewable Energy Laboratory, https://www.nrel.gov/docs/fy11osti/49930.pdf, accessed 1 December 2017.

Couvet, Dennis, Frederic Jiguet, Romain Julliard, Harold Levrel and Anne Teyssedre (2008), 'Enhancing citizen contributions to biodiversity science and public policy', *Interdisciplinary Science Reviews*, **33**(1), 95–103.

Crowston, Kevin, Alison Specht, Carol Hoover, Katherine M. Chudoba and Mary Beth Watson-Manheim (2015), 'Perceived discontinuities and continuities in transdisciplinary scientific working groups', *Science of The Total Environment*, **534**, 159–172.

CTSA (2011), 'Principles of community engagement', CTSA Community Engagement Key Function Committee Task Force on the Principles of Community Engagement, Clinical and Translational Science Awards Consortium, Rockville, MD.

Cumming, Graeme S. and Garry D. Peterson (2017), 'Unifying research on social–ecological resilience and collapse', *Trends in Ecology & Evolution*, **32**(9), 695–713.

Daigger, Glen T. (2008), 'New approaches and technologies for wastewater management' *The Bridge* **38**(3), 38–45.

Dale, Virginia H., Keith L. Kline, Lynn L. Wright, Robert D. Perlack, Mark Downing and Robin L. Graham (2011), 'Interactions among bioenergy feedstock choices, landscape dynamics, and land use', *Ecological Applications*, **21**(4), 1039–1054.

Davies, Bronwyn, Jenny Browne, Susanne Gannon, Eileen Honan and Margaret Somerville (2005), 'Embodied women at work in neoliberal times and places', *Gender, Work & Organization*, **12**(4), 343–362.

Day, J. Chadwick and Thomas I. Gunton (2003), 'The theory and practice of collaborative planning in resource and environmental management', *Environments*, **31**(2), 5–20.

De Bruijn, Hans and Paulien M. Herder (2009), 'System and actor perspectives on sociotechnical systems', *IEEE Transactions on Systems, Man, and Cybernetics – Part A: Systems and Humans*, **39**(5), 981–992.

Denzin, Norman K., Yvonna S. Lincoln and Linda Tuhiwai Smith (eds) (2008), *Handbook of Critical and Indigenous Methodologies*. London: Sage.

Diaz, Robert J. and Rutger Rosenberg (2008), 'Spreading dead zones and consequences for marine ecosystems', *Science*, **321**(5891), 926–929.

Díaz, Sandra, Sebsebe Demissew, Julia Carabias, Carlos Joly, Mark Lonsdale, Neville Ash, Anne Larigauderie, Jay R. Adhikari, Salvator Arico, Andras Baldi, Ann Bartuska, Ivar A. Baste, Adem Bilgin, Eduaurdo Brondizio, Kai M. A. Chan, Viviana E. Figueroa, Anantha Duraiappah, Markus Fischer, Rosemary Hill, Thomas Koetz, Paul Leadley, Philip Lyver, Georgina M. Mace, Berta Martin-Lopez, Michiko Okumura, Diego Pacheco, Unai Pascual, Edgar S. Perez, Belinda Reyers, Evan Roth, Osamu Saito, Roert J. Scholes, Nalini Sharma, Heather Tallis, Randolph Thaman, Robert Watson, Tetsukazu Yahara, Zakir A. Hamid, Callistus Akosim, Yousef Al-Hafedh, Rashad Allahyerdiyey, Edward Amankwah, Stanley T. Asah, Zemede Asfaw, Gabor Bartus, L. Anathea Brooks, Jorge Caillaux, Gemedo Dalle, Dedy Darnaedi, Amanda Driver, Gunay Erpul, Pablo Escobar-Eyzaguirre, Pierre Failler, Ali Moustafa, Mokhtar Fouda, Bojie Fu, Haripriya Gundimeda, Shizuka Hasimoto, Floyd Homer, Sandra Lavorel, Gabriela Lichtenstein, William A. Mala, Wadzanayi Mandivenyi, Piotr Matczak, Carmel Mbizio, Mehrasa Mehrdadi, Jean Paul Metzger, Jean B. Mikissa, Henrik Moller, Harold A. Mooney, Peter Mumby, Harini Nagendra, Cartsen Nesshover, Alfred A. Oteng-Yeboah, Gyorgy Pataki, Marie Roue, Jennifer Rubis, Maria Schultz, Peggy Smith, Rashid Sumaila, Kazuhiko Takeuchi, Spencer Thomas, Madhu Verma, Youn Yeo-Chang and Diana Zlatanova (2015), 'The IPBES Conceptual Framework-connecting nature and people', *Current Opinion in Environmental Sustainability*, **14**, 1–16.

Di Castri, Francesco (1976), 'International, interdisciplinary research in ecology: Some problems of organization and execution. The case of the man and the biosphere (MAB) programme', *Human Ecology*, **4**(3), 235–246.

Dickinson, Janis L., Jennifer Shirk, David Bonter, Rick Bonney, Rhiannon L. Crain, Jason Martin, Tina Phillips and Karen Purcell (2012), 'The current state of citizen science as a tool for ecological research and public engagement', *Frontiers in Ecology and the Environment*, **10**(6), 291–297.

Didou Aupetit, Sylvie and Etienne Gérard (2011), 'El Sistema Nacional de Investigadores en 2009: ¿Un vector para la internacionalización de las élites científicas?', *Perfiles Educativos*, **33**(132), 29–47.

Dietz, Thomas, Gerald T. Gardner, Jonathan Gilligan, Paul C. Stern and Michael P. Vandenbergh (2009), 'Household actions can provide a behavioral wedge to rapidly reduce US carbon emissions', *Proceedings of the National Academy of Sciences*, **106**(44), 18452–18456.

Dillman, Don A., Jolene D. Smyth and Leah Melani Christian (2014), *Internet, Phone, Mail, and Mixed-mode Surveys: The Tailored Design Method*. New York: John Wiley & Sons.

Donatuto, Jamie and Barbara Harper (2008), 'Issues in evaluating fish consumption rates for Native American tribes', *Risk Analysis*, **28**(6), 1497–1506.

Dovers, Stephen (2005), *Environment and Sustainability Policy: Creation, Implementation, Evaluation*. Sydney: Federation Press.

Downey, Liam (2015), *Inequality, Democracy, and the Environment*. New York: NYU Press.

Dozier, André Q., Mazdak Arabi, Benjamin C. Wostoupal, Christopher G. Goemans, Yao Zhang and Keith Paustian (2017), 'Declining agricultural production in rapidly urbanizing semi-arid regions: Policy tradeoffs and sustainability indicators', *Environmental Research Letters*, **12**(8), 085005.

Dressler, Wolfram, Bram Büscher, Michael Schoon, Dan Brockington, Tanya Hayes, Christian A. Kull, James McCarthy and Krishna Shrestha (2010), 'From hope to crisis and back again? A critical history of the global CBNRM narrative', *Environmental Conservation*, **37**(1), 5–15.

Duke, Richard D. and Jac L. A. Geurts (2004), *Policy Games for Strategic Management*. Amsterdam: Rozenberg.

Duran, Bonnie, Nina Wallerstein, Magdalena M. Avila, Lorenda Belone, Meredith Minkler and Kevin Foley (2012), 'Developing and maintaining partnerships with communities', in Barbara A. Israel, Eugenia Eng and Amy J. Schulz (eds) *Methods for Community-based Participatory Research for Health*, 2nd edn. San Francisco, CA: Jossey-Bass, pp. 43–68.

Durham, Catherine A., Bonnie G. Colby and Molly Longstreth (1988), 'The impact of state tax credits and energy prices on adoption of solar energy systems', *Land Economics*, **64**(4), 347–355.

Elliott, Kevin C., Isis H. Settles, Georgina M. Montgomery, Sheila T. Brassel, Kendra Spence Cheruvelil and Patricia A. Soranno (2017), 'Honorary authorship practices in environmental science teams: Structural and cultural factors and solutions', *Accountability in Research*, **24**(2), 80–98.

El Paso Water (2016), 'Service area profile: Geography, history & climate', El Paso Water Utilities, https://epwater.org/UserFiles/Servers/Server_6843404/File/AboutUs/Financial/Reports/_3_COMMUNITY_AND_UTILITY_PROFILE_FY2016-17_9-24.pdf, accessed 5 January 2018.

El Paso Water (2018), 'Advanced purification', El Paso Water: https://www.epwater.org/_water/water_planning/advanced_purification, accessed 24 May 2018.

Emerson, Kirk and Peter Murchie (2011), 'Collaborative governance and climate change', in Rosemary O'Leary, David M. Van Slyke and Soonhee Kim (eds), *The Future of Public Administration around the World: The Minnowbrook Perspective*. Washington, DC: Georgetown University Press, pp. 141–153.

Engels, Anita and Tina Ruschenburg (2008), 'The uneven spread of global science: Patterns of international collaboration in global environmental change research', *Science and Public Policy*, **35**(5), 347–360.

Escobar, Arturo (2011), *Encountering Development: The Making and Unmaking of the Third World*. Princeton, NJ: Princeton University Press.

ExxonMobil (2016), '2016 corporate citizenship report', ExxonMobil, http://corporate.exxonmobil.com/en/community/corporate-citizenship-report/download-the-full-ccr-report-and-highlights/download-the-full-ccr-report-and-highlights, accessed 29 May 2018.

ExxonMobil (2017a), 'About us', ExxonMobil, http://corporate.exxonmobil.com/en/company/about-us, accessed 29 May 2018.

ExxonMobil (2017b), 'Our guiding principles', ExxonMobil, http://corporate.exxonmobil.com/en/company/about-us/guiding-principles, accessed 29 May 2018.

ExxonMobil (2017c), 'Ethics', ExxonMobil, http://corporate.exxonmobil.com/en/investors/corporate-governance/ethics/ethics, accessed 29 May 2018.

ExxonMobil (2017d), 'Environmental performance', ExxonMobil, http://corporate.exxonmobil.com/en/environment/environmental-performance, accessed 29 May 2018.

ExxonMobil (2017e), 'Community', ExxonMobil, http://corporate.exxonmobil.com/en/community/corporate-citizenship-report/download-the-full-ccr-report-and-highlights/download-the-full-ccr-report-and-highlights, accessed 29 May 2018.

Ferrance, Eileen. (2000), 'Action Research', Northeast and Islands Regional Educational Laboratory at Brown University, https://www.brown.edu/academics/education-alliance/sites/brown.edu.academics.education-alliance/files/publications/act_research.pdf, accessed 14 May 2018.

Fiore, Stephen M., Kimberly A. Smith-Jentsch, Eduardo Salas, Norman Warner and Michael Letsky (2010), 'Towards an understanding of macrocognition in teams: Developing and defining complex collaborative processes and products', *Theoretical Issues in Ergonomics Science*, **11**(4), 250–271.

Fischer, Frank (2000), *Citizens, Experts, and the Environment: The Politics of Local Knowledge*. Durham, NC: Duke University Press.

Fischer, Joern, Toby A. Gardner, Elena M. Bennett, Patricia Balvanera, Reinette Biggs, Stephen Carpenter, Tim Daw, Carol Folke, Rosemary Hill, Terry P. Hughes, Tobias Luthe, Manuel Maass, Megan Meacham, Albert V. Norström, Garry Peterson, Cibele Queiroz, Ralf Seppelt, Marja Spierenburg and John Tenhunen (2015), 'Advancing sustainability through mainstreaming a social–ecological systems perspective', *Current Opinion in Environmental Sustainability*, **14**, 144–149.

Flicker, Sarah (2008), 'Who benefits from community-based participatory research? A case study of the positive youth project', *Health Education & Behavior*, **35**(1), 70–86.

Floress, Kristin, Linda S. Prokopy and Shorna B. Allred (2011), 'It's who you know: Social capital, social networks, and watershed groups', *Society and Natural Resources*, **24**(9), 871–886.

Florida Government (2017), 'Gov. Scott: Florida sets another tourism record', http://www.flgov.com/2017/02/16/gov-scott-florida-sets-another-tourism-record-2/, accessed 29 May 2018.

Folke, Carl, Reinette Biggs, Albert V. Norström, Belinda Reyers and Johan Rockström (2016), 'Social–ecological resilience and biosphere-based sustainability science', *Ecology and Society*, **21**(3), 41.

Foucault, Michel (1980), *The History of Sexuality*. New York: Vintage Books.

Freeman, Jody (1997), 'Collaborative governance in the administrative state', *UCLA Law Review*, **45**(1), 1–98.

Freyfogle, Eric T. (2003), *The Land We Share: Private Property and the Common Good*. Washington, DC: Island Press.

Funder, Mikkel and Martin Marani (2015), 'Local bureaucrats as bricoleurs: The everyday implementation practices of county environment officers in rural Kenya', *International Journal of the Commons*, **9**(1), 87–106.

Funkhouser, Erik, Griselda Blackburn, Clare Magee and Varun Rai (2015), 'Business model innovations for deploying distributed generation: The emerging landscape of community solar in the US', *Energy Research & Social Science*, **10**, 90–101.

Gagnon, Valoree S. (2014), 'Synthesis and community brief: A Talking Circles event', Great Lakes Research Center Contribution No. 15, Michigan Technological University, USA.

Gagnon, Valoree S., Hugh S. Gorman and Emma S. Norman (2017), 'Power and politics in research design and practice: Opening space for social equity in interdisciplinary, multi-jurisdictional, and community-based research', *Gateways: Journal of Community Research and Engagement*, **10**(1), 164–184.

Gardner, Gerald T. and Paul C. Stern (2008), 'The short list: The most effective actions U.S. households can take to curb climate change', *Environment*, **50**(5), 12–23.

Gardner, Susan K. (2013), 'Paradigmatic differences, power, and status: A qualitative investigation of faculty in one interdisciplinary research collaboration on sustainability science', *Sustainability Science*, **8**(2), 241–252.

Gardner, Toby A., Joice Ferreira, Jos Barlow, Alexander C. Lees, Luke Parry, Ima Célia Guimarães Vieira, Erika Berenguer, Ricardo Abramovay, Alexandre Aleixo, Christian Andretti, Luiz E. O. C. Aragão, Ivanei Araújo, Williams Souza de Ávila, Richard D. Bardgett, Mateus Batistella, Rodrigo Anzolin Begotti, Troy Beldini, Driss Ezzine de Blas, Rodrigo Fagundes Braga, Danielle de Lima Braga, Janaína Gomes de Brito, Plínio Barbosa de Camargo, Fabiane Campos dos Santos, Vívian Campos de Oliveira, Amanda Cardoso Nunes Cordeiro, Thiago Moreira Cardoso, Déborah Reis de Carvalho, Sergio André Castelani, Júlio Cézar Mário Chaul, Carlos Eduardo Cerri, Francisco de Assis Costa, Carla Daniele Furtado da Costa, Emilie Coudel, Alexandre Camargo Coutinho, Dênis Cunha, Álvaro D'Antona, Joelma Dezincourt, Karina Dias-Silva, Mariana Durigan, Júlio César Dalla Mora Esquerdo, José Feres, Silvio Frosini de Barros Ferraz, Amanda Estefânia de Melo Ferreira, Ana Carolina Fiorini, Lenise Vargas Flores da Silva, Fábio Soares Frazão, Rachel Garrett, Alessandra dos Santos Gomes, Karoline da Silva Gonçalves, José Benito Guerrero, Neusa Hamada, Robert M. Hughes, Danilo Carmago Igliori, Ederson da Conceição Jesus, Leandro Juen, Miércio Junior, José Max Barbosa de Oliveira Junior, Raimundo Cosme de Oliveira Junior, Carlos Souza Junior, Phil Kaufmann, Vanesca Korasaki, Cecília Gontijo Leal, Rafael Leitão, Natália Lima, Maria de Fátima Lopes Almeida, Reinaldo Lourival, Júlio Louzada, Ralph MacNally, Sébastien Marchand, Márcia Motta Maués, Fátima M. S. Moreira, Carla Morsello, Nárgila Moura, Jorge Nessimian, Sâmia Nunes, Victor Hugo Fonseca Oliveira, Renata Pardini, Heloisa Correia Pereira, Paulo Santos Pompeu, Carla Rodrigues Ribas, Felipe Rossetti, Fernando Augusto Schmidt, Rodrigo da Silva, Regina Célia Viana Martins da Silva, Thiago Fonseca Morello Ramalho da Silva, Juliana Silveira, João Victor

Siqueira, Teotônio Soares de Carvalho, Ricardo R. C. Solar, Nicola Savério Holanda Tancredi, James R. Thomson, Patrícia Carignano Torres, Fernando Zagury Vaz-de-Mello, Ruan Carlo Stulpen Veiga, Adriano Venturieri, Cecília Viana, Diana Weinhold, Ronald Zanetti and Jansen Zuanon (2013), 'A social and ecological assessment of tropical land uses at multiple scales: The sustainable Amazon network', *Philosophical Transactions of the Royal Society B: Biological Sciences*, **368**(1619), 20120166.

Garner, Bryan A. (1999), *Black's Law Dictionary*. St. Paul, MN: West Group.

Gaventa, Josh (2004), 'Strengthening participatory approaches to local governance: Learning the lessons from abroad', *National Civic Review*, **93**(4), 16–27.

Gaventa, Josh and Andrea Cornwall (2006), 'Challenging the boundaries of the possible: Participation, knowledge and power', *IDS Bulletin*, **37**(6), 122–128.

Geniusz, Wendy M. (2009), *Our Knowledge is Not Primitive: Decolonizing Botanical Anishinaabe Teachings*. Syracuse, NY: Syracuse University Press.

Gensler, Lauren (2017), 'The world's largest oil And gas companies 2017: Exxon reigns supreme, while Chevron slips', Forbes, https://www.forbes.com/sites/laurengensler/2017/05/24/the-worlds-largest-oil-and-gas-companies-2017-exxon-mobil-reigns-supreme-chevron-slips/#13e5bca84f87, accessed 29 May 2018.

Gerrity, Daniel, Brian Pecson, R. Shane Trussell and R. Rhodes Trussell (2013), 'Potable reuse treatment trains throughout the world', *Journal of Water Supply: Research and Technology-AQUA*, **62**(6), 321–338.

Gewin, Virginia (2015), 'Collaborations: Recipe for a team', *Nature*, **523**(7559), 245–247.

Giang, Amanda and Noelle E Selin (2015), 'Benefits of mercury controls for the United States', *Proceedings of the National Academy of Sciences of the United States of America*, **113**(2), 286–291.

Gibbons, Philip, Charlie Zammit, Kara Youngentob, Hugh P. Possingham and David B. Lindenmeyer (2008), 'Some practical suggestions for improving engagement between researchers and policy-makers in natural resource management', *Ecological Management and Restoration*, **9**(3), 182–186.

Giddens, Anthony (1984), *The Constitution of Society: Outline of the Theory of Structuration*. Berkeley, CA: University of California Press.

Glänzel, Wolfgang and András Schubert (2001), 'Double effort = double impact? A critical view at international co-authorship in chemistry', *Scientometrics*, **50**(2), 199–214.

Glazer-Raymo, Judith (2008), *Unfinished Agendas: New and Continuing Gender Challenges in Higher Education*. Baltimore, MD: Johns Hopkins University Press.

Goddard, Tim, Neil Cranston and Jennie Billot (2006), 'Making it work: Identifying the challenges of collaborative international research', *International Electronic Journal for Leadership in Learning*, **10**(11), http://iejll.journalhosting.ucalgary.ca/iejll/index.php/ijll/article/view/611, accessed 16 November 2018.

Goldkuhl, Goran (2008), 'Practical inquiry as action research and beyond', in *16th European Conference on Information Systems*, Galway, Ireland: ECIS, pp. 3–10.

Goldkuhl, Goran (2012), 'Pragmatism vs interpretivism in qualitative information systems research', *European Journal of Information Systems*, **21**(2), 135–146.

Goodland, Robert and Herman Daly (1996), 'Environmental sustainability: Universal and non-negotiable', *Ecological Applications*, **6**(4), 1002–1017.

Gordon, Eric and Steven Schirra (2011), 'Playing with empathy: Digital role-playing games in public meetings', in *Proceedings of the 5th International Conference on Communities and Technologies*, Brisbane, 29 June to 2 July 2011, New York, NY: Association of Computing Machinery, pp. 179–185.

Goring, Simon J., Kathleen C. Weathers, Walter K. Dodds, Patricia A. Soranno, Lynn C. Sweet, Kendra S. Cheruvelil, John S. Kominoski, Janine Rüegg, Alexandra M. Thorn and Ryan M. Utz (2014), 'Improving the culture of interdisciplinary collaboration in ecology by expanding measures of success', *Frontiers in Ecology and the Environment*, **12**(1), 39–47.

Gould, Kenneth. A., David N. Pellow and Allan Schnaiberg (2004), 'Interrogating the treadmill of production', *Organization and Environment*, **17**(3), 296–316.

Graffy, Elizabeth and Steven Kihm (2014), 'Does disruptive competition mean a death spiral for electric utilities?', *Energy Law Journal,* **35**(1), 1–44.

Gray, Leslie and William Moseley (2005), 'A geographical perspective on poverty–environment interactions', *Geographical Journal,* **171**(1), 9–23.

Graziano, Marcello and Kenneth Gillingham (2015), 'Spatial patterns of solar photovoltaic system adoption: The influence of neighbors and the built environment', *Journal of Economic Geography,* **15**(4), 815–839.

Green, Leslie (2009), 'Legal positivism', in Edward Zalta (ed.), *The Stanford Encyclopedia of Philosophy.* Stanford: The Metaphysics Research Lab Center for the Study of Language and Information Stanford University.

Gregory, Robert, Dan Ohlson and Joseph Arvai (2006), 'Deconstructing adaptive management: Criteria for applications to environmental management', *Ecological Applications,* **16**(6), 2411–2425.

Grewal, David S. (2008). *Network Power: The Social Dynamics of Globalization.* New Haven, CT: Yale University Press.

Griffith, John (1986), 'What is legal pluralism?', *The Journal of Legal Pluralism and Unofficial Law,* **18**(24), 1–55.

Grogan, Paul T. and Sebastian A. Meijer (2017), 'Gaming methods in engineering systems research', *Systems Engineering,* **20**(6), 542–552.

Guerrero, Paul B. (2016), 'Direct potable reuse in El Paso, Texas: Pioneering water resource sustainability in a large urban utility', University of Texas at El Paso, https://digitalcommons.utep.edu/dissertations/AAI10250033, accessed 5 May 2018.

Gunderson, Lance H. and C. S. Holling (2002), *Panarchy: Understanding Transformations in Human and Natural Systems.* Washington, DC: Island Press.

Guruswamy, Lakshman (2010), 'Energy justice and sustainable development', *Colorado Journal of International Environmental Law and Policy,* **21**, 231.

Guruswamy, Lakshman (2016), *Global Energy Justice: Law and Policy.* St Paul, MN: West Academic.

Hacker, Karen (2013), *Community-based Participatory Research.* Los Angeles, CA: Sage.

Hacker, Karen and J. Glover Taylor (2011), 'Community-engaged Research (CEnR) and the Institutional Review Board: Principles, Challenges, and Opportunities', The Harvard Clinical and Translational Science Center, https://catalyst.harvard.edu/pdf/regulatory/CEnR_Webpage_101_Presentation.pdf, accessed 1 May 2018.

Hadorn, Gertrude Hirsch, David Bradley, Christian Pohl, Stephan Rist and Urs Wiesmann (2006), 'Implications of transdisciplinarity for sustainability research', *Ecological Economics,* **60**,119–128.

Hadorn, Gertrude Hirsch, Holger Hoffman-Riem, Susette Biber-Klemm, Walter Grossenbacher-Mansuy, Dominique Joye, Christian Pohl, Urs Wiesmann and Elisabeth Zemp (2008), *Handbook of Transdisciplinary Research.* Cham: Springer.

Haklay, Muki (2013), 'Citizen science and volunteered geographic information: Overview and typology of participation', in Daniel Sui, Sarah Elwood and Michael Goodchild (eds), *Crowdsourcing Geographic Knowledge.* Dordrecht: Springer Netherlands, pp. 105–122.

Hall, Pippa (2005), 'Interprofessional teamwork: Professional cultures as barriers', *Journal of Interprofessional Care,* **19**(1), 188–196.

Hall, Sarah Marie (2013), 'Energy justice and ethical consumption: Comparison, synthesis and lesson drawing', *Local Environment,* **18**(4), 422–437.

Halseth, Greg, Sean Markey, Laura Ryser and Don Manson (2016), *Doing Community-based Research: Perspectives from the Field.* Montreal: McGill–Queen's University Press.

Halvorsen, Kathleen E., Jessie L. Knowlton, Alex S. Mayer, Colin C. Phifer, Tatiana Martins, Erin C. Pischke, Tamara S. Propato, Pablo Cavigliasso, Carlos Garcia, Marta Chiappe, Amarella Eastmond, Julian Licata, Mark Kuhlberg, Rodrigo Medeiros, Valentin Picasso, German Mendez, Patricia Primo, Amanda Frado, Santiago Veron and J. L. Dunn (2016), 'A case study of strategies for fostering international, interdisciplinary research', *Journal of Environmental Studies and Sciences,* **6**(2), 313–323.

Hardy, Scott D. and Tomas M. Koontz (2008), 'Reducing nonpoint source pollution through collaboration: policies and programs across the U.S. states', *Environmental Management*, **41**(3), 301–310.

Harris, Frances and Fergus Lyon (2013), 'Transdisciplinary environmental research: Building trust across professional cultures', *Environmental Science and Policy*, **31**, 109–119.

Harris, Frances and Fergus Lyon (2014), 'Transdisciplinary environmental research: A review of approaches to knowledge co-production', *Nexus Network Think Piece Series*, Paper 2.

Hart, Michael, Silvia Straka and Gladys Rowe (2017), 'Working across contexts: Practical considerations of doing Indigenist/anti-colonial research', *Qualitative Inquiry*, **23**(5), 332–342.

He, Tianwei (2009), 'International scientific collaboration of China with the G7 countries', *Scientometrics*, **80**(3), 571–582.

Heberlein, Thomas (2012), *Navigating Environmental Attitudes*. Oxford: Oxford University Press.

Heffron, Raphael J. and Darren McCauley (2014), 'Achieving sustainable supply chains through energy justice', *Applied Energy*, **123**, 435–437.

Heffron, Raphael J. and Darren McCauley (2017), 'The concept of energy justice across the disciplines', *Energy Policy*, **105**, 658–667.

Hickey, Gordon M. and Craig R. Nitschke (2005), 'Crossing disciplinary boundaries in forest research: An international challenge', *The Forestry Chronicle*, **81**(3), 321–323.

Hilton, Margaret L. and Nancy J. Cooke (eds) (2015), *Enhancing the Effectiveness of Team Science*, Washington, DC: National Research Council.

Hinds, Pamela J. and Diane E. Bailey (2003), 'Out of sight, out of sync: Understanding conflict in distributed teams', *Organization Science*, **14**(6), 615–632.

Hirshberg, Alan and Richard Schoen (1974), 'Barriers to the widespread utilization of residential solar energy: The prospects for solar energy in the US housing industry', *Policy Sciences*, **5**(4), 453–468.

Hodkinson, Phil and Heather Hodkinson (2001), 'The strengths and limitations of case study research', *Learning and Skills Development Agency Conference: Making an Impact on Policy and Practice*, **1**, 1–7.

Holifield, Ryan, Michael Porter and Gordon Walker (2010), *Spaces of Environmental Justice*. Malden: Wiley-Blackwell.

Hollaender, Kirsten, Marie Céline Loibl and Arnold Wilts (2008), 'Management', in Hadorn, Gertrude Hirsch, Holger Hoffman-Riem, Susette Biber-Klemm, Walter Grossenbacher-Mansuy, Dominique Joye, Christian Pohl, Urs Wiesmann and Elisabeth Zemp (eds), *Handbook of Transdisciplinary Research*. Cham: Springer, pp. 385–397.

Hollender, Juliane, Saskia G. Zimmermann, Stephan Koepke, Martin Krauss, Christa S. McArdell, Christoph Ort, Heinz Singer, Urs von Gunten and Hansruedi Siegrist (2009), 'Elimination of organic micropollutants in a municipal wastewater treatment plant upgraded with a full-scale post-ozonation followed by sand filtration', *Environmental Science and Technology*, **43**(20), 7862–7869.

Homer-Dixon, Thomas, Brian Walker, Reinette Biggs, Anne-Sophie Crépin, Carl Folke, Eric Lambin, Garry Peterson, Johan Rockström, Martin Scheffer, Will Steffen and Max Troell (2015), 'Synchronous failure: The emerging causal architecture of global crisis', *Ecology and Society*, **20**(3), 6, http://dx.doi.org/10.5751/ES-07681-200306.

Horowitz, Carol R., Mimsie Robinson and Sarena Seifer (2009), 'Community-based participatory research from the margin to the mainstream: Are researchers prepared?', *Circulation*, **119**(19), 2633–2642.

House-Peters, Lily, Gabriela Alonso-Yanez, Martin Garcia-Cartagena, Jeremy Pittman, Michelle Farfan, Sebastian Bonelli and Ignacio Lorenzo (2015), 'Strengthening teamwork to confront socio-ecological challenges: Generating new knowledge for effective action in the americas', final project report submitted to the Inter-American Institute for Global Change Research (Seed Grant – IAI-TCO-115/2014), Montevideo, Uruguay.

Howe, Cymene and Dominic Boyer (2016), 'Aeolian extractivism and community wind in Southern Mexico', *Public Culture*, **28**(2), 215–235.

Ibarra Colado, Eduardo (2009), 'Impacto de la evaluación en la educación superior Mexicana: Valoración y debates', *Revista de la Educación Superior*, **38**(149), 173–182.

International Energy Agency (2017), 'Global EV outlook 2017: Two million and counting', International Energy Agency, https://www.iea.org/publications/freepublications/publication/GlobalEVOutlook2017.pdf, accessed 29 May 2018.

International Renewable Energy Agency (2017), 'Renewable capacity highlights – 30 March 2017', 30 March: http://www.irena.org/-/media/Files/IRENA/Agency/Publication/2017/Mar/RE_stats_highlights_2017.pdf?la=en&hash=7C535399F0994173AE445772FE62FF8C156D39DE, accessed 26 May 2018.

Interstate Renewable Energy Council (2016), 'Shared renewable energy for low-to-moderate-income consumers: Policy guidelines and model provisions', https://irecusa.org/publications/shared-renewable-energy-for-low-to-moderate-income-consumers-policy-guidelines-and-model-provisions/, accessed 26 May 2018.

Ioris, Antonio A. R. (2015), 'Theorizing state–environment relationships: Antinomies of flexibility and legitimacy', *Progress in Human Geography*, **39**(2), 1–18.

Israel, Barbara A., Susan J. Schurman and Margrit K. Hugentobler (1992), 'Conducting action research: Relationships between organization members and researchers', *The Journal of Applied Behavioral Science*, **28**(1), 74–101.

Israel, Barbara A., Amy J. Schulz, Edith A. Parker and Adam B. Becker (1998), 'Review of community-based research: Assessing partnership approaches to improve public health', *Annual Review of Public Health*, **19**(1), 173–202.

Israel, Barbara A., Edith A. Parker, Zachary Rowe, Alicia Salvatore, Meredith Minkler, Jesus López, Arlene Butz, Adrian Mosley, Lucretia Coates, George Lambert, Paul A. Potito, Barbara Brenner, Maribel Rivera, Harry Romero, Beti Thompson, Gloria Coronado and Sandy Halstead (2005), 'Community-based participatory research: Lessons learned from the Centers for Children's Environmental Health and Disease Prevention Research', *Environmental Health Perspectives*, **113**(10), 1463–1471.

Israel, Barbara A., Amy J. Schulz, Edith A. Parker, Adam B. Becker, Alex. J. Allen III, J. Ricardo Guzman and Richard Lichtenstein (2018), 'Critical issues in developing and following community-based participatory research principles', in Nina Wallerstein, Bonnie Duran, John Oetzel and Meredith Minkler (eds), *Community-based Participatory Research for Health: Advancing Social and Health Equity*. San Francisco, CA: Jossey-Bass, pp. 47–66.

Jacoby, Barbara (ed.) (2003), *Building Partnerships through Service-learning*. Hoboken, NJ: Wiley.

Jahn, Thomas, Matthias Bergmann and Florian Keil (2012), 'Transdisciplinarity: Between mainstreaming and marginalization', *Ecological Economics*, **79**, 1–10.

Jasanoff, Sheila (ed.) (2004), *States of Knowledge: The Co-Production of Science and The Social Order*. London: Routledge.

Jenkins, Kirsten, Darren McCauley, Raphael Heffron, Hannes Stephan and Robert Rehner (2016), 'Energy justice: A conceptual review', *Energy Research and Social Science*, **11**, 174–182.

Jessop, Bob (2008), *State Power: A Strategic–Relational Approach*. Cambridge: Polity Press.

Johnson, David W. and Roger T. Johnson (2003), *Assessing students in groups: Promoting group responsibility and individual accountability*. Thousand Oaks, CA: Corwin Press.

Jones, Benjamin R., Benjamin Sovacool and Roman Sidortsov (2015), 'Making the ethical and philosophical case for "energy justice"', *Environmental Ethics*, **37**, 145–168.

Jones, Christopher M. and Daniel M. Kammen (2011), 'Quantifying carbon footprint reduction opportunities for US households and communities', *Environmental Science and Technology*, **45**(9), 4088–4095.

Kaercher, J. D., Murni Po and B. E. Nancarrow (2003), 'Water recycling community discussion meeting I' (unpublished manuscript). Perth: Australian Research Centre for Water in Society.

Kahn, Brian (2016), 'Earth's CO_2 passes 400 ppm threshold – maybe permanently', *Scientific American*, September 27, https://www.scientificamerican.com/article/earth-s-co2-passes-the-400-ppm-threshold-maybe-permanently/, accessed 4 November 2016.

Kalogirou, Soteris A. (2004), 'Environmental benefits of domestic solar energy systems', *Energy Conversion and Management*, **45**(18–19), 3075–3092.

Kantamneni, Abhilash, Richelle Winkler, Lucia Gauchia and Joshua M. Pearce (2016), 'Emerging economic viability of grid defection in a northern climate using solar hybrid systems', *Energy Policy*, **95**, 378–389.

Kates, Robert W., William C. Clark, Robert Corell, J. Michael Hall, Carlo C. Jaeger, Ian Lowe, James J. McCarthy, Hans Joachim Schellnhuber, Bert Bolin, Nancy M. Dickson, Sylvie Faucheux, Gilberto C. Gallopin, Arnulf Grübler, Brian Huntley, Jill Jäger, Narpat S. Jodha, Roger E. Kasperson, Akin Mabogunje, Pamela Matson, Harold Mooney, Berrien Moore III, Timothy O'Riordan and Uno Svedin (2001), 'Sustainability science', *Science*, **292**(5517), 641–642.

Kayatin, Matthew J., Donald L. Carter, Richard G. Schunk and Jennifer M. Pruitt (2016), 'Upgrades to the ISS Water Recovery System', 46th International Conference on Environmental Systems, 10–14 July, Vienna.

Kimura, Aya H. and Abby Kinchy (2016), 'Citizen science: Probing the virtues and contexts of participatory research', *Engaging Science, Technology, and Society*, **2**, pp. 331–361.

Kingdon, John W. (2011), *Agendas, Alternatives, and Public Policies*, 2nd edn. New York: Pearson.

Kirk-Lawlor, Naomi and Shorna Allred (2017), 'Group development and integration in a cross-disciplinary and intercultural research team', *Environmental Management*, **59**(4), 665–683.

Kirschner, Paul A., Karel Kreijns, Chris Phielix and Jos Fransen (2015), 'Awareness of cognitive and social behavior in a CSCL environment', *Journal of Computer Assisted Learning*, **31**, 59–77.

Klein, Julie Thompson. (2008), 'Evaluation of interdisciplinary and transdisciplinary research: A literature review', *American Journal of Preventative Medicine*, **35**(2S), S116–S123.

Klein, Julie Thompson and Holly J. Falk-Krzesinski (2017), 'Interdisciplinary and collaborative work: Framing promotion and tenure practices and policies', *Research Policy*, **46**(6), 1055–1061.

Klopfer, Eric, Scot Osterweil and Katie Salen (2009), 'Moving learning games forward: Obstacles, opportunities & openness', The Education Arcade, 30 May, https://educators.brainpop.com/printable/moving-learning-games-forward-obstacles-opportunities-openness, accessed 8 June 2018.

Knowlton, Jessie L., Kathleen E. Halvorsen, Robert M. Handler and Michael O'Rourke (2014), 'Teaching interdisciplinary sustainability science teamwork skills to graduate students using in-person and web-based interactions', *Sustainability*, **6**(12), 9428–9440.

Kooiman, Jan, Maarten Bavinck, Ratana Chuenpagdee, Robin Maho and Roger Pullin (2008), 'Interactive governance and governability: An introduction', *The Journal of Transdisciplinary Environmental Studies*, **7**(1), 1–11.

Kraft, Michael E. and Norman J. Vig (2015), 'U.S. environmental policy: Achievements and new directions', in Norman J. Vig and Michael E. Kraft (eds), *Environmental Policy: New Directions for the Twenty-First Century*. Washington, DC: CQ Press, pp. 2–29.

Kristjanson, Patti, Robin S. Reid, Nancy Dickson, William C. Clark, Dannie Romney, Ranjitha Puskur, Susan MacMillan and Delia Grace (2009), 'Linking international agricultural research knowledge with action for sustainable development', *Proceedings of the National Academy of Sciences*, **106**(13), 5047–5052.

Kriz, Willy C. (2003), 'Creating effective learning environments and learning organizations through gaming simulation design', *Simulation & Gaming*, **34**(4), 495–511.

Kuit, Martijn, Igor S. Mayer and Martin de Jong (2005), 'The INFRASTRATEGO game: An evaluation of strategic behavior and regulatory regimes in a liberalizing electricity market', *Simulation & Gaming*, **36**(1), 58–74.

Kumar, A., S. Wu, Y. Huang, H. Liao and J. Kaplan (2017), 'Mercury from wildfires: Global emission inventories and sensitivity to 2000–2050 global change', *Atmospheric Environment*, **173**, 6–15.

Kwan, Calvin Lee (2012), 'Influence of local environmental, social, economic and political variables on the spatial distribution of residential solar PV arrays across the United States', *Energy Policy*, **47**, 332–344.

Lahnsteiner, Josef and G. Lempert (2007), 'Water management in Windhoek, Namibia', *Water Science and Technology*, **55**(1–2), 441–448.

Landon, Adam C., Carena J. van Riper, Nicole F. Angeli, Daniel B. Fitzgerald and Kelsey D. Neam (2015), 'Growing transdisciplinary roots in the Peruvian Amazon: Lessons from the field', *The Journal of Transdisciplinary Environmental Studies*, **14**(1), 2–12.

Lang, Daniel J., Arnim Wiek, Matthias Bergmann, Michael Stauffacher, Pim Martens, Peter Moll, Mark Swilling and Christopher J. Thomas (2012), 'Transdisciplinary research in sustainability science: Practice, principles, and challenges', *Sustainability Science*, **7**(1), 25–43.

Laurance, William F., D. Carolina Useche, Julio Rendeiro, Margareta Kalka, Corey J.A. Bradshaw, Sean P. Sloan, Susan G. Laurance, Mason Campbell, Kate Abernethy, Patricia Alvarez, Victor Arroyo-Rodriguez, Peter Ashton, Julieta Benítez-Malvido, Allard Blom, Kadiri S. Bobo, Charles H. Cannon, Min Cao, Richard Carroll, Colin Chapman, Rosamond Coates, Marina Cords, Finn Danielsen, Bart De Dijn, Eric Dinerstein, Maureen A. Donnelly, David Edwards, Felicity Edwards, Nina Farwig, Peter Fashing, Pierre-Michel Forget, Mercedes Foster, George Gale, David Harris, Rhett Harrison, John Hart, Sarah Karpanty, W. John Kress, Jagdish Krishnaswamy, Willis Logsdon, Jon Lovett, William Magnusson, Fiona Maisels, Andrew R. Marshall, Deedra McClearn, Divya Mudappa, Martin R. Nielsen, Richard Pearson, Nigel Pitman, Jan van der Ploeg, Andrew Plumptre, John Poulsen, Mauricio Quesada, Hugo Rainey, Douglas Robinson, Christiane Roetgers, Francesco Rovero, Frederick Scatena, Christian Schulze, Douglas Sheil, Thomas Struhsaker, John Terborgh, Duncan Thomas, Robert Timm, J. Nicolas Urbina-Cardona, Karthikeyan Vasudevan, S. Joseph Wright, Juan Carlos Arias-G., Luzmila Arroyo, Mark Ashton, Philippe Auzel, Dennis Babaasa, Fred Babweteera, Patrick Baker, Olaf Banki, Margot Bass, Inogwabini Bila-Isia, Stephen Blake, Warren Brockelman, Nicholas Brokaw, Carsten A. Brühl, Sarayudh Bunyavejchewin, Jung-Tai Chao, Jerome Chave, Ravi Chellam, Connie J. Clare, José Clavijo, Robert Congdon, Richard Corlett, H. S. Dattaraja, Chittaranjan Dave, Glyn Davies, Beatriz de Mello Beisiegel, Rosa de Nazaré Paes da Silva, Anthony Di Fiore, Arvin Diesmos, Rodolfo Dirzo, Diane Doran-Sheehy, Mitchell Eaton, Louise Emmons, Alejandro Estrada, Corneille Ewango, Linda Fedigan, François Feer, Barbara Fruth, Jacalyn Giacalone Willis, Uromi Goodale, Steven Goodman, Juan C. Guix, Paul Guthiga, William Haber, Keith Hamer, Ilka Herbinger, Jane Hill, Zhongliang Huang, I Fang Sun, Kalan Ickes, Akira Itoh, Natália Ivanauskas, Betsy Jackes, John Janovec, Daniel Janzen, Mo Jiangming, Chen Jin, Trevor Jones, Hermes Justiniano, Elisabeth Kalko, Aventino Kasangaki, Timothy Killeen, Hen-biau King, Erik Klop, Cheryl Knott, Inza Koné, Enoka Kudavidanage, José Lahoz da Silva Ribeiro, John Lattke, Richard Laval, Robert Lawton, Miguel Leal, Mark Leighton, Miguel Lentino, Cristiane Leonel, Jeremy Lindsell, Lee Ling-Ling, K. Eduard Linsenmair, Elizabeth Losos, Ariel Lugo, Jeremiah Lwanga, Andrew L. Mack, Marlucia Martins, W. Scott McGraw, Roan McNab, Luciano Montag, Jo Myers Thompson, Jacob Nabe-Nielsen, Michiko Nakagawa, Sanjay Nepal, Marilyn Norconk, Vojtech Novotny, Sean O'Donnell, Muse Opiang, Paul Ouboter, Kenneth Parker, N. Parthasarathy, Káátia Pisciotta, Dewi Prawiradilaga, Catherine Pringle, Subaraj Rajathurai, Ulrich Reichard, Gay Reinartz, Katherine Renton, Glen Reynolds, Vernon Reynolds, Erin Riley, Mark-Oliver Rödel, Jessica Rothman, Philip Round, Shoko Sakai, Tania Sanaiotti, Tommaso Savini, Gertrud Schaab, John Seidensticker, Alhaji Siaka, Miles R. Silman, Thomas B. Smith, Samuel Soares de Almeida, Navjot Sodhi, Craig Stanford, Kristine Stewart, Emma Stokes, Kathryn E. Stoner, Raman Sukumar, Martin Surbeck, Mathias Tobler, Teja Tscharntke, Andrea Turkalo, Govindaswamy Umapathy, Merlijn van Weerd, Jorge Vega Rivera, Meena Venkataraman, Linda Venn, Carlos Verea, Carolina Volkmer de Castilho, Matthias Waltert, Benjamin Wang, David Watts, William Weber, Paige West, David Whitacre, Ken Whitney, David Wilkie, Stephen Williams, Debra D. Wright, Patricia Wright, Lu Xiankai, Pralad Yonzon, Franky Zamzani (2012), 'Averting biodiversity collapse in tropical forest protected areas', *Nature* **489**(7415), 290–294.

Lavis, John N., Dave Robertson, Jennifer M. Woodside, Christopher B. McLeod and Julia Abelson (2003), 'How can research organizations more effectively transfer research knowledge to decision makers?', *Milbank Quarterly*, **81**(2), 221–248.

Lazarus, Richard J. (2008), 'Super wicked problems and climate change: Restraining the present to liberate the future', *Cornell Law Review*, **94**, 1153–1233.

Leach, William D. (2006), 'Collaborative public management and democracy: Evidence from Western Watershed Partnerships', *Public Administration Review*, **66**(s1), 100–110.

Leavy, Patricia (2016), *Essentials of Transdisciplinary Research: Using Problem-centered Methodologies*. London: Routledge.

Ledyaev, Valeri (2001), 'Power: A conceptual analysis', *Polis. Political Studies*, **1**(1).

Leiter, Brian (2001), 'Legal realism and legal positivism reconsidered', *Ethics*, **11**(2), 278–301.

Lemos, Maria Carmen and Arun Agrawal (2006), 'Environmental governance', *Annual Review of Environment and Resources*, **31**(1), 297–325.

Lemos, Maria Carmen and Barbara J. Morehouse (2005), 'The co-production of science and policy in integrated climate assessments', *Global Environmental Change*, **15**(1), 57–68.

Levi, Daniel J. (2016), *Group Dynamics for Teams*, 5th edn. Thousand Oaks, CA: Sage.

Levin, Kelly, Benjamin Cashore, Steven Bernstein and Graeme Auld (2012), 'Overcoming the tragedy of super wicked problems: Constraining our future selves to ameliorate global climate change', *Policy Sciences*, **45**(2), 123–152.

Lipsky, Michael (1980), *Street-level Bureaucracy: Dilemmas of the Individual in Public Services*. New York: Russell Sage Foundation.

Little, Meg M., Catherine A. St Hill, Kenric B. Ware, Michael T. Swanoski, Scott A. Chapman, M. Nawal Lutfiyya and Frank B. Cerra (2016), 'Team science as interprofessional collaborative research practice: A systematic review of the science of team science literature', *Journal of Investigative Medicine*, **65**(1), 15–22.

Liu, Jianguo, Thomas Dietz, Stephen R. Carpenter, Marina Alberti, Carl Folke, Emilio Moran, Alice N. Pell, Peter Deadman, Timothy Kratz, Jane Lubchenco, Elinor Ostrom, Zhiyun Ouyang, William Provencher, Charles L. Redman, Stephen H. Schneider and William W. Taylor (2007), 'Complexity of coupled human and natural systems', *Science*, **317**(5844), 1513–1516.

Loaeza, Soledad (2005), 'La ciencia política: El pulso del cambio Mexicano', *Revista De Ciencia Política*, **25**(1), 192–203.

Lobel, Ruben and Georgia Perakis (2011), 'Consumer choice model for forecasting demand and designing incentives for solar technology', MIT Sloan Research Paper no. 4872-11. http://dx.doi.org/10.2139/ssrn.1748424

Loftus, Alex (2009), 'Rethinking political ecologies of water', *Third World Quarterly*, **30**(5), 953–968.

Lomas, Jonathan (2000), 'Connecting research and policy', *Canadian Journal of Policy Research*, **1**(1), 140–144.

Louisiana Department of Health (2010), 'Louisiana LDH releases oil spill-related exposure information', Louisiana Department of Health, 10 June, http://new.dhh.louisiana.gov/index.cfm/newsroom/detail/124, accessed 29 May 2018.

Lukes, Steven (2005), *Power: A Radical View*, 2nd edn. Basingstoke: Palgrave Macmillan.

Lyon, Oren (1978), 'An Iroquois perspective', in Christopher Vecsey and Robert W. Venables (eds), *American Indian Environments: Ecological Issues in Native American History*. Syracuse, NY: Syracuse University Press, pp. 171–174.

Madsen, Henning and John P. Ulhøi (2015), 'Stakeholder pressures, environmental impact and managerial initiatives of SMEs: A longitudinal study', *The Journal of Transdisciplinary Environmental Studies*, **14**(1), 13–26.

Mahdizadeh, Mousa, Abbas Heydari and Hossien Karimi Moonaghi (2015), 'Clinical interdisciplinary collaboration models and frameworks from similarities to differences: A systematic review', *Global Journal of Health Science*, **7**(6), 170–180.

Mandelker, Daniel R. (1989), 'Controlling nonpoint source water pollution: Can it be done?', *Chicago-Kent Law Review*, **65**(2), 479–502.

Mantel, Sukhmani, Dennis Cheung, Richard Welford and Peter Hills (2007), 'Cooperation for environmental reform', *Journal of Corporate Citizenship*, **27**, 91–106.

Margolis, Robert and Jarrett Zuboy (2006), 'Nontechnical barriers to solar energy use: Review of recent literature', no. NREL/TP-520-40116, National Renewable Energy Laboratory, Golden, USA.

Marshall, Anne and Suzanne Batten (2004), 'Researching across cultures: Issues of ethics and power', *Forum: Qualitative Social Research*, **5**(3), Article 39.

Martin, Jean-Louis, Virginie Maris and Daniel S. Simberloff (2016), 'The need to respect nature and its limits challenges society and conservation science', *Proceedings of the National Academy of Sciences*, **113**(22), 6105–6112.

Marvier, Michelle (2014), 'New conservation is true conservation', *Conservation Biology*, **28**(1), 1–3.

Maseeh, George P., Caroline G. Russell, Sanaan Lair Villalobos, John E. Balliew and Gilbert Trejo (2015), 'El Paso's advanced water purification facility: A new direction in potable reuse', *Journal of the American Water Works Association*, **107**(11), 36–45.

Mauser, Wolfram, Gernot Klepper, Martin Rice, Bettina Susanne Schmalzbauer, Heide Hackmann, Rik Leemans and Howard Moore (2013), 'Transdisciplinary global change research: The co-creation of knowledge for sustainability', *Current Opinions in Environmental Sustainability*, **5**, 420–431.

Max-Neef, Manfred A. (2005), 'Foundations of transdisciplinarity', *Ecological Economics*, **53**(1), 5–16.

Mayer, Audrey L., Pekka E. Kauppi, Per K. Angelstam, Yu Zhang and Paivi M. Tikka (2005a), 'Importing timber, exporting ecological impact', *Science* **308**(5720), 359–360.

Mayer, Igor S., Ellen M. van Bueren, Pieter W. G. Bots, Haiko van der Voort and Robin Seijdel (2005b), 'Collaborative decision making for sustainable urban renewal projects: A simulation–gaming approach', *Environment and Planning B: Planning and Design*, **32**(3), 403–423.

McCarthy, James (2004), 'Privatizing conditions of production: Trade agreements as neoliberal environmental governance', *Geoforum*, **35**(3), 327–341.

McCauley, Darren A., Raphael J. Heffron, Hannes Stephan, Kirsten Jenkins (2013), 'Advancing energy justice: the triumvirate of tenets', *International Energy Law Review*, **32**(3) pp. 107–110.

McCauley, Douglas (2006), 'Selling out on nature', *Nature*, **443**(7107), 27–28.

MDHHS (Michigan Department of Health and Human Services) (2016), 'Eat safe fish guide, Upper Peninsula', Eat Safe Fish Guides, State of Michigan, MI.

MEA (Millennium Ecosystem Assessment) (2005), *Ecosystems and Human Well-being: Current Status and Trends*. Cambridge: Cambridge University Press.

Mead, George H. (1934), *Mind, Self and Society*, Vol. 111. Chicago, IL: University of Chicago Press.

Mead, George H. and David L. Miller (1982), *The Individual and the Social Self*. Chicago, IL: University of Chicago Press.

Mebratu, Desta (1998), 'Sustainability and sustainable development: Historical and conceptual review', *Environmental Impact Assessment Review*, **18**(6), 493–520.

Mehran, Ali, Amir AghaKouchak, Navid Nakhjiri, Michael J. Stewardson, Murray C. Peel, Thomas J. Phillips, Yoshihide Wada and Jakin K. Ravalico (2017), 'Compounding impacts of human-induced water stress and climate change on water availability', *Scientific Reports*, **7**(1), 6282.

Merry, Sally E. (1988), 'Legal pluralism', *Law and Society Review*, **22**(5), 869–896.

Meyer, Erin (2014), *The Culture Map: Breaking through the Invisible Boundaries of Global Business*. New York: Hachette Book Group.

Meyer, John M. (2015), *Engaging the Everyday: Environmental Social Criticism and the Resonance Dilemma*. Cambridge, MA: MIT Press.

Mills, Bradford F. and Joachim Schleich (2009), 'Profits or preferences? Assessing the adoption of residential solar thermal technologies', *Energy Policy*, **37**(10), 4145–4154.

Minkler, Meredith and Nina Wallerstein (2008), *Community-based Participatory Research for Health: From Process to Outcomes*. San Francisco, CA: Jossey-Bass.

Mirchi, Ali, David W. Watkins Jr, Casey J. Huckins, Kaveh Madani and Peder Hjorth (2014), 'Water resources management in a homogenizing world: Averting the growth and underinvestment trajectory', *Water Resources Research*, **50**(9), 7515–7526.

Mitchell, Timothy (1991), 'The limits of the state: Beyond statist approaches and their critics', *American Political Science Review*, **85**, 77–96.

Montalvo, Vania (2015), 'In Mexico, tackling climate change starts with corruption', *Devex*, 22 July: https://www.devex.com/news/in-mexico-tackling-climate-change-starts-with-corruption-86574, accessed 16 November 2018.

Montrie, Chad (2011), *A People's History of Environmentalism in the United States*. London: Continuum.

Moore, Jason W. (2015) *Capitalism in the Web of Life: Ecology and the Accumulation of Capital*. New York: Verso.

Moore, Scott T. (1987), 'The theory of street-level bureaucracy: A positive critique', *Administration and Society*, **19**(1), 74–94.

Moran, Robert T., Neil Remington Abramson and Sarah V. Moran (2007), *Managing Cultural Differences*. London: Routledge.

Morley, Louise (2007), 'Sister-matic: Gender mainstreaming in higher education', *Teaching in Higher Education*, **12**(5–6), 607–620.

Morris, Peter (2012), *Power: A Philosophical Analysis*. Manchester: Mancester University Press.

Morse, Wayde C., Max Nielsen-Pincus, Jo Ellen Force and J. D. Wulfhorst (2007), 'Bridges and barriers to developing and conducting interdisciplinary graduate-student team research', *Ecology & Society*, **12**(2), 1–14.

Moseley, William G. (2005), 'Global cotton and local environmental management: The political ecology of rich and poor smallhold farmers in southern Mali', *The Geographical Journal*, **171**(1), 36–55.

Moser, Christine, Tina Hildebrandt and Robert Bailis (2014), 'International sustainability standards and certification', in Barry D. Solomon and Robert Bailis (eds), *Sustainable Development of Biofuels in Latin America and the Caribbean*. New York: Springer, pp. 27–69.

Nadasdy, Paul (2004), *Hunters and Bureaucrats: Power, Knowledge, and Aboriginal-State Relations in the Southwest Yukon*. Vancouver: UBC Press.

Narin, Francis, Kimberly Stevens and Edith S. Whitlow (1991), 'Scientific co-operation in Europe and the citation of multinationally authored papers', *Scientometrics*, **21**(3), 313–323.

NAS (National Academy of Sciences) (2005), *Facilitating interdisciplinary research*. Washington, DC: National Academies Press.

Nasiritousi, Naghmeh, Mattias Hjerpe and Björn-Ola Linnér (2016), 'The roles of non-state actors in climate change governance: Understanding agency through governance profiles', *International Environmental Agreements: Politics, Law and Economics*, **16**(1), 109–126.

National Commission. (2011). 'Deep water: The Gulf Oil disaster and the future, report to the President', National Commission on the BP Deepwater Horizon Oil Spill and Offshore Drilling, https://www.gpo.gov/fdsys/pkg/GPO-OILCOMMISSION/pdf/GPO-OILCOMMISSION.pdf, accessed 29 May 2018.

National Oceanic and Atmospheric Administration (2016), 'Damage assessment, remediation, and restoration program, Deepwater Horizon', National Oceanic and Atmospheric Administration, https://darrp.noaa.gov/oil-spills/deepwater-horizon, accessed 29 May 2018.

National Research Council (2008), 'International collaborations in behavioral and social sciences research: Report of a workshop', Board on International Scientific Organizations. Washington, DC: The National Academies Press.

National Research Council (2012), *Water Reuse: Potential for Expanding the Nation's Water Supply Through Reuse of Municipal Wastewater*. Washington, DC: The National Academies Press.

Nelson, Geoffrey, Isaac Prilleltensky and Heather MacGillivary (2001), 'Building value-based partnerships: Toward solidarity with oppressed groups', *American Journal of Community Psychology*, **29**(5), 649–677.

Neumann, Roderick P. (1998), *Imposing Wilderness: Struggles over Livelihood and Nature Preservation in Africa*. Berkeley, CA: University of California Press.

Neumann, Roderick P. (2005), *Making Political Ecology*. London: Hodder Education.

Newfont, Kathryn (2012), *Blue Ridge Commons: Environmental Activism and Forest History in Western North Carolina*. Athens, GA: University of Georgia Press.

Newig, Jens and Oliver Fritsch (2009), 'Environmental governance: Participatory, multi-level and effective?', *Environmental Policy and Governance*, **19**(3), 197–214.

Newman, Greg, Andrea Wiggins, Alycia Crall, Eric Graham, Sarah Newman and Kevin Crowston (2012), 'The future of citizen science: Emerging technologies and shifting paradigms', *Frontiers in Ecology and the Environment*, **10**(6), 298–304.

Newman, Mark E. J. (2001), 'The structure of scientific collaboration networks', *Proceedings of the National Academy of Sciences*, **98**(2), 404–409.

Noll, Daniel, Colleen Dawes and Varun Rai (2014), 'Solar community organizations and active peer effects in the adoption of residential PV', *Energy Policy*, **67**, 330–343.

Norris, Patricia, Michael O'Rourke, Alex Mayer and Kathleen E. Halvorsen (2016), 'Doubling down: Transdisciplinary research team formation as a wicked problem', *Landscape and Urban Planning*, **154**:115–122.

Northmore, Simon and Angie Hart (2011), 'Sustaining community–university partnerships', *Gateways: International Journal of Community Research and Engagement*, **4**, 1–11.

Nowotny, Helga (2003), 'Democratising expertise and socially robust knowledge', *Science and Public Policy*, **30**(3), 151–156.

Oakes, J. Michael, Ann Forsyth, Mary O. Hearst and Kathryn H. Schmitz. (2009), 'Recruiting participants for neighborhood effects research: Strategies and outcomes of the Twin Cities walking study', *Environment and Behavior*, **41**(6), 787–805.

OCEP (Office of Community Engagement and Partnerships) (2015), 'Community-engaged scholarship toolkit', University of Southern Florida, http://www.usf.edu/engagement/faculty/community-engaged-scholarship-toolkit.aspx#anchor3, accessed 14 January 2018.

O'Fallon, Liam R. and Allen Dearry (2002), 'Community-based participatory research as a tool to advance environmental health sciences', *Environmental Health Perspectives*, **110**(suppl 2), 155–159.

Oldekop, Johan A., George Holmes, W. Edwin Harris and Karl L. Evans (2016), 'A global assessment of the social and conservation outcomes of protected areas', *Conservation Biology*, **30**(1), 133–141.

O'Neill, Catherine A. (2004), 'Mercury, risk, and justice', *Environmental Law Reporter*, **34**, 11070–11115.

Onyango, L., Greg L. Leslie and James G. Wood (2014), 'Global potable reuse case study 5: Torreele/St. Andre, Koksijde Belgium', Australian Water Recycling Centre of Excellence, Brisbane, Australia.

O'Rourke, Michael and Stephen J. Crowley (2013), 'Philosophical intervention and cross-disciplinary science: The story of the toolbox project', *Synthese*, **190**(11), 1937–1954.

O'Rourke, Michael R., Stephen J. Crowley, Sanford D. Eigenbrode and J. D. Wulfhorst (2014), 'Introduction', in Michael R. O'Rourke, Stephen Crowley, Sanford D. Eigenbrode and J. D. Wulfhorst (eds), *Enhancing Communication and Collaboration in Interdisciplinary Research*. Thousand Oaks, CA: Sage, pp. 1–10.

Ostrom, Elinor (1996), 'Crossing the great divide: Coproduction, synergy, and development', *World Development*, **24**(6), 1073–1087.

O'Toole Jr, Laurence J. and Kenneth J. Meier (2004), 'Public management in intergovernmental networks: Matching structural networks and managerial networking', *Journal of Public Administration Research and Theory*, **14**(4), 469–494.

Paletz, Susannah B. F. and Christian D. Schunn (2010), 'A social-cognitive framework of multidisciplinary team innovation', *Topics in Cognitive Science*, **2**(1), 73–95.

Paletz, Susannah B. F., Christian D. Schunn and Kevin H. Kim (2011), 'Intragroup conflict under the microscope: Micro-conflicts in naturalistic team discussions', *Negotiation and Conflict Management Research*, **4**(4), 314–351.

Paletz, Susannah B. F., Christian D. Schunn and Kevin H. Kim (2013), 'The interplay of conflict and analogy in multidisciplinary teams', *Cognition*, **126**(1), 1–19.

Paletz, Susannah B. F., Joel Chan and Christian D. Schunn (2016), 'Uncovering uncertainty through disagreement', *Applied Cognitive Psychology*, **30**(3), 387–400.

Palmer, Margaret A., Jonathan G. Kramer, James Boyd and David Hawthorne (2016), 'Practices for facilitating interdisciplinary synthetic research: The national socioenvironmental synthesis center (SESYNC)', *Current Opinion in Environmental Sustainability*, **19**, 111–122.

Pannell, David J. (2004), 'Effectively communicating economics to policy makers', *Australian Journal of Agricultural and Resource Economics*, **48**(3), 535–555.

Parenti, Christian (2014), 'Rethinking the state', *New Politics*, **14**(4), 11.

Pascual, Unai, Jacob Phelps, Eneko Garmendia, Katrina Brown, Esteve Corbera, Adrian Martin, Erik Gomez-Baggethun and Roldan Muradian. (2014), 'Social equity matters in payments for ecosystem services', *Bioscience*, **64**(11), 1027–1036.

Paulos, Bentham (2017), 'Bringing the benefits of solar energy to low-income consumers: A guide for states and municipalities', Clean Energy States Alliance, Montpelier, USA.

Paulson, Susan and Lisa L. Gezon (2005), *Political Ecology Across Spaces, Scales, and Social Groups*. New Brunswick, NJ: Rutgers University Press.

Pearce, Joshua M. (2009), 'Expanding photovoltaic penetration with residential distributed generation from hybrid solar photovoltaic. Combined heat and power systems', *Energy*, **34**(11), 1947–1954.

Pecson, Brian M., R. Shane Trussell, Aleks N. Pisarenko and R. Rhodes Trussell (2015), 'Achieving reliability in potable reuse: The four Rs', *Journal of the American Water Works Association*, **107**(3), 48–58.

Peet, Richard, Paul Robbins and Michael Watts (2011), *Global Political Ecology*. London: Routledge.

Peluso, Nancy L. (1992), *Rich Forests, Poor People: Resource Control and Resistance in Java*. Berkeley, CA: University of California Press.

Peng, Wei, Mira Lee and Carrie Heeter (2010), 'The effects of a serious game on role taking and willingness to help', *Journal of Communication*, **60**(4), 723–742.

Pennington, Deana (2008), 'Cross-disciplinary collaboration and learning', *Ecology and Society*, **13**(2), 8.

Pennington, Deana D., Gary L. Simpson, Marjorie S. McConnell, Jeanne M. Fair and Robert J. Baker (2013), 'Transdisciplinary research, transformative learning, and transformative science', *BioScience*, **63**(7), 564–573.

Perlinger, Judith A., Hugh S. Gorman, Emma S. Norman, Daniel Obrist, Noelle E. Selin, Noel R. Urban and Shiliang Wu (2016), 'Viewpoint: Measurement and modeling of atmosphere–surface exchangeable pollutants (ASEPs) to understand their environmental cycling and planetary boundaries', *Environmental Science & Technology*, **50**(17), 8932–8934.

Perlinger, Judith A., Noel R. Urban, Amanda Giang, Noelle E. Selin, Ashley N. Hendricks, Han Zhang, Aditya Kumar, Shiliang Wu, Valoree S. Gagnon, Hugh S. Gorman and Emma S. Norman, (2018), 'Responses of deposition and bioaccumulation in the Great Lakes region to policy and other large-scale drivers of mercury emissions', *Environmental Science: Processes and Impacts*, **20**(1), 195–209.

Persson, Olle, Wolfgang Glänzel and Rickard Danell (2004), 'Inflationary bibliometric values: The role of scientific collaboration and the need for relative indicators in evaluative studies', *Scientometrics*, **60**(3), 421–432.

Perz, Stephen, G. (2016), *Crossing Boundaries for Collaboration: Conservation and Development Projects in the Amazon*. New York: Lexington Books.

Perz, Stephen G., Silvia Brilhante, I. Foster Brown, Andrea Chavez Michaelsen, Elsa Mendoza, Veronica Passos, Raul Pinedo, Juan Fernando Reyes, Daniel Rojas and Galia Selaya (2010), 'Crossing boundaries for environmental science and management: Combining interdisciplinary, interorganizational and international collaboration', *Environmental Conservation*, **37**(4), 419–431.

Peters, Scott, Arjen E. J. Wals (2013), 'Learning and knowing in pursuit of sustainability: Concepts and tools for trans-disciplinary environmental research', in Marianne E. Krasny and Justin Dillon (eds), *Trading Zones in Environmental Education: Creating Trans-disciplinary Dialogue*, New York: Peter Lang, pp. 79–104.

PetroChina (2017a), 'About PetroChina', PetroChina Company Limited, http://www.petrochina.com.cn/ptr/gsjj/gsjs_common.shtml, accessed 29 May 2018.

PetroChina (2017b), 'Sustainability report', PetroChina Company Limited, http://www.petrochina.com.cn/ptr/shyhj/index20150326.shtml, accessed 29 May 2018.

Phillipson, Jeremy, Philip Lowe, Amy Proctor and Eric Ruto (2012), 'Stakeholder engagement and knowledge exchange in environmental research', *Journal of Environmental Management,* **95**(1), 56–65.

Phinney, Robin (2013), 'Exploring residential mobility among low-income families', *Social Service Review,* **87**(4), 780–815.

Pischke, Erin C., Jessie L. Knowlton, Colin C. Phifer, Jose Gutierrez Lopez, Tamara S. Propato, Amarella Eastmond, Tatiana Martins de Souza, Mark Kuhlberg, Valentin Picasso Risso, Santiago R. Veron, Carlos Garcia, Marta Chiappe and Kathleen E. Halvorsen (2017), 'Barriers and solutions to conducting large international, interdisciplinary research projects', *Environmental Management,* **60**(6), 1011–1021.

Pischke, Erin C., Lucía Pérez Volkow, Mayra Fragoso-Medina and Laura Aguirre Franco (2018), 'Practicing what we preach: Reflections on the pros and cons of transdisciplinary research in Erongarícuaro, Mexico', *Revista Vínculos,* **3**(1), 17–21.

Pittman, Jeremy, Holm Tiessen and Elma Montaña (2016), 'The evolution of interdisciplinarity over 20 years of global change research by the IAI', *Current Opinion in Environmental Sustainability,* **19**, 87–93.

Piven, Frances F. (2008), 'Can power from below change the world?' *American Sociological Review,* **73**(1), 1–14.

Po, Murni, Juliane D. Kaercher and Blair E. Nancarrow (2003), 'Literature review of factors influencing public perceptions of water reuse', CSIRO Land and Water Technical Report 54/03, Canberra, Australia.

Polasky, Stephen, Stephen R. Carpenter, Carl Folke and Bonnie Keeler (2011), 'Decision-making under great uncertainty: Environmental management in an era of global change', *Trends in Ecology & Evolution,* **26**(8), 398e404.

Pradhan, Prajal, Dominik E. Reusser and Jeurgen P. Kropp (2013), 'Embodied greenhouse gas emissions in diets', *PloS One,* **8**(5), e62228.

Prince, John D. (1904), 'Review: The Code of Hammurabi', *The American Journal of Theology,* **8**(3), 601–609.

Probe Research Inc. (2015), '2015 Water issues public opinion poll, prepared for San Diego County Water Authority', San Diego, CA.

Pure Water San Diego (PWSD) (2017), 'North City Pure Water Project Title 22 engineering report', Pure Water San Diego, San Diego, CA.

Rai, Varun, D. Cale Reeves and Robert Margolis (2016), 'Overcoming barriers and uncertainties in the adoption of residential solar PV', *Renewable Energy,* **89**, 498–505.

Ranco, D. and D. Suagee (2007), 'Tribal sovereignty and the problem of difference in environmental regulation: Observations on "Measured Separatism" in Indian Country', *Antipode,* **39**(4), 691–707.

Rantala, Salla, Reem Hajjar and Margaret Skutsch (2014), 'Multilevel governance for forests and climate change: Learning from Southern Mexico', *Forests,* **5**(12), 3147–3168.

Raudsepp-Hearne, Ciara, Garry D. Peterson, Maria Tengö, Elena M. Bennett, Tim Holland, Karina Benessaiah, Graham K. MacDonald and Laura Pfeifer (2010), 'Untangling the environmentalist's paradox: Why is human well-being increasing as ecosystem services degrade?', *BioScience,* **60**(8), 576–589.

Reed, Mark S. (2008), 'Stakeholder participation for environmental management: A literature review', *Biological Conservation,* **141**(10), 2417–2431.

Reid, Walter V., Harold A. Mooney (2016), 'The Millennium Ecosystem Assessment: Testing the limits of interdisciplinary and multi-scale science', *Current Opinion in Environmental Sustainability,* **19**, 40–46.

Robbins, Paul (2012), *Political Ecology: A Critical Introduction.* Malden: John Wiley and Sons.

Robbins, Paul, Katharine Meehan, Hannah Gosnell and Susan J. Gilbertz (2009), 'Writing the new west: A critical review', *Rural Sociology,* **74**(3), 356–382.

Rodela, Romina and Dušan Alašević (2017), 'Crossing disciplinary boundaries in environmental research: Interdisciplinary engagement across the Slovene research community', *Science of The Total Environment,* **574**(1), 1492–1501.

Rogers, Everett M. (2010), *Diffusion of Innovations*. New York: Simon and Schuster.

Romero-Lankao, Patricia, Mercy Borbor-Cordova, Rosana Abrutsky, Griselda Günther, Eduardo Behrentz and Laura Dawidowsky (2013), 'ADAPTE: A tale of diverse teams coming together to do issue-driven interdisciplinary research', *Environmental Science and Policy*, **26**, 29–39.

Rosenbloom, David H. (1983), 'Public administrative theory and the separation of powers', in Jay M. Shafritz and Albert C. Hyde (eds), *Classics of Public Administration*. Boston, MA: Wadsworth, pp. 442–453.

Ross, Abraham S. (1984), 'Practical problems associated with programme evaluation in third world countries', *Evaluation and Program Planning*, **7**(3), 211–218.

Ross, Suzanne, John Lavis, Charo Rodriguez, Jennifer Woodside and Jean-Louis Denis (2003), 'Partnership experiences: Involving Decision-makers in the research process', *Journal of Health Services Research and Policy*, **8**, 26–34.

Rothausen, Sabrina G. S. A. and Declan Conway (2011), 'Greenhouse-gas emissions from energy use in the water sector', *Nature Climate Change*, **1**(4), 210–219.

Roux, Dirk J., Kevin H. Rogers, Harry C. Briggs, Peter J. Ashton and Anne Sargeant (2006), 'Bridging the science–management divide: Moving from unidirectional knowledge transfer to knowledge interfacing and sharing', *Ecology and Society*, **11**(1), 4.

Rowbotham, Samantha, Merryn McKinnon, Joan Leach, Rod Lamberts and Penelope Hawe (2017), 'Does citizen science have the capacity to transform population health science?', *Critical Public Health*, 1–11.

Russell, Bertrand (1937), *Power*. London: George Allen and Unwin.

Sanchez Garcia, Diego Armando (2017), 'Household water consumption in El Paso, Texas: Perceptions and behaviors towards water in urban households', ETD Collection for University of Texas, El Paso. AAI10688397. https://digitalcommons.utep.edu/dissertations/AAI10688397

Sarthou, Nerina (2013), 'Los sistemas de evaluación de la investigación y la universidad en América Latina: ¿Distintos sistemas para un mismo fin', *Gestion Universitaria*, **6**(1), 1–20.

Sarzynski, Andrea, Jeremy Larrieu and Gireesh Shrimali (2012), 'The impact of state financial incentives on market deployment of solar technology', *Energy Policy*, **46**, 550–557.

Sasser, Bill (2010), 'Despite BP oil spill, Louisiana still loves Big Oil', *The Christian Science Monitor*, https://www.csmonitor.com/USA/2010/0524/Despite-BP-oil-spill-Louisiana-still-loves-Big-Oil, accessed 29 May 2018.

Schelly, Chelsea (2010), 'Testing residential solar thermal adoption', *Environment and Behavior*, **42**(2), 151–170.

Schelly, Chelsea (2014), 'Residential solar electricity adoption: What motivates, and what matters? A case study of early adopters', *Energy Research and Social Science*, **2**, 183–191.

Schelly, Chelsea (2017). *Dwelling in Resistance: Living with Alternative Technologies in America*. New Brunswick, NJ: Rutgers University Press.

Schelly, Chelsea and Aparajita Banerjee (2018), *Environmental Policy and the Pursuit of Sustainability*. London: Routledge.

Schelly, Chelsea, Edward P. Louie and Joshua M. Pearce (2017), 'Examining interconnection policy and net metering policy for distributed generation in the United States', *Renewable Energy Focus*, **22–23**, 10–19.

Schmidt, Charles (2011), 'Occupational health: Study to examine health effects in Deepwater Horizon oil spill cleanup workers', *Environmental Health Perspectives*, **119**(5), A204.

Schmidt, Laura and Michael Pröpper (2017), 'Transdisciplinarity as a real-world challenge: A case study on a North–South collaboration', *Sustainability Science*, **12**(3), 365–379.

Schneider, Anne and Helen Ingram (1990), 'Behavioral assumptions of policy tools', *The Journal of Politics*, **52**(2), 510–529.

Schor, Juliet B. (2008), *The Overworked American: The Unexpected Decline of Leisure*. New York: Basic Books.

Schouten, Greetje and Pieter Glasbergen (2011), 'Creating legitimacy in global private governance: The case of the Roundtable on Sustainable Palm Oil', *Ecological Economics*, **70**(11), 1891–1899.

Scott, James C. (1985), *Weapons of the Weak: Everyday Forms of Peasant Resistance*. New Haven, CT: Yale University Press.

Scott, James C. (1990), *Domination and the Arts of Resistance: Hidden Transcripts*. New Haven, CT: Yale University Press.

Scott, John (2001), *Power*. Cambridge: Polity Press.

Scruggs, Caroline E. and Bruce M. Thomson (2017), 'Opportunities and challenges for direct potable water reuse in arid inland communities', *Journal of Water Resources Planning and Management*, **143**(10), 04017064.

Selin, Henrik (2014), 'Global environmental law and treaty-making on hazardous substances: The Minamata Convention and mercury abatement', *Global Environmental Politics*, **14**(1), 1–19.

Selin, Henrik and Stacy D. VanDeveer (2009), 'Climate leadership in northeast North America', in Henrik Selin and Stacy D. VanDeveer (eds), *Changing Climates in North American Politics: Institutions, Policymaking, and Multilevel Governance*. Cambridge, MA: MIT Press, pp. 111–136.

Sener, Can and Vasilis Fthenakis (2014), 'Energy policy and financing options to achieve solar energy grid penetration targets: Accounting for external costs', *Renewable and Sustainable Energy Reviews*, **32**, 854–868.

Seyfang, Gill (2005), 'Shopping for sustainability: Can sustainable consumption promote ecological citizenship?' *Environmental Politics*, **14**(2), 290–306.

Sharma, Ardhana and Akhil Gupta (2006), 'Introduction: Rethinking theories of the state in an age of globalization', in Ardhana Sharma and Akhil Gupta (eds) *The Anthropology of the State: A Reader*. Malden: Blackwell, pp. 1–42.

Shea, Marybeth and Cameron Mozafari (2014), 'Communicating complexity in transdisciplinary science teams for policy: Applied stasis theory for organizing and assembling collaboration', *Communication Design Quarterly Review*, **2**(3), 20–24.

Shell Global (2017a), 'About us', Shell Global, http://www.shell.com/about-us/who-we-are.html, accessed 29 May 2018.

Shell Global (2017b) 'Sustainability, communities', Shell Global, http://www.shell.com/sustainability/communities.html, accessed 29 May 2018.

Sheng, Zhuping (2005), 'An aquifer storage and recovery system with reclaimed wastewater to preserve native groundwater resources in El Paso, Texas', *Journal of Environmental Management*, **75**(4), 367–377.

Sheng, Zhuping (2013), 'Impacts of groundwater pumping and climate variability on groundwater availability in the Rio Grande Basin', *Ecosphere*, **4**(1), 1–25.

Shove, Elizabeth (2004), *Comfort, Cleanliness, and Convenience: The Social Organization of Normality*. New York: Berg.

Shove, Elizabeth (2010), 'Beyond the ABC: Climate change policy and theories of social change', *Environment and Planning A*, **42**(6), 1273–1285.

Shwom, Rachael and Janet A. Lorenzen (2012), 'Changing household consumption to address climate change: Social scientific insights and challenges', *Wiley Interdisciplinary Reviews: Climate Change*, **3**(5), 379–395.

Sidortsov, Roman and Benjamin Sovacool (2015), 'Left out in the cold: Energy justice and Arctic energy research', *Journal of Environmental Studies and Sciences*, **5**(3), 302–307.

Sillitoe, Paul (2004), 'Interdisciplinary experiences: Working with indigenous knowledge in development', *Interdisciplinary Science Reviews*, **29**, 6–23.

Silva Payró, Martha Patricia, Verónica García Martínez and Silvia Patricia Aquino Zúñig (2016), 'Retos de crecimiento del Sistema Nacional de Investigadores (SNI) del consejo Nacional de Ciencia y Tecnología (Conacyt) en México', *Actualidades Investigativas en Educación*, **16**(2), 1–24.

Simon, David and Friedrich Schiemer (2015), 'Crossing boundaries: Complex systems, transdisciplinarity and applied impact agendas', *Current Opinion in Environmental Sustainability*, **12**, 6–11.

Simon, David, Duncan McGregor, Kwasi Nsiah-Gyabaah and Donald Thompson (2003), 'Poverty elimination, North–South research collaboration, and the politics of participatory development', *Development in Practice*, **13**(1), 40–56.

Simpson, Genevieve (2018), 'Looking beyond incentives: The role of champions in the social acceptance of residential solar energy in regional Australian communities', *Local Environment*, **23**(2), 127–143.

Smart Electric Power Alliance (2018), 'Avoiding the growing pains of community solar', https://sepapower.org/event/avoiding-growing-pains-community-solar/, accessed 5 April 2018.

Smeds, Riitta (1997), 'Organizational learning and innovation through tailored simulation games: Two process re-engineering case studies', *Knowledge and Process Management*, **4**(1), 22–33.

Solar Energy Industries Association (2017), 'Solar market insight report 2017 Q4', https://www.seia.org/research-resources/solar-market-insight-report-2017-q4, accessed 15 October 2017.

Solomon, Barry and Valerie A. Luzadis (2008), *Renewable Energy from Forest Resources in the United States*. New York: Routledge.

Solomon, Barry D., Aparajita Banerjee, Alberto Acevedo, Kathleen E. Halvorsen and Amarella Eastmond (2015), 'Policies for the sustainable development of biofuels in the pan American region: A review and synthesis of five countries', *Environmental Management*, **56**(6), 1276–1294.

Soulé, Michael E. (2013), 'The "new conservation"', *Nature* **27**(5), 895–897.

Sovacool, Benjamin K. (2009), 'The intermittency of wind, solar, and renewable electricity generators: Technical barrier or rhetorical excuse?', *Utilities Policy*, **17**(3–4), 288–296.

Sovacool, Benjamin K. and Michael H. Dworkin (2014), *Global Energy Justice: Problems, Principles, and Practices*. Cambridge: Cambridge University Press.

Sovacool, Benjamin, Roman Sidortsov and Benjamin Jones (2014), *Energy Security, Equality, and Justice*. New York: Routledge.

Sovacool, Benjamin K., Raphael J. Heffron, Darren McCauley and Andreas Goldthau (2016), Energy decisions reframed as justice and ethical concerns', *Nature Energy*, **1**, 16024.

Spaargaren, Gert (2003), 'Sustainable consumption: A theoretical and environmental policy perspective', *Society & Natural Resources*, **16**(8), 687–701.

Spaargaren, Gert (2011), 'Theories of practices: Agency, technology, and culture: Exploring the relevance of practice theories for the governance of sustainable consumption practices in the new world-order', *Global Environmental Change*, **21**(3), 813–822.

Spash Clive L. and Lulie Aslaksen (2015), 'Re-establishing an ecological discourse in the policy debate over how to value ecosystems and biodiversity', *Journal of Environmental Management*, **159**, 245–253.

SSHRC (Social Sciences and Humanities Research Council) (2017), 'Guidelines for Effective Knowledge Mobilization', Government of Canada, http://www.sshrc-crsh.gc.ca/funding-financement/policies-politiques/knowledge_mobilisation-mobilisation_des_connaissances-eng.aspx, accessed 14 January 2018.

Stanley, Kevin G., Ian Livingston, Alan Bandurka, Robert Kapiszka and Regan L. Mandryk (2010), 'PiNiZoRo: A GPS-based exercise game for families', *International Academic Conference on the Future of Game Design and Technology*, Vancouver, 6–7 May 2010, pp. 243–246.

Stattman, Sarah L. and Arthur P. Mol (2014), 'Social sustainability of Brazilian biodiesel: The role of agricultural cooperatives', *Geoforum*, **54**, 282–294.

Steingröver, Eveliene G., Willemien Geertsema and Walter K. R. E. van Wingerden (2010), 'Designing agricultural landscapes for natural pest control: A transdisciplinary approach in the Hoeksche Waard (The Netherlands)', *Landscape Ecology*, **25**, 825–838.

Stevens, Ed and Annaleise Depper (2016), 'Engaging with policymakers: Top tips and relevant resources'. University of Bath Press, 20 April 2016, http://www.bath.ac.uk/marketing/public-engagement/get-involved/pe-conversations, accessed 6 May 2018.

Stevens, Matthias, Michalis Vitos, Julia Altenbuchner, Gillian Conquest, Jerome Lewis and Muki Haklay (2014), 'Taking participatory citizen science to extremes', *IEEE Pervasive Computing*, **13**(2), 20–29.

Stoecker, Randy (2009), 'Are we talking the walk of community-based research?', *Action Research*, **7**(4), 385–404.

Stoecker, Randy (2012), *Research Methods for Community Change: A Project-based Approach*. Washington, DC: Sage.

Stokols, Daniel (2006), 'Toward a science of transdisciplinary action research', *American Journal of Community Psychology*, **38**(1–2), 79–93.

Stokols, Daniel, Kara L. Hall, Brandie K. Taylor and Richard P. Moser (2008), 'The science of team science: Overview of the field and introduction to the supplement', *American Journal of Preventative Medicine*, **35**, 2S.

Strand, Kerry, Sam Marullo, Nick Cutforth, Randy Stoecker and Patrick Donohue (2003), *Community-based Research and Higher Education: Principles and Practices*. San Francisco, CA: Jossey-Bass.

Streets, D. G., Q. Zhang and Y. Wu (2009), "Projections of global mercury emissions in 2050', *Environmental Science and Technology*, **43**(8), 2983–2988.

Strober, Myra H. (2006), 'Habits of the mind: Challenges for multidisciplinary engagement', *Social Epistemology*, **20**(3–4), 315–331.

Sullivan-Bolyai, Susan, Carol Bova, Janet A. Deatrick, Kathy Knafl, Margaret Grey, Katherine Leung and Allison Trudeau (2007), 'Barriers and strategies for recruiting study participants in clinical settings', *Western Journal of Nursing Research*, **29**(4), 486–500.

Sumaila, U. Rashid, Andrés M. Cisneros-Montemayor, Andrew Dyck, Ling Huang, William Cheung, Jennifer Jacquet, Kristin Kleisner, Vicky Lam, Ashley McCrea-Strub, Wilf Swartz, Reg Watson, Dirk Zeller and Daniel Pauly (2012), 'Impact of the Deepwater Horizon well blowout on the economics of US Gulf fisheries', *Canadian Journal of Fisheries and Aquatic Sciences*, **69**(3), 499–510.

Tchobanoglous, George, Harold Leverenz, Margaret H. Nellor and James Crook (2011), 'Direct potable reuse: A path forward', WateReuse Research Foundation, WateReuse California, Alexandria, CA.

Tchobanoglous, George, Joseph Cotruvo, James Crook, Ellen McDonald, Adam Olivieri, Andrew Salveson and R. Shane Trussell (2015), 'Framework for direct potable reuse', WateReuse Research Foundation, Alexandria, CA.

Texas Water Development Board (2017), '2017 Texas State Water Plan', Texas Water Development Board, https://2017.texasstatewaterplan.org/county/El%20Paso, accessed 5 January 2018.

Thompson, Jessica L. (2009), 'Building collective communication competence in interdisciplinary research teams', *Journal of Applied Communication Research*, **37**, 278–297.

Tocqueville, Alexis de (1835/2004), *Democracy in America* (translated by Arthur Goldhammer). New York: Library of America.

Tourism Economics (2011), 'The impact of the BP Oil Spill on visitor spending in Louisiana: Revised estimates based on data through 2010 Q4', Louisiana Office of Tourism, https://www.crt.state.la.us/Assets/Tourism/research/documents/2011-2012/Oil_Spill_Impacts_201106.pdf, accessed 29 May 2018.

Tritter, Jonathan Q. and Alison McCallum (2006), 'The snakes and ladders of user involvement: Moving beyond Arnstein', *Health Policy*, **76**, 156–168.

Tuckman, Bruce W. and Mary Ann C. Jensen (1977), 'Stages of small-group development revisited', *Group & Organization Studies*, **2**(4), 419–427.

Turner, Billie L., II (2003), 'A framework for vulnerability analysis in sustainability science', *Proceedings of the National Academy of Sciences*, **100**(14), 8074–8079.

Turner, Billie L., Karen J. Esler, Peter Bridgewater, Joshua Tewksbury, Nadia Sitas, Brent Abrahams, F. Stuart Chapin III, Rinku Roy Chowdhury, Patrick Christie, Sandra Diaz, Penny Firth, Corrine N. Knapp, Jonathan Kramer, Rik Leemans, Margaret Palmer, Diana Pietri, Jeremy Pittman, José Sarukhán, Ross Shackleton, Reinmar Seidler, Brian van Wilgen and Harold Mooney (2016), 'Socio-environmental systems (SES) research: What have we learned and how can we use this information in future research programs', *Current Opinion in Environmental Sustainability*, **19**, 160–168.

United Nations General Assembly (1972), 'Report of the United Nations Conference on the Human Environment', United Nations, Stockholm.

United Nations General Assembly (1992), 'Summary of the United Nations Conference on Environment and Development. Annex 1: Rio Declaration on Environment and Development', United Nations, Rio de Janeiro.

United Nations General Assembly (2000), 'United Nations Millennium Declaration', Geneva.

United Nations General Assembly (2015), 'The Millennium Development Goals Report: 2015', Geneva.

United Nations General Assembly (2017), 'Who we are. Retrieved from United Nations Global Compact', https://www.unglobalcompact.org/what-is-gc, accessed 29 May 2018.

United States Environmental Protection Agency (US EPA) (1990), 'Clean Air Act, Title IV: Acid Deposition Control', 40 CFR Parts 72–78. Washington, DC.

United States Environmental Protection Agency (US EPA) (2011), *'A National Evaluation of the Clean Water Act Section 319 Program'*. Office of Wetlands, Oceans, & Watersheds. Assessment & Watershed Protection Division, Nonpoint Source Control Branch, USEPA, November 2011, https://www.epa.gov/sites/production/files/2015-09/documents/319evaluation.pdf, accessed 15 November 2017.

United States Environmental Protection Agency (US EPA) (2013), 'Nonpoint source program and grants guidelines for states and territories', USEPA, April 2013, https://www.epa.gov/sites/production/files/2015-09/documents/319-guidelines-fy14.pdf, accessed 29 May 2018.

United States Environmental Protection Agency (US EPA) (2016), *Our Nation's Air: Status and Trends through 2015*. Washington, DC: United States Environmental Protection Agency.

United States Environmental Protection Agency (US EPA) (2017), *Our Nation's Air: Status and Trends through 2016*. Washington, DC: United States Environmental Protection Agency, https://gispub.epa.gov/air/trendsreport/2016/, accessed 16 November 2018.

Unruh, Gregory C. (2000), 'Understanding carbon lock-in', *Energy Policy,* **28**(12), 817–830.

Unruh, Gregory C. (2002), 'Escaping carbon lock-in', *Energy Policy,* **30**(4), 317–325.

Upper Occoquan Service Authority (2017), 'Treatment process', Upper Occoquan Service Authority, https://www.uosa.org/DisplayContentUOSA.asp?ID=490, accessed 31 December 2017.

Urban N. R., J. A. Perlinger, E. Sokol, H. Wang, H. Lin, A. Hendricks, W. Alakayak and M. Priyadarshini (2016), 'Contaminants within the landscape mosaic of lakes, from small to great: Health in space and time', paper presentation, International Symposium on Society and Resource Management, Houghton, MI.

US Census Bureau (2012–2016), 'American community survey 5-year estimates', https://factfinder.census.gov/faces/tableservices/jsf/pages/productview.xhtml?src=CF, accessed 10 October 2017.

USCG (United States Coast Guard) (2011), 'Report on the investigation into the circumstances surrounding the explosion, fire, sinking and loss of eleven crew members aboard the mobile offshore drilling unit Deepwater Horizon', https://www.bsee.gov/newsroom/library/deepwater-horizon-reading-room/joint-investigation-team-report, accessed 16 November, 2018.

US Department of the Interior (2010), 'Notice to lessees and operators of federal oil and gas leases in the outer Continental Shelf regions of the Gulf of Mexico and the Pacific to implement the directive to impose a moratorium on all drilling of deepwater wells, NTL no. 2010-N04', US Department of the Interior, Minerals Management Service, https://www.doi.gov/sites/doi.gov/files/migrated/news/pressreleases/upload/MORATORIUM_NTL.pdf, accessed 29 May 2018.

US Energy Information Administration (EIA) (2018), 'Levelized cost and levelized avoided cost of new generation', Energy Information Administration Annual Energy Outlook, https://www.eia.gov/outlooks/aeo/pdf/electricity_generation.pdf, accessed 29 May 2018.

US Government Publishing Office (2011), 'Title 26 Internal Revenue Code Subpart E, Sec 48', US Government Publishing Office, https://www.gpo.gov/fdsys/pkg/USCODE-2011-title26/pdf/USCODE-2011-title26-subtitleA-chap1-subchapA-partIV-subpartE-sec48.pdf, accessed 25 October 2017.

US Internal Revenue Service (2018), 'Governmental information letter', 13 February, https://www.irs.gov/government-entities/federal-state-local-governments/governmental-information-letter, accessed 26 May 2018.

Uzochukwu, Benjamin, Obinna Onwujekwe, Chinyere Mbachu, Chinenye Okwuosa, Enyi Etiaba, Monica E. Nyström, and Lucy Gilson (2016), 'The challenge of bridging the gap between researchers and policy makers: Experiences of a health policy research group in engaging policy makers to support evidence informed policy making in Nigeria', *Globalization and Health*, **12**(1), 67.

Van den Brink, Marieke and Yvonne Benschop (2012), 'Slaying the seven-headed dragon: The quest for gender change in academia', *Gender, Work & Organization*, **19**(1), 71–92.

Van Pelt, Saskia C., Marjolijin Haasnoot, Bas Arts, Fulco Ludwig, Rob Swart and Robert Biesbroek (2015), 'Communicating climate (change) uncertainties: Simulation games as boundary objects', *Environmental Science and Policy*, **45**, 41–52.

Vatn, Arild (2016), *Environmental Governance: Institutions, Policies and Actions*. Cheltenham, UK and Northampton, MA, USA: Edward Elgar Publishing.

Venhoeven, Leonie A., Jan Willem Bolderdijk and Linda Steg (2016), 'Why acting environmentally-friendly feels good: Exploring the role of self-image', *Frontiers in Psychology*, **7**, 1846.

Viardot, Eric (2013), 'The role of cooperatives in overcoming the barriers to adoption of renewable energy', *Energy Policy*, **63**, 756–764.

Virapongse, Arika, Samantha Brooks, Elizabeth Covelli Metcalf, Morgan Zedalis, Jim Gosz, Andrew Kliskey and Lilian Alessa (2016), 'A social–ecological systems approach for environmental management', *Journal of Environmental Management*, **178**, 83–91.

Vos, Robert O. (2007), 'Defining sustainability: A conceptual orientation', *Journal of Chemical Technology and Biotechnology*, **82**(4), 334–339.

Wagner, Caroline S., Travis A. Whetsell and Loet Leydesdorff (2017), 'Growth of international collaboration in science: Revisiting six specialties', *Scientometrics*, **110**(3), 1633–1652.

Walshe, Kieran and Thomas G. Rundall (2001), 'Evidence-based management: From theory to practice in health care', *Milbank Quarterly*, **79**(3), 429–457.

Wania, F. and D. Mackay (1996), 'Tracking the distribution of persistent organic pollutants', *Environmental Science & Technology*, **30**(9), 390–396.

Watkins, David (2016), 'Coupled production-consumption systems for climate change mitigation: designing equitable food, energy, and water conservation strategies', product of a Workshop held at Michigan Technological University, Houghton, Michigan, 16–17 October 2015. Sponsored by the National Science Foundation (award no. 1541816).

Watkins Jr., David, D. Buyung Agusdinata, Eric Bahel, Jennifer Becker, Analena Bruce, Morey Burnham, . . . and Tingzhu Zhu (2016), 'Coupled production–consumption systems for climate change mitigation: Designing equitable food, energy, and water conservation strategies', Workshop Report, National Science Foundation, Washington, DC.

Weber, Maz (1978), *Economy and Society: An Outline of Interpretive Sociology* (edited by Guether Roth and Claus Wittich). Berkeley, CA: University of California Press.

Weible, Christopher M. (2008), 'Expert-based information and policy subsystems: A review and synthesis', *Policy Studies Journal*, **36**(4), 615–635.

Wenz, Peter (1988), *Environmental Justice*. Albany: SUNY Press.

Wenzler, Ivo, Rob Willems and Alexander M. van't Noordeinde (1995), 'A policy exercise for the Dutch power industry', in David Crookall and Kiyoshi Arai (eds), *Simulation and Gaming across Disciplines and Cultures*. Thousand Oaks: Sage, pp. 143–149.

West, Jodie, Ian Bailey and Michael Winter (2010), 'Renewable energy policy and public perceptions of renewable energy: A cultural theory approach', *Energy Policy*, **38**(10), 5739–5748.

White, Damian F., Alan P. Rudy, Brian J. Gareau (2015), *Environments, Natures and Social Theory: Towards a Critical Hybridity*. London: Palgrave Macmillan.

Whyte, William F. (1991), *Participatory Action Research*. Newbury Park, CA: Sage.

Wickson, Fern, Anna L. Carew and Alice W. Russell (2006), 'Transdisciplinary research: Characteristics, quandaries and quality', *Futures*, **38**(9), 1046–1059.

Wiek, Arnim, Alexander J. Walter (2009), 'A transdisciplinary approach for formalized integrated planning and decision-making in complex systems', *European Journal of Operational Research,* **197**, 360–370.

Wiesmann, Urs, Susette Biber-Klemm, Walter Grossenbacher-Mansuy, Gertrude Hirsch Hadorn, Holger Hoffmann-Riem, Dominique Joye, Christian Pohl and Elisabeth Zemp (2008), 'Enhancing transdisciplinary research: A synthesis in fifteen propositions', in, Gertrude Hirsch Hadorn, Holger Hoffman-Riem, Susette Biber-Klemm, Walter Grossenbacher-Mansuy, Dominique Joye, Christian Pohl, Urs Wiesmann and Elisabeth Zemp (eds), *Handbook of Transdisciplinary Research.* Cham: Springer, pp. 433–441.

Wilkinson, Paul, Kirk R. Smith, Michael Davies, Heather Adair, Ben G. Armstrong, Mark Barrett, Nigel Bruce, Andy Haines, Ian Hamilton, Tadj Oresczyn, Ian Ridley, Cathryn Tonne and Zaid Chalabi (2009), 'Public health benefits of strategies to reduce greenhouse-gas emissions: Household energy', *The Lancet,* **374**(9705), 1917–1929.

Willis, Margaret M. and Juliet B. Schor (2012), 'Does changing a light bulb lead to changing the world? Political action and the conscious consumer', *Annals of the American Academy of Political and Social Science,* **644**(1), 160–190.

Wilson, James Q. (2000), *Bureaucracy: What Government Agencies Do and Why They Do It.* New York: Basic Books.

Winkler, Richelle (2013), 'Living on lakes: Segregated communities and inequality in a natural amenity destination', *The Sociological Quarterly,* **54**(1), 105–129.

Winkler, Richelle, Lorri Oikarinen, Heather Simpson, Melissa Michaelson and Mayra S. Gonzalez (2016), 'Boom, bust and beyond: Arts and sustainability in Calumet, Michigan', *Sustainability,* **8**(3), 284.

World Commission on Environment and Development (1987), *Our Common Future.* Oxford: Oxford University Press.

Wright, Christopher and Daniel Nyberg (2017), 'An inconvenient truth: How organizations translate climate change into business as usual', *Academy of Management Journal,* **60**(5), 1633–1661.

Wüstenhagen, Rolf, Maarten Wolsink and Mary Jean Bürer (2007), 'Social acceptance of renewable energy innovation: An introduction to the concept', *Energy Policy,* **35**(5), 2683–2691.

Zahran, Sammy, Samuel D. Brody, Arnold Vedlitz, Michael G. Lacy and Chelsea Lynn Schelly (2008), 'Greening local energy: Explaining the geographic distribution of household solar energy use in the United States', *Journal of the American Planning Association,* **74**(4), 419–434.

Zaring, David (1996), 'Agriculture, nonpoint source pollution, and regulator control: The Clean Water Act's bleak present and future', *Harvard Environmental Law Review,* **20**, 515, pp. 515–528.

Zhang H., C. D. Holmes and S. Wu (2016), 'Impacts of changes in climate, land use, and land cover on atmospheric mercury', *Atmospheric Environment,* **141**, 230–224.

Zhou, Qiqi, Geertje Bekebrede, Igor Mayer, Jeroen Warmerdam and Maxim Knepflé (2013), 'The climate game: Connecting water management and spatial planning through simulation gaming', in Nancy Bressers (ed.), *Water Governance as Connective Capacity.* London: Routledge, pp. 109–127.

Zimmerer, Karl S. and Thomas J. Bassett (2003), *Political Ecology: An Integrative Approach to Geography and Environment-development Studies.* New York: Guilford Press.

Zooniverse (2018), 'GalaxyZoo', https://www.zooniverse.org/projects/zookeeper/galaxy-zoo/, accessed 5 January 2018.

Index